Judicializing the Administrative State

A basic feature of the modern US administrative state taken for granted by legal scholars but neglected by political scientists and historians is its strong judiciality. Formal, or courtlike, adjudication was the primary method of first-order agency policy making during the first half of the twentieth century. Even today, most US administrative agencies hire administrative law judges and other adjudicators conducting hearings using formal procedures autonomously from the agency head. No other industrialized democracy has even come close to experiencing the systematic state judicialization that took place in the United States.

Why did the American administrative state become highly judicialized, rather than developing a more efficiency-oriented Weberian bureaucracy? Legal scholars argue that lawyers as a profession imposed the judicial procedures they were the most familiar with on agencies. But this explanation fails to show why the judicialization took place only in the United States at the time it did. Okayama demonstrates that the American institutional combination of common law and the presidential system favored policy implementation through formal procedures by autonomous agencies and that it induced the creation and development of independent regulatory commissions explicitly modeled after courts from the late nineteenth century. These commissions judicialized the state not only through their proliferation but also through the diffusion of their formal procedures to executive agencies over the next half century, which led to a highly fairness-oriented administrative state.

Hiroshi Okayama is Professor of Political Science in the Faculty of Law at Keio University, Tokyo, Japan.

Routledge Research in Public Administration and Public Policy

Administrative Ethics and Executive Decisions
Channeling and Containing Administrative Discretion
Chad B. Newswander

Citizen Participation in the Age of Contracting
When Service Delivery Trumps Democracy
Anna A. Amirkhanyan and Kristina T. Lambright

Community Development and Public Administration Theory
Promoting Democratic Principles to Improve Communities
Edited by Ashley E. Nickels and Jason D. Rivera

Contextualizing Compliance in the Public Sector
Individual Motivations, Social Processes, and Institutional Design
Saba Siddiki, Salvador Espinosa, and Tanya Heikkila

The Politics of Fracking
Regulatory Policy and Local Community Responses
to Environmental Concerns
Sarmistha R. Majumdar

The Data Economy
Implications from Singapore
Sree Kumar, Warren B. Chik, See-Kiong Ng, and Sin Gee Teo

Corruption Prevention and Governance in Hong Kong
Ian Scott and Ting Gong

Judicializing the Administrative State
The Rise of the Independent Regulatory Commissions
in the United States, 1883–1937
Hiroshi Okayama

For more information about this series, please visit: www.routledge.com/Routledge-Research-in-Public-Administration-and-Public-Policy/book-series/RRPAPP.

Judicializing the Administrative State

The Rise of the Independent Regulatory Commissions in the United States, 1883–1937

Hiroshi Okayama

Routledge
Taylor & Francis Group
LONDON AND NEW YORK

First published 2019
by Routledge
2 Park Square, Milton Park, Abingdon, Oxon OX14 4RN

and by Routledge
605 Third Avenue, New York, NY 10017

First issued in paperback 2021

Routledge is an imprint of the Taylor & Francis Group, an informa business

Publisher's Note
The publisher has gone to great lengths to ensure the quality of this reprint but points out that some imperfections in the original copies may be apparent.

British Library Cataloguing-in-Publication Data
A catalogue record for this book is available from the British Library

Library of Congress Cataloging-in-Publication Data
Names: Okayama, Hiroshi, 1972– author.
Title: Judicializing the administrative state : the rise of the independent regulatory commissions in the United States, 1883–1937 / Hiroshi Okayama.
Description: Abingdon, Oxon ; New York, NY : Routledge, 2020. | Series: Routledge research in public administration and public policy | Includes bibliographical references and index.
Identifiers: LCCN 2019004637 | ISBN 9781138306653 (hardback) | ISBN 9781315141886 (e-book)
Subjects: LCSH: Independent regulatory commissions—United States.—History. | Administrative courts—United States.—History. | United States—Politics and government—1865–1933.
Classification: LCC KF5417 .O53 2020 | DDC 342.73/0664—dc23
LC record available at https://lccn.loc.gov/2019004637

Typeset in Galliard
by Apex CoVantage, LLC

ISBN 13: 978-1-03-209266-9 (pbk)
ISBN 13: 978-1-138-30665-3 (hbk)

For Naho and Mone

Contents

Acknowledgments

This book has taken much longer to write than I envisioned at the outset of the research. The project was rather innocently conceived as an inquiry into the introduction of policy expertise into US policy making through the lens of independent regulatory commissions, but it morphed into a quest for the origins of the courtlike administrative state, which required much additional research and self-teaching. It is a joy to be able to finally thank those who have supported me along the way.

I have taught at the University of Tokyo and Keio University while working on this book, and the two academic homes have provided a working environment in which I could balance teaching and research. At the University of Tokyo, I was fortunate to have Yasuo Endo, Jun Furuya, Sheila Hones, Masako Notoji, Toru Umezaki, Yujin Yaguchi, and Daizaburo Yui in American studies guiding me in different aspects of academic life as a full-time faculty member. After moving to Keio, the friendship and advice of those in the faculty of law's Area Studies and Comparative Politics section, Kazuaki Inoue, Naoya Izuoka, Yuko Kasuya, Ryosei Kokubun, Hiroshi Tomita, Shinji Yokote were indispensable in my settling in quickly and continuing working on this project.

It would not have been possible to complete the research for this book without the sabbatical at the University of Virginia School of Law. I very much appreciate the hospitality its faculty and staff extended to me. Naoyuki Agawa, Ryosei Kokubun, Paul Mahoney, Akiyo Okuda, Elizabeth Sanders, and Olivier Zunz played critical roles in making the stay happen, and I am deeply obliged for their support. At UVA, I also benefited much from attending occasional academic events at the Miller Center, and I thank Brian Balogh and Sidney Milkis for being such kind hosts. Befriending Adrienne and Colin Bird, Claudia Brühwiler, and Daniel Häusermann was among the best things that happened to me during the visit. I also cherish the memories of the fun time George, Lois, and Christina Westerlund; the late Jim Kauzlarich; and the folks from the "Saturday Coffee Group" shared with me and my family.

Many organizations extended generous support for this research, for which I am grateful. The two JSPS Grants-in-Aid for Scientific Research, 19730106 and 23530162, and the Sakuradakai Foundation grants in 2010 and 2018 constituted the primary fund for the research. The Keio Gijuku Fukuzawa Memorial Fund supported my sabbatical. Travel grants from the American Studies Foundation and the Japanese Political Science Association enabled the conference travels to the United States. The archival research for the book became much easier thanks to the archivists and librarians at the Albert and Shirley Small Special Collections Library, University of Virginia; the University of Michigan's Bentley Historical Library; the Booth Family Center for Special Collections at Georgetown University; the Briscoe Center for American History at the University of Texas at Austin; the University of Chicago's Special Collections Research Center; Yale University's Sterling Memorial Library; the Special Collections Library at George Mason University; the Herbert Hoover Presidential Library; the Hoover Institution; the John F. Kennedy Presidential Library; the Franklin D. Roosevelt Presidential Library; the Library of Congress's Manuscript Reading Room; and the National Archives at College Park.

Parts of the research for this book were presented at various venues, including the conferences of the American Political Science Association, the International Political Science Association, Japan Association for Comparative Politics, the Midwest Political Science Association, the Policy History Conference, and the Southern Political Science Association and also at the seminars sponsored by Hokkaido University, the University of Tokyo, and the US Politics Study Group. Of the feedbacks I received at such occasions, I particularly appreciate the questions and comments from Hisashi Aizawa, Richard Bensel, Stephen Bragaw, Daniel Carpenter, Daniel Ernst, Judge Glock, Takeshi Ito, Shoko Kohama, Guy Peters, Joseph Postell, Jesse Rhodes, Gretchen Ritter, Hironori Sasada, Mamoru Sorai, Bartholomew Sparrow, and Yu Uchiyama.

The introduction and the first two chapters contain portions of Hiroshi Okayama's "The Interstate Commerce Commission and the Genesis of America's Judicialized Administrative State," *Journal of the Gilded Age and Progressive Era* 15 (2016): 29–48, in revised form. I thank Cambridge University Press for the permission to reproduce the material in this book. The suggestions for the original article from the coeditors of the journal at the time, Benjamin Johnson and Robert Johnston, and the two anonymous reviewers were extremely helpful in honing the argument of this book.

I am fortunate to have colleagues who kindly took time and effort to read all or part of my manuscript with care and offer comments at various stages, helping me make this book a better one: Seito Hayasaki, Sheila Hones, Jacques Hymans, Naoya Izuoka, Rieko Kage, Keigo Komamura, Fumiaki Kubo, Lee Hwansung, Shunichi Matsuda, Masaru Nishikawa, Sayuri Shimizu, Kensuke Takayasu, and Rikuo Tsukuda. All remaining errors are my own.

Simon Bates and the editorial staff at Routledge including Tan ShengBin and Anandan Bommen have made sure that the editorial process of this book goes smoothly. I have also greatly benefited from the very detailed comments and advice from the anonymous reviewer commissioned by the press.

My only regret about not having completed this book earlier is that Takeshi Igarashi and Joel H. Silbey, my Japanese and American mentors, did not live to see it. They taught me how to do US political history and enjoy it. I hope this book lives up to their expectations.

I have been lucky to be part of a caring family who have put up with me while I have been too much distracted in researching for this book for too long. My parents, Kei and Chieko Okayama, and my in-laws, Toru and Yuko Ishiwari, have extended unwavering support to me and my family over the years, for which I cannot thank them enough. Last but not least, this book is dedicated to the two women who have not just endured but cheered for its production.

Abbreviations

ABA	American Bar Association
AC	administrative commission
ACUS	Administrative Conference of the United States
AJ	administrative judge
ALJ	administrative law judge
APA	Administrative Procedure Act
CAA	Civil Aeronautics Administration
CAB	Civil Aeronautics Board
FCC	Federal Communications Commission
FPC	Federal Power Commission
FRB	Federal Reserve Board
FRC	Federal Radio Commission
FRS	Federal Reserve System
FTC	Federal Trade Commission
ICC	Interstate Commerce Commission
IRC	independent regulatory commission
ITC	Interstate Trade Commission
NLRB	National Labor Relations Board
NTC	National Transportation Committee
SEC	Securities and Exchange Commission
USSB	United States Shipping Board

Introduction

On January 8, 1937, the President's Committee on Administrative Management, known as the Brownlow Committee after its chair, submitted its final report on federal executive branch reorganization to President Franklin D. Roosevelt. For more than six months the three-member committee and its staff had worked on the project with the aim of devising a reorganization plan that would make the administrative state – a collective term for all policy-implementing government bodies outside the three constitutional branches – more efficient and executive centered.

While the Committee's proposals offered "to make democracy work" in the United States dealt with many aspects of the administrative state, there were two core messages. The first was that "[t]he president needs help": organizational support for the president had to be considerably enhanced. The chief executive's role had expanded so much in the past century and a half since the formation of the federal government that it could no longer be filled by a single individual. In addition to increasing the president's staff, the Committee proposed the creation of the Executive Office of the President, which would assist the president in decision-making. The second message was that, according to the Committee, the workings of administrative agencies were too cumbersome and likely to produce inconsistent policy outputs. The administrative state ought to be streamlined and more responsive to the president, who represented the people of the United States.[1]

The view that the American state lacks order has long been widely shared among political scientists. The same year the Committee was at work, E. Pendleton Herring noted that "the federal administrative services have not been fused into a unified and responsible whole." They were no more than "a conglomeration of service agencies, independent regulatory commissions, and ill-proportioned bureaus and departments." With the hierarchical Weberian state in mind, scholars have described it as "the crazy quilt" and "the Rube Goldberg state." From this standpoint, it should not be surprising that the Committee's prescriptions called

1 The President's Committee on Administrative Management, *Report of the Committee, with Studies of Administrative Management in the Federal Government* (Washington, DC: Government Printing Office, 1937) (hereafter *PCAM Report*), 4, 5. For FDR's executive reorganization, see Richard Polenberg, *Reorganizing Roosevelt's Government: The Controversy over Executive Reorganization, 1936–1939* (Cambridge, MA: Harvard University Press, 1966).

for consolidating some hundred federal agencies into twelve executive departments, two of which were new.[2]

The agencies that would have been most heavily affected were those the Committee termed "the independent regulatory commissions" (IRCs). While the report itself does not offer a precise definition, IRCs are regulatory agencies characterized by such institutional features as multimember panel form, the immunity of members from removal at the president's discretion, and the members' staggered terms that are longer than the four-year term of the president. They are also noted for their case-by-case approach to decision-making and courtlike administrative procedures. Robert Cushman, a political scientist who analyzed the IRCs for the Brownlow Committee, counted ten IRCs starting with the Interstate Commerce Commission (ICC), established in 1887, in his report to the Committee.[3]

For the Brownlow Committee, which was pursuing an efficient administrative state tightly organized around the president, it was only natural for IRCs to be the primary target. In addition to pointing out the clumsiness of the commissions' policy implementation due to its courtlike policy making, the Committee questioned their lack of accountability and unwillingness to cooperate with the administration. This reluctance was what led to the inconsistent outputs for which the president was held responsible. In a well-known passage, the Committee described the IRCs as "a headless 'fourth branch' of the Government" and denounced them as "a haphazard deposit of irresponsible agencies and uncoordinated powers." The Committee's proposed solution to "the problem of the independent regulatory commissions" was to assimilate every IRC into an executive department. Each commission was to be divided into a judicial part conducting formal, courtlike hearings and an administrative part responsible for other policy-making functions and "housekeeping." Both were to be absorbed into an executive department as its bureaus, although the commission's judicial part would retain its autonomy in conducting adjudication.[4]

Curiously, however, the IRC reorganization plan, once described as "the most important by the committee," was not included in the Roosevelt administration's legislative proposals based on the report. The Executive Reorganization

2 Colin Campbell, "The Complex Organization of the Executive Branch: The Legacies of Competing Approaches to Administration," in *The Executive Branch*, ed. Joel D. Aberbach and Mark A. Peterson (New York: Oxford University Press, 2005), 252; Elisabeth S. Clemens, "Lineages of the Rube Goldberg State: Building and Blurring Public Programs, 1900–1940," in *Rethinking Political Institutions: The Art of the State*, ed. Ian Shapiro, Stephen Skowronek, and Daniel Galvin (New York: New York University Press, 2006), 187–215; E. Pendleton Herring, *Public Administration and the Public Interest* (New York: McGraw-Hill, 1936), 9.

3 Mark Allen Eisner, Jeff Worsham, Evan J. Ringquist, and Franchesca Nestor, *Contemporary Regulatory Policy*, 3rd ed. (Boulder: Lynne Rienner, 2018), 37; Robert E. Cushman, "The Problem of Independent Regulatory Commissions," in *PCAM Report*, 208. Also see Paul R. Verkuil, "The Purposes and Limits of Independent Agencies," *Duke Law Journal* 1988 (1988): 257–279.

4 *PCAM Report*, 5, 40.

Act of 1939 materializing some of the Committee proposals also exempted major IRCs from the president's reorganization authority. The Brownlow Committee was still successful in stigmatizing IRCs. The members and staff of the Committee were experts in public administration, where the hierarchical Weberian bureaucracy was becoming the dominant model of the state. In no time, the IRCs were perceived as institutional outliers in the federal bureaucracy. It became commonplace to refer to their difference from other agencies using the expression "quasi-judicial." Aside from describing the courtlike form and procedures of the commissions, the modifier implies that the commissions belied the constitutional separation of powers by its use of quasi-judicial or even all three powers of the government. Cushman's massive *The Independent Regulatory Commissions*, originating in his research for the Committee and published in 1941, was crucial in establishing the IRCs as a distinct – and anomalous – category of government bodies.[5]

As a result, social science research on IRCs stalled after World War II. When the commissions were taken up, it was often in the context of harsh criticism. From the 1950s, influential political scientists such as Samuel Huntington and Merver Bernstein accused IRCs of becoming "captured" by the industries they were supposed to oversee. As administrative law scholar Louis Jaffe notes in his review of Bernstein's work, the attack on the commissions went so far as to make them "a scapegoat."[6] Numerous books and articles with such titles as *The Crisis of the Regulatory Commissions* and *The Interstate Commerce Omission* argued that the commissions, enjoying considerable autonomy in policy making, were either captured by the regulated industries or simply incapable of devising sound regulatory policy. Later political scientists have taken up IRCs more often, but not in ways that highlighted their distinctiveness. Many works treat an IRC as just another administrative agency. Even when the IRC as a category is the focus of attention, researchers more often than not emphasize how much the commissions have

5 Barry D. Karl, *The Uneasy State: The United States from 1915 to 1945* (Chicago: University of Chicago Press, 1983), 157; John A. Rohr, *To Run a Constitution: The Legitimacy of the Administrative State* (Lawrence: University Press of Kansas, 1986), 152–153; Robert E. Cushman, *The Independent Regulatory Commissions* (New York: Oxford University Press, 1941). For an overview of the IRCs' constitutional status, see Louis Fisher, *The Politics of Shared Power: Congress and the Executive*, 4th ed. (College Station: Texas A&M University Press, 1998).

6 Samuel P. Huntington, "The Marasmus of the ICC: The Commission, the Railroads, and the Public Interest," *Yale Law Journal* 61 (1952): 467–509; Marver H. Bernstein, *Regulating Business by Independent Commission* (Princeton: Princeton University Press, 1955), 291–296; Michael Nelson, "A Short, Ironic History of American National Bureaucracy," *Journal of Politics* 44 (1982): 770–772; Louis L. Jaffe, "The Independent Agency: A New Scapegoat," *Yale Law Journal* 65 (1956): 1068; Louis L. Jaffe, "The Effective Limits of the Administrative Process: A Reevaluation," *Harvard Law Review* 67 (1954): 1105–1135. William Novak offers a critical new look at the development of the capture thesis in "A Revisionist History of Regulatory Capture," in *Regulatory Capture: Special Interest Influence and How to Limit It*, ed. Daniel Carpenter and David A. Moss (New York: Cambridge University Press, 2014), 25–48.

in common with executive departments, downplaying their autonomy from the president. The long academic indifference to IRCs is manifested in the fact that more than seven decades after its publication, Cushman's tome is still by far the most cited work on the subject.[7]

Such inattention to IRCs, however, is unfortunate. After all, FDR and the Brownlow Committee attacked the commissions and demanded more oversight from the president because of their enormous presence in the administrative state. The commissions were, and remain, far from peripheral; for most of the twentieth century they collectively controlled such important policy domains as finance, the securities market, antitrust issues, labor relations, energy, transportation, and telecommunication. The presence of such powerful IRCs by the New Deal derived from the fact that they had been considered prototypical agencies ideally suited for regulation. Mark Allen Eisner argues that the commissions were primary regulators of the regulatory regime he calls the "market regime" from the late nineteenth century to the 1920s. Even Bernstein, known for his vicious attack on the commissions, still concedes that they were the most significant regulatory mechanism before 1940. While the most powerful commissions appeared before World War II, IRCs were also popular among postwar legislators; David Lewis reports that almost one in five new federal agencies created during the half century after the war was an independent commission. Although executive agencies undoubtedly grew in importance in the twentieth century, it is impossible to make sense of American state building without taking IRCs fully into account.[8]

7 Bernard Schwartz, *The Professor and the Commissions* (New York: Alfred A. Knopf, 1959); Robert C. Fellmeth, *The Interstate Commerce Omission, the Public Interest and the ICC: The Ralph Nader Study Group Report on the Interstate Commerce Commission* (New York: Viking Press, 1970); Paul W. MacAvoy, ed., *The Crisis of the Regulatory Commissions: An Introduction to a Current Issue of Public Policy* (New York: W. W. Norton, 1970); William E. Brigman, "The Executive Branch and the Independent Regulatory Agencies," *Presidential Studies Quarterly* 11 (1981): 244–261; Lisa Schultz Bressman and Robert B. Thompson, "The Future of Agency Independence," *Vanderbilt Law Review* 63 (2010): 599–672; Charles R. Shipan, *Designing Judicial Review: Interest Groups, Congress, and Communications Policy* (Ann Arbor: University of Michigan Press, 2000); Terry M. Moe, "Regulatory Performance and Presidential Administration," *American Journal of Political Science* 26 (1982): 197–224; Charles T. Goodsell and Ceferina C. Gayo, "Appointive Control of Federal Regulatory Commissions," *Administrative Law Review* 23 (1971): 291–303; Verkuil, "Purposes and Limits"; James O. Freedman, *Crisis and Legitimacy: The Administrative Process and American Government* (New York: Cambridge University Press, 1978), 62–69. But see Marshall J. Breger and Gary J. Edles, *Independent Agencies in the United States: Law, Structure, and Politics* (New York: Oxford University Press, 2015).

8 Mark Allen Eisner, *Regulatory Politics in Transition*, 2nd ed. (Baltimore: Johns Hopkins University Press, 2000); Bernstein, *Regulating Business*, 6. Also see Frederick F. Blachly and Miriam E. Oatman, *Federal Regulatory Action and Control* (Washington, DC: Brookings Institution, 1940), 42; Morton Keller, *Regulating a New Economy: Public Policy and Economic Change in America, 1900–1933* (Cambridge, MA: Harvard University Press, 1990); Robert L. Rabin, "Federal Regulation in Historical Perspective," *Stanford Law Review* 38 (1986): 1188–1326; David E. Lewis, *Presidents and the Politics of Agency Design: Political Insulation in the United States Government Bureaucracy, 1946–1997* (Palo Alto: Stanford University Press, 2003), 45.

How did quasi-judicial IRCs develop and come to play central roles in the United States? In what ways did they impact the course of state building? These important questions have not received sufficient attention either from public administration scholars or political scientists. Cushman's work details the growth of IRCs over the half century from the 1880s to the 1930s. Because of its origin as a staff report for the Brownlow Committee, the work is a compilation of legislative histories of statutes establishing IRCs and modifying their functions and the historical and constitutional background of their emergence and development. While the book is an excellent guide to the politics of IRCs – hence its continuing popularity – Cushman stops short of offering a comprehensive explanation of their institutional growth.[9]

The same could be said of the students of American political development who have analyzed the IRCs out of interest in state building. Even though the scholars of the subfield's founding generation such as Stephen Skowronek, Scott James, and Elizabeth Sanders have greatly contributed to elucidating the rise of major IRCs including the ICC and the Federal Trade Commission (FTC), they do not differentiate the commissions from other types of agencies, just like political science research on contemporary IRCs. As best exemplified in Skowronek's classic *Building a New American State*, they treat them as an early form of "national bureaucracy." This approach to state building invited criticism from Daniel Carpenter, who charged that their attention to IRCs was excessive. Contending that the commissions "figured little in the American policy state" in the twentieth century, he encouraged researchers to analyze executive bureaucracy, as he did in his work. Although Carpenter's assessment that IRCs were inconsequential must be taken with a grain of salt, he has a point. There is not much point in concentrating on IRCs if one sees no meaningful difference between them and executive departments.[10]

This book contends not only that there is indeed such a difference but that it has mattered a great deal to US state building. To make this point, it analyzes the institutional development of IRCs from their emergence in the 1880s to the commissions' institutional consolidation as an established category of agencies in the 1930s. Although Cushman's work covers this half century, this study is original in its treatment of the era and IRCs. It consciously asks why the commissions adopted the courtlike features that made them the chief target of the Brownlow

9 Cushman, *Independent Regulatory Commissions.*

10 Stephen Skowronek, *Building a New American State: The Expansion of National Administrative Capacities, 1877–1920* (New York: Cambridge University Press, 1982); Scott C. James, *Presidents, Parties, and the State: A Party System Perspective on Democratic Regulatory Choice, 1884–1936* (New York: Cambridge University Press, 2000); Elizabeth Sanders, *Roots of Reform: Farmers, Workers, and the American State, 1877–1917* (Chicago: University of Chicago Press, 1999); Daniel P. Carpenter, *The Forging of Bureaucratic Autonomy: Reputations, Networks, and Policy Innovation in Executive Agencies* (Princeton: Princeton University Press, 2001), 8–9; However, see Desmond King and Robert C. Lieberman, "The American State," in *The Oxford Handbook of American Political Development*, ed. Richard M. Valelly, Suzanne Mettler, and Robert C. Lieberman (New York: Oxford University Press, 2016), 238–239.

Committee and how their judicialization impacted administrative state building. Whereas researchers, including Cushman, have tended to explain IRCs' strong judiciality as imposed by the judiciary, this book demonstrates that the ICC, the first IRC, was explicitly modeled after courts in Congress and that its judiciality was inherited by other commissions and executive agencies, largely through legislation.

In addition, this book traces the development of courtlike IRCs in the judicialization of the US administrative state that it promoted. Because of the large presence of IRCs in the administrative state and their status as prototypical agencies, their judicialization had considerable impact on the workings of other parts of the government. Although little known outside legal scholarship, American administrative agencies have been judicialized to a degree unexperienced elsewhere in the world. As discussed in the next chapter, researchers have attributed this to the political clout of American lawyers internalizing the common-law principle of the supremacy of law (or the rule of law) guaranteeing the right to resolve legal conflicts in judicial courts. While admitting that the profession was critical in state judicialization, this book argues that the separation-of-powers system in the United States was equally consequential. It will be shown that the process was kicked off by the creation of the ICC and that the later proliferation of regulation by IRCs into different policy domains led to the dissemination of IRCs' judiciality to executive departments.

This book's primary contribution is to the study of American political development. It provides a new explanation of how the administrative state came to be characterized by judiciality, which has been virtually unnoticed in the social sciences. In doing so, it looks at the hitherto marginalized IRCs in a new light and situates them at the core of America's courtlike administrative state. The research on the administrative state used to be interested in the capacity of state apparatus and how it developed, analyzing such elements as policy expertise and autonomy from elected politicians, and this has also been the case with the United States.[11] The focus was on *what* the state could do. In contrast, many of the more recent works on administrative state building, both in political science and legal history, are interested in how agencies implement policy. For instance, Sean Farhang and Quinn Mulroy demonstrate how the Department of Justice promoted the use of litigation in achieving the improvement of African American civil rights in the 1960s. Legal historians such as Daniel Ernst and Joanna Grisinger have also explored the legal and political battles over administrative procedures. As Grisinger notes, they are primarily interested in *how* the state operates. This book joins forces with these scholars in investigating the different manners in which the state functions, but it goes further in arguing that institutional form also matters; the modern American state from the turn of the twentieth century not only

11 Peter B. Evans, Dietrich Rueschemeyer, and Theda Skocpol, eds., *Bringing the State Back In* (Cambridge: Cambridge University Press, 1985); Kenneth Finegold and Theda Skocpol, *State and Party in America's New Deal* (Madison: University of Wisconsin Press, 1995); Skowronek, *Building a New American State*; Carpenter, *Forging of Bureaucratic Autonomy*.

has done things in ways similar to courts but also was designed like them for the purpose.[12]

That is not all this book has to offer, however. As a study of the judicialized administrative state, it makes an innovation in the scholarship on its two elements, judicialization and the administrative state. This book adds a new dimension to the research on the judicialization of politics. In studying the phenomenon commonly observed around the globe today, scholars invariably focus on the expanding role of judicial courts in the political process. That is not the only way in which politics could be judicialized, though. As this book shows, the political process could also bear attributes of court proceedings through the judicialization of nonjudicial government bodies. The case of the US administrative state judicialization taken up in this study clearly illustrates that the judicialization of politics had taken place in such a way long before it appeared elsewhere.

This book also shows a new way of analyzing administrative state building. The scholarship of comparative state building has perceived the American state as a "laggard" because of the late arrival and limited penetration of the hierarchical Weberian bureaucracy characterized by efficiency and accountability to the chief executive. This study demonstrates that the United States instead saw the rise of a highly developed courtlike state. Major US administrative agencies took after judicial courts and became government bodies prioritizing the pursuit of fairness in decision-making through their formal procedures and autonomy. The literature has failed to grasp the significance of such a fairness-oriented administrative state, antithetical to the efficiency-oriented Weberian bureaucracy that has been the standard model of the administrative state. This book argues that fairness, widely considered a core value of public administration along with efficiency, should be taken more seriously in studies of administrative state building. The United States is an excellent example of the significance of fairness as a goal of administrative state building.[13]

From the next chapter, this book explores how the modern US administrative state became judicialized primarily through the institutional development of the IRCs, from their emergence in the 1880s to the New Deal. As such, this book focuses on the adjudicatory functions of the commissions, even though

12 Sean Farhang, *The Litigation State: Public Regulation and Private Lawsuits in the U.S.* (Princeton: Princeton University Press, 2010); Quinn Mulroy, "Public Regulation through Private Litigation: The Regulatory Power of Private Lawsuits and the American Bureaucracy." (Ph.D. diss., Columbia University, 2012); Daniel R. Ernst, *Tocqueville's Nightmare: The Administrative State Emerges in America, 1900–1940* (New York: Oxford University Press, 2014); Joanna L. Grisinger, *The Unwieldy American State: Administrative Politics since the New Deal* (New York: Cambridge University Press, 2012), 4. Also see Joanna Lynn Grisinger, "Reforming the State: Reorganization and the Federal Government, 1937–1964." (Ph.D. diss., University of Chicago, 2005), 31.

13 In its emphasis on the departure of the American administrative state from the Weberian model, see Clemens, "Rube Goldberg State"; Nicholas R. Parrillo, *Against the Profit Motive: The Salary Revolution in American Government, 1780–1940* (New Haven: Yale University Press, 2013), esp. 359–361.

they also engage in a wide range of activities such as investigation and policy-related research. While this definitely is a limitation of this work, quasi-judicial and quasi-legislative policy making through formal hearings was the most powerful way in which agencies influenced society, at least until the mid-twentieth century, and deserves its own study. In the course of discussion, several important but unanswered questions on the origins and development of major commissions will be tackled.

After recasting this book's research question in terms of the judicialization of the US administrative state, Chapter One reviews the literature on the causes of the judicialization and explains how this book overcomes its limitations. While this study agrees with the previous research that the influence of common-law lawyers seeking to impose judiciality on administrative agencies was an important cause, it shows that existing scholarship cannot fully explain why extensive judicialization took place solely in the United States and only from the late nineteenth century. The chapter complements them by proposing that the institutional combination of the common law and the separation of powers differentiated the United States from other countries in the degree of state judicialization. It also argues that judicialization was triggered by the establishment of the ICC modeled after judicial courts and then promoted by the institutional development of IRCs.

Chapter Two begins the historical analysis by revisiting the origins and early workings of the ICC, which was introduced to regulate railroad rates. The IRCs have been treated as an institutional outlier in the US administrative state under the assumption that the ICC, the first IRC, resembled state-level railroad commissions. Through an intensive reinvestigation of the legislative creation of the 1887 act that established the ICC, the chapter demonstrates that such a view is unfounded. Although inspired by state-level commissions, the ICC was actually designed with judicial courts in mind out of concern for the supremacy of law and was intentionally operated in a courtlike fashion from its early years. By the Progressive Era, the ICC was widely considered a model administrative agency because of its strong judiciality. The administrative state judicialization was initiated by the creation and development of the commission.

Chapter Three shows that the ICC came to be viewed as a model for other government bodies in the early twentieth century because of its judiciality by looking at the creation of the Federal Reserve System (FRS) in 1913. It pays close attention to the institutional construction of the Federal Reserve Board (FRB), categorized as an IRC despite being part of a central banking system. Although it now has a firm footing in the federal government, the reason for Americans' acceptance of the creation of a new central banking system in spite of their strong hatred of powerful bankers in the aftermath of the Panic of 1907 has remained a mystery. This chapter argues that agency judiciality was the key. The Woodrow Wilson administration sold the FRS to the Americans by describing the FRB as an ICC-like regulator overseeing the reserve banks. In doing so, the administration treated the ICC as a tribunal just as authoritative as the US Supreme Court. The fact that the FRB, with almost no adjudicatory functions, could still be linked to the ICC and the Supreme Court without pressure from lawyers confirms that the courtlike ICC was already accepted as the dominant model of administrative agencies among the contemporaries.

Despite their popularity, IRCs soon faced powerful challengers. Chapter Four takes up the years from the mid-1910s to the Herbert Hoover administration, when the IRCs underwent gradual retrenchment as the federal government introduced a variety of new regulations. The attack on IRCs came from all three branches of the government. The presidents either attempted to limit the autonomy of new IRCs or sought to give the new regulatory authority to executive departments to gain control over policy implementation. Although the judiciality of IRCs was highly regarded in Congress, many members feared that creating an IRC for every new regulation was too irresponsible fiscally and began to back the presidential proposals. The Supreme Court dealt a blow to the IRCs in the 1926 *Myers v. United States* decision by declaring that the chief executive had the constitutional power to fire any IRC member at will.

Chapter Five analyzes how the IRCs not only regained autonomy from the president but also consolidated their position in the federal government during the New Deal. The Supreme Court decision in *Myers* made the presidents tolerant of the now-nonindependent commissions, and this ironically led to the addition of powerful commissions. Furthermore, the Court unexpectedly reversed its position in 1935 and reinstated the commissions' autonomy from the chief executive. Furious with the ruling, FDR instructed the Brownlow Committee, formed in 1936, to come up with a reorganization plan including a scheme to abolish IRCs. The advisory committee and its staff composed of experts in public administration, however, were unable to justify the replacement of IRCs with executive departments, as any such reform would come at the cost of procedural fairness in administrative policy making. While FDR insisted that the committee go forward with the plan to absorb IRCs into executive departments, he faced strong opposition, and it never even appeared in the administration's reorganization bills. The failure of FDR's attack on IRCs confirmed that the commissions had become a permanent fixture in the federal government.

In the next ten years, the pendulum swung further toward state judicialization. The conclusion shows how the joint effort made by congressional conservatives and the leaders of the American Bar Association resulted in the adoption of the Administrative Procedure Act (APA) of 1946, which included provisions on formal adjudication and hearing examiners, both modeled after those of IRCs. This book closes with a discussion of the lasting impact of the IRC-centered judicialized administrative state established in the first half of the twentieth century, despite the gradual loss of judiciality it would experience later in the century.

1 Why did the US administrative state judicialize?

In the United States today, around 150,000 removal cases that will determine the fate of asylum seekers and noncitizens suspected of unlawfully staying in, or attempting to enter, the country are annually completed by some three hundred immigration judges distributed among more than 50 immigration courts around the country. The courts hold formal hearings presided by the judges who are given such powers as administering oaths and subpoenaing witnesses. The courtrooms are configured to hold adversarial hearings, and the judges wear black robes, hold gavels, and make full records of proceedings. Immigration courts and judges, however, are not part of the judicial branch prescribed in Article III of the US Constitution. Technically speaking, the judges are administrative officers, and since 1983, the tribunals have been affiliated with the Executive Office for Immigration Review, a division of the Department of Justice.[1]

Immigration is not the only policy domain in which agency decisions are made in a courtlike manner. US administrative agencies employ approximately two thousand administrative law judges (ALJs), experienced lawyers charged with presiding over formal hearings. The most extensive role played by the ALJ corps is the conduct of hearings on retirement, survivors, disability insurance, and supplemental securities income benefits at the Social Security Administration (SSA), with which four in five ALJs are affiliated. Once named by the Supreme Court of the United States as "the largest adjudicative agency in the western world," the ALJs receive more than 700,000 requests for hearings each year today.[2] While

1 US Department of Justice, Executive Office for Immigration Review, *Statistics Yearbook, Fiscal Year 2017* (2017), www.justice.gov/eoir/statistical-year-book (last accessed Dec. 4, 2018), 13; For a good overview of the immigration judiciary, see Arnold & Porter LLP, *Reforming the Immigration System* (Washington, DC: American Bar Association Commission on Immigration, 2010), Pt. 2. Also see Paul Grussendorf, *My Trials: Inside America's Deportation Factories*, 2nd ed. (North Charleston, SC: CreateSpace Publishing, 2012). On the historical background of the judicialization of deportation proceedings, see Lucy E. Salyer, *Laws Harsh as Tigers: Chinese Immigrants and the Shaping of Modern Immigration Law* (Chapel Hill: University of North Carolina Press, 1995), esp. Pt. 2.

2 "Administrative Law Judges," US Office of Personnel Management website, www.opm.gov/services-for-agencies/administrative-law-judges/#url=ALJs-by-Agency (last accessed Dec. 26, 2018); *Heckler v. Campbell*, 461 U.S. 458 (1983), at 461, n. 2, quoting Jerry L. Mashaw,

their proceedings are not strictly adversarial and their procedures less formal than those of judicial courts, the hearings are still considered very courtlike. The ALJs, said to constitute America's "hidden" or "invisible" judiciary, enjoy considerable autonomy from other agency officers, including agency heads, in making decisions. Although not as extensive as the protection extended to Article III judges, they also receive substantial status protection regarding tenure and salaries. The hiring agency cannot instruct its ALJs to conduct investigative and prosecutorial functions or review their performance. They can be removed only for good cause, after a formal hearing by the Merit Systems Protection Board, an independent quasi-judicial agency.[3]

While not widely known, quasi-judicial adjudication has long been a hallmark of US public administration. In arguing that the Americans historically "kept administration largely in the courts and in *private* hands," William Forbath points out that even "where non-judicial *public* officials did gain authority, we *judicialized* the way these public officials exercise administrative power" [emphases in original]. Agency judiciality has two components: institutionalized autonomy of agency members from elected public officials, especially the president, and formal, courtlike procedures usually featuring adversarial settings, cross-examination of witnesses, and the taking of full records.[4] The ALJs and formal hearings are both prescribed in the APA that covers all federal agencies. Most formal hearings

---

Charles J. Goetz, Frank I. Goodman, Warren F. Schwartz, Paul R. Verkuil, and Milton M. Carrow, *Social Security Hearings and Appeals: A Study of the Social Security Administration Hearing System* (Lexington, MA: Lexington Books, 1978), xi; US Government Accountability Office, *Social Security Disability: Additional Measures and Evaluation Needed to Enhance Accuracy and Consistency of Hearings Decisions* (Washington, DC: Government Accountability Office, 2017), 11.

3 Chris Guthrie, Jeffrey J. Rachlinski, and Andrew J. Wistrich, "The 'Hidden Judiciary': An Empirical Examination of Executive Branch Justice," *Duke Law Journal* 2009 (2009): 1477–1530; William D. Schreckhise, Daniel E. Chand, and Nicholas P. Lovrich, "Decision Making in the Hidden Judiciary: Institutions, Recruitment, and Responsiveness Among U.S. Administrative Law Judges," *Administrative Theory and Praxis* 40 (2018): 119–142; Jeffrey S. Lubbers, "Federal Administrative Law Judges: A Focus on Our Invisible Judiciary," *Administrative Law Review* 33 (1981): 109–131; Daniel L. Skoler, "The Administrative Law Judiciary: Change, Challenge, and Choices," *Annals of the American Academy of Political and Social Science* 462 (1982): 34–47; Kent Barnett, "Why Bias Challenges to Administrative Adjudication Should Succeed," *Missouri Law Review* 81 (2016): 1025–1026; Jeffrey B. Litwak, ed., *A Guide to Federal Agency Adjudication*, 2nd ed. (Chicago: American Bar Association, 2012), Ch. 10.

4 William E. Forbath, "The Long Life of Liberal America: Law and State-Building in the U.S. and England," *Law and History Review* 24 (2006): 183; Ernst, *Tocqueville's Nightmare*, 2–5. Different from some works, the influence of judicial courts on administrative agencies is not included in the definition of judiciality, as it is widely considered a *cause* of agency judiciality. Loren A. Smith, "Judicialization: The Twilight of Administrative Law," *Duke Law Journal* 1985 (1985): 428. Ralph F. Fuchs, "Fairness and Effectiveness in Administrative Agency Organization and Procedures," *Indiana Law Journal* 36 (1960): 26–27. While agency independence could take different forms, this book concentrates on the adjudicators' protection from discretionary removal because of its interest in agency judiciality. See *Free Enterprise Fund v. Public Company Accounting Oversight Board*, 561 U.S. 477 (2010).

today are conducted by ALJs and other officers generically known as administrative judges (AJs). Immigration judges are among the most prominent example of AJs. The use of courtlike hearings, however, has not always been limited to those conducted by such officers specializing in adjudication. Until the mid-twentieth century, formal adjudication was the primary mode of agency policy making in the United States. The origins of the ALJ system could be traced to the hearing examiners introduced by the Hepburn Act of 1906. The examiners were to hold formal hearings regarding railroad regulation on behalf of the members of the ICC who, after two decades of officiating all hearings themselves, were no longer able to catch up with increasingly heavy caseloads. Other agencies soon followed suit, although heads of executive agencies also conducted formal hearings. Agencies have used courtlike hearings not just to carry out the quasi-judicial function of discretionary interpretation and application of law to individual cases but also for quasi-legislative rulemaking, such as setting new railroad tariffs.[5]

The United States is the only industrialized democracy in which formal, courtlike adjudication ever became the primary mode of making policy decisions at major administrative agencies. As Bernard Schwartz and H. W. R. Wade comment in their comparative study of British and American administrative law, "[a]dministrative procedure in the United States has acquired most of the attributes of courtroom procedure" to the degree that "must strike a foreign observer forcibly."[6] American administrative agencies have had a pronounced tendency to make policy using courtlike hearings. True, formal hearings have been used extensively elsewhere in the world by government bodies reviewing agency decisions such as the French *Conseil d'État* and the Administrative Appeals Tribunal in Australia. But arguably, no country has come close to the judicialization of first-order agency decision-making in the United States. As will be discussed in the conclusion, the judiciality of the American administrative process has eroded since the mid-twentieth century but still characterizes the US public administration in a profound way.[7]

5 Paul R. Verkuil, "Reflections upon the Federal Administrative Judiciary," *UCLA Law Review* 39 (1992): 1341–1363; For an overview of AJs, see Michael Asimow, *Adjudication Outside the Administrative Procedure Act* (Washington, DC: Administrative Conference of the Unite States, 2016) and Kent H. Barnett and Russell Wheeler, "Non-ALJ Adjudicators in Federal Agencies: Status, Selection, Oversight, and Removal," *Georgia Law Review* 53 (2019): 1–127; Blachly and Oatman, *Federal Regulatory Action and Control*, 59–65; Kent Barnett, "How the Supreme Court Derailed Formal Rulemaking," *George Washington Law Review Arguendo* 85 (2017): 1–24.

6 Bernard Schwartz and H. W. R. Wade, *Legal Control of Government: Administrative Law in Britain and the United States* (Oxford: Clarendon Press, 1972), 107; Bernard Schwartz, *American Administrative Law* (London: Sir Isaac Pitman & Sons, 1950); H. W. R. Wade, *Towards Administrative Justice* (Ann Arbor: University of Michigan Press, 1963), 52–53.

7 Frederick Davis, "Judicialization of Administrative Law: The Trial-type Hearing and the Changing Status of the Hearing Officer," *Duke Law Journal* 1977 (1977): 389–408; Marshall E. Dimock, *Law and Dynamic Administration* (New York: Praeger, 1980), Chs. 1 and 10; Peter Cane, "Judicial Review and Merits Review: Comparing Administrative Adjudication by Courts and Tribunals," in *Comparative Administrative Law*, ed. Susan Rose-Ackerman

Why and how did the United States alone come to experience this exceptionally high degree of administrative state judicialization? This is an intriguing question, as the judiciality in administrative decision-making strongly affects American governance, and not all of its features are popular. Consuming much more time and other types of costs before reaching a decision than other modes of policy making, courtlike adjudication has been frequently criticized for its inefficiency. Immigration courts have produced backlogs of hundreds of thousands of cases, and on average, it now takes around five hundred days to process a case. Although such a logjam definitely owes much to increasing caseloads and the government's failure to supply the courts with sufficient organizational and human resources, there is no doubt that the formality of proceedings is a principal cause of the prolonged wait time. The situation is similar for disability hearings at the SSA. An average applicant for pension payment must wait for more than a year before being heard by an ALJ after the denial of the initial claim by an SSA state office.[8]

Courtlike agencies have also been susceptible to inconsistency. Even if each adjudicator decides cases consistently, their autonomy impedes coherence among adjudicators. As a result, the state inevitably lacks uniformity in policy. The disposition and allowance rates for ALJ adjudication on disability insurance at the SSA and deportation rates for immigration judges, for instance, have very high variation across judges. Certain personal attributes of the ALJs, such as gender, party affiliation, and previous career, are known to have strong correlation with their conclusions. Some ALJs stand out for unusually high rates of overturning state office decisions, even raising the suspicion that they are not interpreting the law and facts carefully. Significant variation has also been found between immigration courts and ALJs in different states. There is a marked difference in the proportion of deportation decisions not only between immigration judges with different personalities but also between immigration courts in different regions. This haphazardness regarding deportation proceedings has been described as "refugee roulette." While some inconsistency is unavoidable in similar institutional

---

and Peter L. Lindseth (Cheltenham, UK: Edward Elgar, 2010), 426–448; Reuel Schiller, "The Historical Origins of American Regulatory Exceptionalism," in *Comparative Law and Regulation*, ed. Francesca Bignami and David Zaring (Cheltenham, UK: Edward Elgar, 2016), 55–72; Michael Asimow and Jeffrey S. Lubbers, "The Merits of 'Merits Review': A Comparative Look at the Australian Administrative Appeals Tribunal," *AIAL Forum* 67 (2011): 58–79; Daniel L. Skoler and Cynthia E. Weixel, "Social Security Adjudication in Five Nations," *Administrative Law Review* 33 (1981): 281; Peter Cane, *Administrative Tribunals and Adjudication* (Portland, OR: Hart Publishing, 2009), esp. Ch. 1.

8 For latest figures, see Transactional Records Access Clearinghouse, "Average Time Pending Cases Have Been Waiting in Immigration Courts," http://trac.syr.edu/phptools/immigration/court_backlog/apprep_backlog_avgdays.php (last accessed Dec. 26, 2018); Transactional Records Access Clearinghouse, "Backlog of Pending Cases in Immigration Courts as of December 2017," http://trac.syr.edu/phptools/immigration/court_backlog/apprep_backlog.php (last accessed Dec. 26, 2018); US Social Security Administration, *Leading the Hearings and Appeals Process into the Future: A Plan for Compassionate and Responsive Service* (2016), www.gao.gov/assets/690/688824.pdf (last accessed Dec. 26, 2018).

settings – judicial courts are also known for it – it has been a point of attack from those who prefer more centralized policy making.[9]

Criticisms of inefficiency and inconsistency of courtlike administrative adjudication have been heard from both within and outside the government. The Brownlow Committee was an early example. In an attempt to increase efficiency, in April 1961 President John F. Kennedy created the Administrative Conference of the United States (ACUS), an advisory committee of experienced administrators and scholars of public administration and administrative law, and instructed it to study administrative procedures and suggest improvements. In the executive order announcing its establishment, Kennedy cited the "increasing concern over the efficiency and adequacy of department and agency procedures" as a chief reason for his action. The ACUS was made a permanent body in 1964 through legislation, and the improvement of both immigration and disability claim adjudications has been an important part of its agenda over the years.[10]

Why were the agencies given judiciality if there were such serious drawbacks? The courtlike government bodies have also been accused of being unaccountable and elitist because of their autonomy. Despite its long tradition and deep roots in the American state, judicialization has received little scholarly attention. In public administration, the judiciality of American agencies has largely gone unnoticed. An important exception is research by David Rosenbloom and the "constitutional school" in which he has played a leading role. Giving the Constitution and the supremacy of law the status of the "central legitimating forces that hold the American administrative state together," scholars often take note of the courtlike character of American agencies in their research.[11] Still, in his work

9 Mashaw et al., *Social Security Hearings and Appeals*; Harold J. Krent and Scott Morris, *Achieving Greater Consistency in Social Security Disability Adjudication: An Empirical Study and Suggested Reforms* (Washington, DC: Administrative Conference of the United States, 2013); Social Security Advisory Board, *Aspects of Disability Decision Making: Data and Materials* (2012), available at www.ssab.gov/Details-Page/ArticleID/217/CHARTBOOK-Aspects-of-Disability-Decision-Making-Data-and-Materials-February-2012 (last accessed Dec. 4, 2018); US Government Accountability Office, *Social Security Disability*; Jaya Ramji-Nogales, Andrew I. Schoenholtz, and Philip G. Schrag, *Refugee Roulette: Disparities in Asylum Adjudication and Proposals for Reform* (New York: New York University Press, 2009); Rebecca Hamlin, *Let Me Be a Refugee: Administrative Justice and the Politics of Asylum in the United States, Canada, and Australia* (New York: Oxford University Press, 2014), 70–75; Banks Miller, Linda Camp Keith, and Jennifer S. Holmes, *Immigration Judges and U.S. Asylum Policy* (Philadelphia: University of Pennsylvania Press, 2015); Arnold & Porter LLP, *Reforming the Immigration System*.

10 John F. Kennedy, Executive Order 10934, Establishing the Administrative Conference of the United States, April 13, 1961; Paul R. Verkuil, "A Study of Immigration Procedures," *UCLA Law Review* 31 (1984): 1141–1207; Paul R. Verkuil, "Meeting the Mashaw Test for Consistency in Administrative Decision-Making," in *Administrative Law from the Inside Out: Essays on Themes in the Work of Jerry L. Mashaw*, ed. Nicholas R. Parrillo (New York: Cambridge University Press, 2017), 239–246.

11 Stephanie P. Newbold and David H. Rosenbloom, eds., *The Constitutional School of American Public Administration* (New York: Routledge, 2017), 3; Douglas F. Morgan, Kent

on Congress's effort to create "legislative-centered" public administration after World War II, Rosenbloom simply notes that before the adoption of the APA, administrative agencies were not required to "adhere to legislative or judicial values" when performing quasi-legislative or quasi-judicial functions, which suggests that agencies were not heavily judicialized before the war. The situation is not much different in political science despite the discipline's strong interest in the judicialization of politics. Students of American political development have paid scant attention to administrative state judiciality. Sarah Staszak's chapter-long discussion on the judicialized agency policy making after World War II is an important exception, but it does not explore how and why administrative state judicialization occurred.[12]

In stark contrast to the neglect from social scientists, the strong judiciality of US agencies has been common knowledge in legal studies. But systematic investigation on its origins has just begun. To many legal scholars whose gold standard of hearings is court proceedings, American administrative hearings highly judicialized in comparative terms do not seem courtlike enough to make their judiciality a subject that merits deep inquiry. The lawyers' standard perception of administrative state judicialization is not a positive one of strong judiciality of agencies but, as James Freeman notes, a negative one of "departure from judicial norms." In their eyes, the procedures of administrative adjudication not only look informal but also often involve the notorious judge-prosecutor combination that is unthinkable in a judicial trial. In accordance with such a view, Staszak discusses the significant role judicialized agencies played after the war in the context of judicial retrenchment and deprivation of access to the judiciary. The decline of formal agency hearings from the mid-twentieth century has certainly strengthened the lawyers' impression that administrative state judiciality is not worthy of their attention.[13]

Daniel Ernst's *Tocqueville's Nightmare* stands out in its focus on judicialization and its cause. Ernst argues that Americans relied on common law's "court-centered notion of the rule of law" that had been inherited from England in their attempt to tame the administrative state and that it resulted in the pervasion of legalism in the state emergent in the twentieth century. This legal conception, according to Ernst, was made popular among American lawyers through English constitutional scholar Albert V. Dicey's *Lectures Introductory to the Study of the*

A. Kirwan, John A. Rohr, David H. Rosenbloom, and David Lewis Schaefer, "Recovering, Restoring, and Renewing the Foundations of American Public Administration," *Public Administration Review* 70 (2010): 621–633; David H. Rosenbloom, *Public Administration and Law*, 3rd ed. (Boca Raton, FL: CRC Press, 2010).

12 David H. Rosenbloom, *Building a Legislative-Centered Public Administration: Congress and the Administrative State, 1946–1999* (Tuscaloosa: University of Alabama Press, 2000), 147. Also see David H. Rosenbloom, "Retrofitting the Administrative State to the Constitution: Congress and the Judiciary's Twentieth-Century Progress," *Public Administration Review* 60 (2000): 39–46; Sarah Staszak, *No Day in Court: Access to Justice and the Politics of Judicial Retrenchment* (New York: Oxford University Press, 2015), Ch. 5.

13 Freedman, *Crisis and Legitimacy*, Ch. 3; Staszak, *No Day in Court*; Grisinger, *Unwieldy American State*, 20.

Law of the Constitution originally published in 1885. Ernst argues for what he calls "procedural (or institutional) Diceyism," the notion that the procedures in administrative hearings should emulate those of courts, which came to form the basis of American lawyers' foundational view on the topic. He demonstrates how courts and lawyers worked together to make sure that public administration "approximated the structure, procedures, and logic of the judiciary."[14]

Ernst is not the first to point out the impact of the supremacy of law principle and the role of Dicey and his work in American administrative state building. Still, offering critical episodes in which leading jurists inside and outside the judiciary strove to make and keep administrative agencies judicialized during the first four decades of the twentieth century, his is the most granular and sophisticated study on the subject to date. According to the principle, as Dicey and others have emphasized, citizens are entitled to have their legal disputes adjudicated by judicial courts, which are in charge of determining the individuals' rights and liberties through litigation. Also, everyone, including government officials, must be subjected to the same set of laws. The supremacy of law constitutes the fundamental doctrine in the Anglo-American legal tradition. It signifies that government bodies other than judicial courts are not supposed to rule, at least not with finality. This is why adjudication by administrative agencies "strikes the Anglo-American lawyer as such a novel and challenging thing."[15]

While Ernst's explanation of US state judicialization stressing the impact of the supremacy of law makes much sense, it also leaves a question unanswered: why didn't the same thing happen in other common-law jurisdictions? Although administrative state judicialization did take place in some other jurisdictions, such as England and Canada, it was limited in its depth and persistence compared to that of the United States. The administrative state has been much more judicialized in the United States than in fellow common-law jurisdictions, both quantitatively and qualitatively. One reason is that administrative decisions tend to be made using procedures that are more courtlike by agencies more autonomous from other government officials in the United States. In her study of refugee policy-making process taking up the cases of Australia, Canada, the United Kingdom, and the United States, Rebecca Hamlin shows that the American style of removal proceedings involving the immigration courts is much more courtlike than the other three cases.[16]

14 Ernst, *Tocqueville's Nightmare*, 2–3, 5, 30–33; Daniel R. Ernst, "Morgan and the New Dealers," *Journal of Policy History* 20 (2008): 447–481; Albert V. Dicey, *Lectures Introductory to the Study of the Law of the Constitution* (London: Macmillan, 1885); James M. Landis, *The Administrative Process* (New Haven: Yale University Press, 1938), 124. See G. Edward White, *The Constitution and the New Deal* (Cambridge, MA: Harvard University Press, 2000), Ch. 4, for an excellent overview of the judiciary's early involvement in administrative procedures.

15 Dicey, *Law of the Constitution*, 174–218; Ernst, *Tocqueville's Nightmare*, 30; John Dickinson, *Administrative Justice and the Supremacy of Law in the United States* (New York: Russell and Russell, 1927), 6, 32–35.

16 Schwartz and Wade, *Legal Control of Government*; Henry Parris, *Constitutional Bureaucracy: The Development of British Central Administration since the Eighteenth Century* (London: George Allen & Unwin, 1969); Henry M. Bates, "Trends in American Government," in

Another reason is that judicialization in the United States extends to different types of administrative agencies, including those "multi-function" agencies that exercise all three powers of the government, such as executive departments and IRCs. The fact that the APA prescribing formal hearings and ALJs applies to all agencies signifies it. In contrast, most of the courtlike agencies in other jurisdictions have been mono-function ones only engaging in quasi-judicial adjudication; multi-function agencies have rarely thrived in other common-law jurisdictions. Their proliferation in the United Kingdom was short lived, and their large presence in Canada since World War II is often attributed to the influence of the United States.[17]

The influence of the supremacy of law principle – called "natural justice" in other common-law countries – cannot explain different degrees of administrative state judicialization between common-law jurisdictions. Then why does the "legality" of American administrative process stand out even among Anglo American countries, as Guy Peters and others suggest?[18]

One possibility is the difference in the magnitude of political influence of lawyers as a profession. The impact of the common-law principle may have been different between jurisdictions due to the varying political impact of its agents. In fact, there is a tacit understanding that the political clout of lawyers was behind agency judicialization in the United States. America, according to Bernard Schwartz, is a "lawyer-dominated society," and the profession has imposed judicial procedures on administrative agencies out of a strong preference for, and stakes in, court proceedings. The lawyers' deep involvement in the adoption of the Administrative Procedure Act of 1946 through the American Bar Association (ABA), its national organ, is a most notable case. The ABA itself later stated that "Familiarity of lawyers with formal courtroom procedures led them to assume that these or some close approximation are the only proper way to reach an official decision."[19] This view is shared by legal historians studying administra-

Morrison Foundation Lectures, ed. State Bar of California (San Francisco: Alexander F. Morrison Lectureship Foundation, 1940), 98; G. Bruce Doern, Michael J. Prince, and Richard J. Schultz, *Rules and Unruliness: Canadian Regulatory Democracy, Governance, Capitalism, and Welfarism* (Montreal: McGill-Queen's University Press, 2014), Ch. 5; Hamlin, *Let Me Be a Refugee*.

17 Cane, *Administrative Tribunals and Adjudication*, 69–70; Peter Cane, *Controlling Administrative Power: A Historical Comparison* (Cambridge: Cambridge University Press, 2016), 39–42; Ron Ellis, *Unjust by Design: Canada's Administrative Justice System* (Vancouver: UBC Press, 2013), 35; Richard Schultz, "Regulatory Agencies and the Dilemmas of Delegation," in *The Administrative State in Canada: Essays in Honour of J. E. Hodgetts*, ed. O. P. Dwivedi (Toronto: University of Toronto Press, 1982), 89–106.

18 Frederick F. Schauer, "English Natural Justice and American Due Process: An Analytical Comparison," *William and Mary Law Review* 18 (1976): 47–72; B. Guy Peters, "Administrative Traditions and the Anglo-American Democracies," in *Civil Service Systems in Anglo-American Countries*, ed. John Halligan (Cheltenham, UK: Edward Elgar, 2003), 10–26; C. D. Foster, *Privatization, Public Ownership and the Regulation of Natural Monopoly* (Oxford: Blackwell, 1992), esp. Chs. 2 and 7; Asimow and Lubbers, "Merits of 'Merits Review.'"

19 Bernard Schwartz, *Administrative Law* (Boston: Little, Brown, 1976), 292; Ronen Shamir, *Managing Legal Uncertainty: Elite Lawyers in the New Deal* (Durham: Duke University

tive state building. Morton Horwitz argues in his classic work that the degree of judiciality in administrative adjudications was a major point of negotiation in the politics of the administrative state in the twentieth century. He notes the "enormous influence" of law and lawyers in American society and the "unusual power" the courts have wielded in American government and treats them as a given in his analysis. Ernst's work offers a nuanced explanation of how and why common-law lawyers, a "powerful profession," sought to judicialize the administrative state.[20]

This book does not dispute the impact of common law and lawyers internalizing its principles on the judicialization of the US administrative state. Many, if not most, of the major actors who appear in this book's historical narrative are lawyers. But it also contends that their influence alone cannot explain why and how only the United States experienced extensive administrative state judicialization. Given the generally high social prestige of the legal profession around the globe, especially in industrialized states, the power of lawyers cannot in itself show why extreme judicialization took place only in the United States. For instance, Alastair Davidson stresses the power of lawyers in explaining state building in Australia. There also is the difficulty of measuring the political influence of lawyers. After all, constructing a shared definition of the profession across jurisdictions is an intellectual challenge in itself.[21]

It would be unfair, however, to judge the power of the legal profession as an explanatory variable without factoring in its intended scope, which undoubtedly is confined to the United States. Moreover, the influence of common-law

---

Press, 1995); Bernstein, *Regulating Business*, 15; George B. Shepard, "Fierce Compromise: The Administrative Procedure Act Emerges from New Deal Politics," *Northwestern University Law Review* 90 (1996): 1557–1683; Nicholas S. Zeppos, "The Legal Profession and the Development of Administrative Law," *Chicago-Kent Law Review* 72 (1997): 1119–1157; Dimock, *Dynamic Administration*, Ch. 1. Also see William C. Chase, *The American Law School and the Rise of Administrative Government* (Madison: University of Wisconsin Press, 1982); Jerold S. Auerbach, *Unequal Justice: Lawyers and Social Change in Modern America* (New York: Oxford University Press, 1976); Commission on Law and the Economy, American Bar Association, *Federal Regulation: Roads to Reform* (Chicago: American Bar Association, 1979), 10.

20 Morton J. Horwitz, *The Transformation of American Law, 1870–1960: The Crisis of Legal Orthodoxy* (New York: Oxford University Press, 1992), 221–222; Skowronek, *Building a New American State*; Grisinger, *Unwieldy American State*, 6. Also see John A. Rohr, *Civil Servants and Their Constitutions* (Lawrence: University Press of Kansas, 2002), 80; Williamjames Hull Hoffer, *To Enlarge the Machinery of Government: Congressional Debates and the Growth of the American State, 1858–1891* (Baltimore: Johns Hopkins University Press, 2007), 198–199; Ernst, *Tocqueville's Nightmare*, 5.

21 A large majority of members of Congress during the period studied in this book was lawyers. Howard W. Allen and Robert Slagter, "Congress in Crisis: Changes in Personnel and the Legislative Agenda in the U.S. Congress in the 1890s," *Social Science History* 16 (1992): 407. Robert Harrison, *Congress, Progressive Reform, and the New American State* (New York: Cambridge University Press, 2004), 14; Alastair Davidson, *The Invisible State: The Formation of the Australian State, 1788–1901* (Melbourne: Cambridge University Press, 1991); Dietrich Rueschemeyer, *Lawyers and Their Society: A Comparative Study of the Legal Profession in Germany and in the United States* (Cambridge, MA: Harvard University Press, 1973).

lawyers cannot fully account for the American case. The problem is with the *timing* of judicialization. When the legal-profession explanation of state judiciality appeared, there was a consensus that the administrative state did not appear in the United States until the late nineteenth century. But recent scholarship has firmly established that some form of the administrative state has been present since the early republic. While the explanation would still hold had the American state been judicialized in the nineteenth century, that was not the case. Jerry Mashaw's magisterial work unearthing a rich tradition of discretionary administrative adjudication and rulemaking during the nineteenth century demonstrates that agencies developed sophisticated "internal administrative law." Their procedures, however, were far from judicialized, although some agencies individually came to conduct hearings in a courtlike manner. Systematic state judicialization in the United States did not begin until the turn of the twentieth century.[22]

If this is the case, the question about the cause of American state judicialization must be rephrased: why and how did the American administrative state undergo a major shift in its mode of operation from procedural diversity in the nineteenth century to judicialization in the twentieth? The collective influence of common-law lawyers clearly cannot be the explanation, as they were at least as influential in nineteenth-century America as later. In reviewing the literature on the nineteenth-century administrative state, Ernst notes that the administrators' "prerogative power" came to be widely recognized as a possible threat to the American society in the early twentieth century, suggesting that such a change in perception set off judicialization. This makes sense, but the systematic and rapid judicialization from the turn of the twentieth century strongly suggests a more specific cause.[23]

This book pinpoints such a cause and proposes a new explanation that compensates for the legal-profession theory's comparative and chronological shortcomings. In order to account for the extraordinary degree of administrative state judicialization in the United States, one must look for the conditions under which a range of political actors, not just lawyers as agents of the common law, would back strong judiciality in administrative agencies. This study finds that cause in the separation-of-powers (or the presidential) system, the constitutional arrangement in which executive power is exercised by the chief executive who is elected separately from the legislature. Most common-law jurisdictions have adopted the parliamentary system. The presence of the presidential system in combination

22 Jerry L. Mashaw, *Creating the Administrative Constitution: The Lost One Hundred Years of American Administrative Law* (New Haven: Yale University Press, 2012), 310; Jerry L. Mashaw, "The American Model of Federal Administrative Law: Remembering the First One Hundred Years," *George Washington Law Review* 78 (2010): 975–992. It should be kept in mind, however, that the adversarial legal culture became fully developed in the postbellum period. Amalia D. Kessler, *Inventing American Exceptionalism: The Origins of American Adversarial Legal Culture, 1800–1877* (New Haven: Yale University Press, 2017).

23 Skowronek, *Building a New American State*; Ernst, *Tocqueville's Nightmare*, 158, n. 2.

with common law, this book argues, was the key factor in making the American state alone a highly courtlike one.[24]

The separation of powers in the United States promotes state judiciality in two ways. The separation of powers as a constitutional principle induces the judicialization of agencies in tandem with the supremacy of law principle. Many actors, including lawyers, came to believe that administrative agencies ought not to come under exclusive control of any of the three branches of the government if they were to be delegated quasi-legislative and/or quasi-judicial authorities so that no constitutional branch would exercise multiple powers. It was also thought that the autonomy of agencies would lead to impartial policy making. Such a view gained popularity among political elites by the Progressive Era but did not become a consensus. There were also those who believed that the separation of powers required that agencies unsanctioned in the Constitution should either be abolished or controlled by the president if they were to exist as policy-implementing devices. The latter view, now known as the unitary executive theory, became popular among chief executives and conservative lawyers.[25]

While there is no single agreed-upon view of what constitutes separation of powers, the principle nonetheless has had a critical impact on the judicialization of the administrative state. Whereas independent agencies in the United States including the IRCs do not belong to any of the three branches of the government, in some jurisdictions such as the United Kingdom and Canada, the line between agencies and judicial courts is often blurred, rendering the discussion of courtlike agencies itself somewhat irrelevant.[26] Many courtlike agencies in other common-law jurisdictions have in fact been treated as part of the judiciary. Some administrative commissions in these countries were to have one or more judges

24 The trouble with this explanation is that the rarity of the institutional combination among states with long state-building tradition prevents the testing of its validity outside the case of the United States. While the Philippines inheriting many institutional features of the US constitutional system from the Progressive Era taken up in this book is an interesting case in this respect, the fact that the case is strongly impacted by the United States and that it is a mixed jurisdiction of common and Roman law makes the comparison a difficult one. Patricio N. Abinales, "Progressive-Machine Conflict in Early-Twentieth-Century U.S. Politics and Colonial-State Building in the Philippines," in *The American Colonial State in the Philippines: Global Perspectives*, ed. Julian Go and Anne L. Foster (Durham: Duke University Press, 2003), 148–181.

25 Freedman, *Crisis and Legitimacy*, 60; J. David Alvis, Jeremy D. Bailey, and F. Flagg Taylor, IV, *The Contested Removal Power, 1789–2010* (Lawrence: University Press of Kansas, 2013), 144–150; Steven G. Calabresi and Christopher S. Yoo, *The Unitary Executive: Presidential Power from Washington to Bush* (New Haven: Yale University Press, 2008).

26 Cane, *Administrative Tribunals and Adjudication*, 44–48; Cane, *Controlling Administrative Power*, 52–54, 160, 330–332; Andrew J. Roman, "Regulatory Law and Procedure," in *The Regulatory Process in Canada*, ed. G. Bruce Doern (Toronto: Macmillan, 1978), esp. 80. The case of Australia, where the strict enforcement of separation of powers written in the federal constitution, influenced by the US Constitution, precludes the use of multi-function agencies, shows the impact of separation of powers on state judicialization in a different way. Asimow and Lubbers, "Merits of the 'Merits Review,'" 64–65; Cane, *Controlling Administrative Power*, 134–135.

as their members, as did the English Railway and Canal Commission established in 1888. Technically speaking, many administrative commissions in these jurisdictions are special courts despite their aggressive regulatory actions; the "judicialization of administrative agencies" took the form of judicial encroachment on agencies. It should not be surprising that the judiciality of courtlike agencies in these jurisdictions did not diffuse to other administrative agencies.[27]

Even more importantly, the separation of powers as a constitutional system gave key political actors the incentive to judicialize administrative agencies. When compared to the parliamentary system, the presidential system works in favor of agency autonomy. Among the three powers of the government, the executive primarily responsible for the appointment of agency officers has the biggest influence on their day-to-day workings. But the actual scope of executive control over agencies depends much on how constitutional powers are distributed in the political system. In a parliamentary system, the chief executive is almost always supported by the legislative majority, and the fusion of powers gives the legislature little motivation to restrain the executive's dealings with agencies. The fusion also discourages the judiciary from checking the executive power, as doing so would only result in retaliation from the other two branches. Because many common-law jurisdictions have traditionally had two-party systems, the executive-legislative tie in the parliamentary systems has also been reinforced by that of co-partisans.

The situation is quite different in the United States. Having its own policy preferences distinct from the president's, Congress is motivated to rein in the executive branch, especially under divided government. The separation of the two branches also gives the judiciary the incentive to intervene in a president's possible abuse of power. Such an institutional arrangement induces both the legislative and judicial branches to keep administrative agencies with strong discretionary powers at arm's length from the president, and judicialization is an ideal institutional template for the purpose. This is why judicialized administrative agencies with strong agency autonomy could enjoy wider support in the United States than elsewhere in the common-law world.[28]

David Lewis's study of the institutional design of administrative bodies in the United States after World War II illustrates the validity of this logic. He shows that the ideological distance between the president and Congress is positively correlated to the degree of institutional autonomy given to newly created agencies. When the two branches think alike, a new agency is more likely to be part of

27 S. J. McLean, "The English Railway and Canal Commission of 1888," *Quarterly Journal of Economics* 20 (1905): 1–58; R. E. Wraith and P. G. Hutchesson, *Administrative Tribunals* (London: George Allen and Unwin, 1973); Ellis, *Unjust by Design*. Similarly, the Immigration Judges affiliated with the British Asylum and Immigration Tribunal, an administrative tribunal, are considered members of the judiciary. Robert Thomas, *Administrative Justice and Asylum Appeals: A Study of Tribunal Adjudication* (Oxford: Hart Publishing, 2011), Ch. 2.

28 Cane, *Administrative Tribunals and Adjudication*, 70. Peter Cane offers a comparative analysis of common-law jurisdictions based on how government power is diffused or concentrated. See Cane, *Controlling Administrative Power*.

an executive department accountable to the president, whereas Congress chooses more autonomous forms such as independent commissions and government corporations when the gap between the preferences of the two branches is wider. Although Lewis's work covers only the United States, it is not difficult to see that legislatures in parliamentary systems would be much less motivated to keep new agencies autonomous from the prime minister.[29]

While the rare combination of the common law and the presidential system in the United States encourages administrative state judicialization, it does not fully account for the judicialization that actually took place in America. As is the case with the legal-profession thesis, the explanation is silent on the timing of judicialization; the pair of institutions had always been present in the republic. If the set of institutions creates a political condition favorable to state judicialization but does not immediately produce courtlike administrative agencies, how did judicialization happen in the United States when it did? This is where quasi-judicial IRCs, the quintessential courtlike administrative agencies, enter the equation. The core argument of this book is that it took the rise of IRCs for the US administrative state to initiate systematic judicialization, which started in the late nineteenth century and came full circle with the commissions' institutional consolidation during the New Deal. In regulating the railroads, the nation's largest industry at the time, members of Congress in the 1880s fiercely debated the institutional form of new regulation with the supremacy of law and separation of powers in mind and designed the ICC taking after judicial courts. After its creation, the ICC established a reputation as the prototypical administrative agency, and its judiciality was inherited not only by IRCs modeled after it but also by executive departments, although to a lesser degree. While the IRCs experienced a serious setback due to challenges from those frustrated by their autonomy, especially the president, they were fully institutionalized by the New Deal, occupying a central position in the now-judicialized administrative state.

The ascent of the IRCs was not accidental. Compared to their predecessors, members of Congress from the late nineteenth century had additional reasons to install judicialized agencies with extensive discretion and strict procedures in formulating national regulation. While Congress still occupied the central role in policy making in what William Novak calls the "legislative state," it was becoming increasingly clear that the legislature lacked the policy expertise necessary to produce self-enforcing legislations effectively addressing the problems arising from the rapidly nationalizing economy and society. This meant that Congress was unable to control agency discretion through detailed legislation, a standard tactic to prevent agencies from deviating from congressional will today.[30] The

29 Lewis, *Politics of Agency Design*.

30 William Novak, "Making the Modern American Legislative State," in *Living Legislation: Durability, Change, and the Politics of American Lawmaking*, ed. Jeffery A. Jenkins and Eric M. Patashnik (Chicago: University of Chicago Press, 2012), 20–43; Mathew D. McCubbins, Roger G. Noll, and Barry R. Weingast, "Administrative Procedures as Instruments of Political Control," *Journal of Law, Economics, and Organization* 3 (1987): 243–277;

absence of congressional policy expertise was manifest in the poor organizational support for legislators. Few staffers were assigned to members and committees, and Congress was yet to develop its research arms such as the Congressional Research Service and Congressional Budget Office. Congressional committees were provided with permanent professional staff only after the passage of the Legislative Reorganization Act of 1946. Without the ability to communicate its policy preference persuasively to agencies, Congress could only impose strict, formal procedures to limit agency discretion.[31]

In addition to this legislative challenge, lawmakers had to deal with the presidents who were becoming increasingly defiant. It was once thought that pre–New Deal presidents refrained from taking initiative in the policy process. But, as presidential scholars such as Jeffrey Tulis and Peri Arnold have demonstrated, some Progressive-Era chief executives were much more eager to realize their policy goals than their predecessors. Facing such presidents the legislators felt it necessary to insulate agencies from their influence. This is why, as the Brownlow Committee complained, Congress was "always tempted to turn each new regulatory function over to a new independent commission."[32]

This book's explanation of administrative state judicialization is original in its understanding of the development of IRCs. In stark contrast to the dominant view that sees the commissions as peripheral in the US administrative state, this book demonstrates that they were in fact the backbone of the judicialized state, at least until the mid-twentieth century. The politics of state judicialization from the late nineteenth century was to a large extent that of the institutional development of courtlike IRCs. The commissions became model administrative agencies whose judiciality spread to the entire administrative state. This may sound striking, but the commissions were considered the representative administrative agencies matching best to the US constitutional system and were rarely criticized openly before the Brownlow Committee stigmatized them in the late 1930s.[33]

McNollgast, "The Political Origins of the Administrative Procedure Act," *Journal of Law, Economics, and Organization* 15 (1999): 180–217; David Epstein and Sharyn O'Halloran, *Delegating Powers: A Transaction Cost Approach to Policy Making under Separate Powers* (New York: Cambridge University Press, 1999); John D. Huber and Charles R. Shipan, *Deliberate Discretion? The Institutional Foundations of Bureaucratic Autonomy* (New York: Cambridge University Press, 2002).

31 Alexander Bolton and Sharece Thrower, "Legislative Capacity and Executive Unilateralism," *American Journal of Political Science* 60 (2016): 649–663; Rosenbloom, *Building a Legislative-Centered Public Administration*, 72, 78. The Legislative Reference Service, the predecessor to the Congressional Research Service, was established in 1914.

32 Jeffrey Tulis, *The Rhetorical Presidency* (Princeton: Princeton University Press, 1987); James, *Presidents, Parties, and the State*, 23–25; Peri E. Arnold, *Remaking the Presidency: Roosevelt, Taft, and Wilson, 1901–1916* (Lawrence: University Press of Kansas, 2009). Also see William G. Howell, *Thinking about the Presidency: The Primacy of Power* (Princeton: Princeton University Press, 2013); *PCAM Report*, 41.

33 Bernard Schwartz, "Administrative Law: The Third Century," *Administrative Law Review* 29 (1977): 293.

This book's explanation that US state judicialization occurred through the rise of IRCs under the institutional combination of the common law and presidential system also urges the rethinking of the role of lawyers and courts in the process. As noted earlier, previous research in legal history, including Ernst's, treats agency judiciality as something imposed by lawyers, especially judges and leaders of the bar. They sought to curtail the power of agencies by delimiting the scope of agency adjudication and imposing expansive judicial review out of belief that the agencies were not sufficiently courtlike to adjudicate properly. It is true that the judiciary and lawyers were intent on constraining agencies; traditionally, administrative law was defined as the set of tools with which the courts regulate administrative agencies, not as the law created by agencies.[34] But as this book shows, such lawyer-centered explanation falls short of accurately capturing judicialization. Most importantly, from their inception the IRCs adopted their courtlike features. Also, as has been pointed out, the Supreme Court was initially receptive to the administrative agencies in the early twentieth century, at least until it began striking down New Deal policies in 1935. Early on, the judicial review on agencies mostly had to do with the scope of review rather than the administrative procedures. This study sees state judicialization primarily as a political process driven by Congress trying to regulate in accordance with the constitutional system, with the judiciary playing the role of legitimizing the courtlike public administration it created. This is a significant, but not radical, departure from the literature. Ernst argues that lawyers and politicians came to cooperate in the judicialization of the administrative state in the 1930s.[35] This book demonstrates that such a joint enterprise had been going on for a long time.

In order to achieve its goal, this book analyzes the politics of IRCs from the 1880s to the 1930s. To explain the judicialization of the American state, this book departs from Cushman's work that covers the same period. In contrast to Cushman's general overview of IRCs' political and constitutional backgrounds and their development, this study focuses on the commissions' judiciality and offers a comprehensive explanation of how they developed over the half century. As such, much of the narrative of this book will be devoted to Congress's creation of major IRCs with particular attention to the institutional choices made during the legislative processes. In doing so, this book looks not only at what promoted IRCs but at the obstacles to their institutionalization, including the attack by FDR and the Brownlow Committee in which Cushman himself was central. In addition, because this book sees the IRCs as the engine of administrative state

34 For early attempts to define the administrative law, see Oscar Kraines, *The World and Ideas of Ernst Freund: The Search for General Principles of Legislation and Administrative Law* (University: University of Alabama Press, 1974), 64–76. Also see Kenneth Culp Davis, *Administrative Law Treatise* (St. Paul: West Publishing, 1958), 1:1–4.

35 White, *Constitution and the New Deal*, 108–109; Paul R. Verkuil, "The Emerging Concept of Administrative Procedure," *Columbia Law Review* 78 (1978): 258–329; Horwitz, *Transformation of American Law*; Ernst, *Tocqueville's Nightmare*, 5, 77; Grisinger, *Unwieldy American State*, 6–7, 28.

judicialization, it also discusses how the commissions' judiciality diffused to other agencies. From the 1920s, several executive departments were authorized to conduct adjudications using IRC-like procedures. This study explains why and how the departments, and not IRCs, were given such authority and what it meant to state building.

This book's focus on the legislative process of the creation of IRCs and agency judiciality may seem old fashioned and inappropriate in studying administrative state building. In his study of bureaucratic autonomy, Daniel Carpenter states that the way in which the administrative state becomes hard wired cannot be observed through the analysis of legislation. Similarly, Joanna Grisinger warns that by concentrating on the way new agencies are made, scholars could fail to see how they actually operate. While these are valid pieces of advice, this book's goal is to elucidate the way in which America's modern administrative state was designed, with much emphasis on how agencies ought to operate. As Lewis Meriam argues, the observation in the early twentieth century that the administrative state "like Topsy, it just 'growed'" is not accurate. Although there admittedly was no grand design for state building, "both the Congress and the Presidents in establishing new agencies have given much time and thought to matters of organization: where the new agency shall be placed with relation to the President and to existing agencies and often as to what its internal structure should be." This book shows how the state judicialized through their interaction.[36]

In explaining the political process of IRC institutionalization within the context of administrative state judicialization, this book makes an analytical innovation. Discussions of the historical development of IRCs by existing works generally take the presence of the commissions as a category of government bodies as granted. Although Cushman notes that the IRCs "evolved by the process of trial and error," he does not explain the cause of the variety in institutional form across the commissions created during or before the 1930s. Such a view, however, is biased by hindsight. As Mark Eisner notes, the IRCs experienced much institutional transformation during the Progressive Era. Once the ICC established its reputation as regulator early in the twentieth century, the commission form of government was challenged by political forces preferring executive departments, which led to the substitution of IRCs with executive departments as new regulators from the early 1920s. There was no guarantee that the commissions would survive as quasi-judicial regulators, let alone come to constitute a class of agencies. In addition, in the course of the development, the commissions' judiciality was at times severely undermined. The analysis must deal squarely with the trajectory of IRCs' institutional development and the diversity of their organizational forms.[37]

36 Carpenter, *Forging of Bureaucratic Autonomy*, 11; Grisinger, *Unwieldy American State*, 251; Lewis Meriam and Laurence F. Schmeckebier, *Reorganization of the National Government: What Does It Involve?* (Washington, DC: Brookings Institution, 1939), 12–13.

37 Cushman, *Independent Regulatory Commissions*, 419; Bernstein, *Regulating Business*; Eisner, *Regulatory Politics*, 48.

In fact, the institutional variety among commissions is so extensive that it is inadequate to use the label "independent regulatory commissions" for the period taken up in this study. The commissions during the half century did not always fit the standard definition of the IRC. For instance, the original Federal Power Commission established in 1920 consisted of three cabinet officers, effectively subordinating the commission to the president. Also, the members of all commissions lost protection from presidential removal for an entire decade from 1926 due to a Supreme Court decision, making it awkward to describe them as "independent." More importantly, it must be remembered that the term is both historical and political, coined by the Brownlow Committee to castigate the commissions beyond presidential control. As will be discussed in Chapter Five, the adoption of the term in itself significantly contributed to the institutionalization of the commissions. The use of the expression for the period before its diffusion would therefore be misleading, as it generates a false impression that the commissions had already been fully institutionalized. For the sake of historical accuracy and to better capture the institutional fluidity of the commissions, the term "IRC" will not be used in this historical narrative. In its place, this book employs the term "administrative commission" (AC) when referring to the commissions. This expression has the dual merit of being sufficiently broad to cover all types of commissions that appeared and already being in use by the turn of the twentieth century.

To capture the institutional vicissitudes of the IRCs, this book uses the concept of creative syncretism developed by Gerald Berk and Dennis Galvan. Whereas historical institutionalist research tends to explain the birth and development of institutions with models such as lock in and path dependence emphasizing institutional continuity, Berk and Galvan argue that the processes could actually be much more creative and extemporaneous.[38] Even when a new institution is modeled upon an existing one, the former may not simply be a copy of the latter as the theory of institutional isomorphism suggests. The proposers of the new institution could actually be relying on multiple models taken from different institutional domains. Even after its creation, the form of a government body may not always become fixed immediately as the conventional institutionalist theories suggest; it could instead undergo further adjustments and metamorphosis. Berk himself shows that the creation and development of the FTC involved creative syncretism. The process shepherded by Louis Brandeis with input from many other policy entrepreneurs was much more complex than the straightforward adoption of the ICC model regarding both the new commission's authorities and

38 Gerald Berk and Dennis Galvan, "How People Experience and Change Institutions: A Field Guide to Creative Syncretism," *Theory and Society* 38 (2009): 543–580; Gerald Berk and Dennis C. Galvan, "Processes of Creative Syncretism: Experiential Origins of Institutional Order and Change," in *Political Creativity: Reconfiguring Institutional Order and Change*, ed. Gerald Berk, Dennis C. Galvan, and Victoria Hattam (Philadelphia: University of Pennsylvania Press, 2013), 29–54; Gerald Berk, *Louis D. Brandeis and the Making of Regulated Competition, 1900–1932* (New York: Cambridge University Press, 2009), Ch. 1.

regulatory style. This study goes a step further and analyzes the evolution and institutionalization of IRCs as a long-term process of creative syncretism in the creation of the "experimentalist state."[39]

From such a perspective, how can the politics of IRC institutionalization and state judicialization be understood? During the half century from the 1880s, IRCs with autonomy from the chief executive and courtlike procedures enjoyed widespread popularity. Dissatisfied with the sluggishness and lack of policy expertise of judicial courts, most political actors, including many lawyers, came to realize the merit of assigning the regulation of industries to courtlike agencies with relevant knowledge, if only as a necessary evil at first.[40] This did not mean everyone became judicialists who advocated the administrative state organized around courtlike agencies such as IRCs. Leaving aside those who opposed extensive federal intervention to the society regardless of its institutional form, two contrasting groups of challengers to judicialized administrative policy making appeared. The first group consisted of those who rejected IRCs out of conviction that their autonomy and adjudication infringed on the principles of the supremacy of law and separation of powers. In contrast to regular judicialists who looked favorably upon courtlike public administration, these extreme judicialists were unable to cast off the "sense of uneasiness as to its [the administrative process's] fundamental fairness" and strove to weaken or terminate administrative adjudication in general. As easily imagined, conservative lawyers had the largest presence among them. In addition, IRCs were attacked by those preferring executive agencies directed by cabinet secretaries accountable to the president to implement public policy. The presidents seeking control over administrative agencies and executive department officials wishing to retain or expand their turf were the most ardent supporters of this executivist notion of state building.[41]

The politics of state judicialization from the late nineteenth century, this book argues, played out along the extreme judicialist-executivist spectrum, with judicialists and courtlike IRCs situated at its center. The extreme judicialists and executivists attacked judicialists, respectively seeking further judicialization and dejudicialization of the courtlike state. Frederick Blachly and Miriam Oatman, who analyzed executive reorganization for Congress concurrently with the Brownlow Committee, found three conflicting doctrines in public administration: the doctrine of executive management, which asserts that all administrative activities should be controlled by the president; the doctrine of the judicial formula claiming that administrative policy making must follow the judicial formula and be made subject to meticulous judicial review; and the revisionist doctrine affirming the administration of law through independent boards and commissions. These positions, respectively corresponding to those held by the executivists, extreme

39 Paul J. DiMaggio and Walter W. Powell, "The Iron Cage Revisited: Institutional Isomorphism and Collective Rationality in Organizational Fields," *American Sociological Review* 48 (1983): 147–160; Berk, *Making of Regulated Competition*, 2–3.

40 Ernst, *Tocqueville's Nightmare*, 5–7, 32–33; Bernstein, *Regulating Business*, 192.

41 Freedman, *Crisis and Legitimacy*, 21.

judicialists, and judicialists in this book, had developed and influenced the politics of public administration over the preceding half century. Excluding the extreme judicialists denying the legitimacy of the administrative state, the battle over the type of administrative state to be built took the form of the clash between the two visions of the administrative state, a judicialist one promoting courtlike IRCs and an executivist one in support of hierarchical bureaucracy.[42]

To call the judicialist view in favor of IRCs a distinct vision of the administrative state building may seem striking, as autonomous commissions operating with court-like procedures do not fit the standard model of the bureaucratic state. Max Weber himself argued that hierarchical agencies staffed by career bureaucrats responsive to the chief executive could achieve "[p]recision, speed, unambiguity, knowledge of the files, continuity, discretion, unity, strict subordination, reduction of friction and of material and personal costs" to "the optimum point," compared to other forms of administration, including the collegial one. As Lewis Meriam notes, "When emphasis is placed on speed or instantaneous action, commissions, boards, and committees are taboo." If so, does the administrative state organized around IRCs qualify as an alternative model of the state? Isn't the American state just a "laggard"? This study argues that the judicialist vision of the state deserves to be taken seriously, as it suggests the limits of the yardstick for the executive, Weberian state in measuring administrative state building not just of the courtlike state but of administrative states in general.[43]

In his well-known article on public administration theory, David Rosenbloom argues that there are three conflicting approaches to the nature and goal of public administration in the United States, all promoting different values and organizational structures. In addition to the "managerial approach" emphasizing efficiency in policy implementation and the use of Weberian bureaucracy, he identifies two approaches: the "political approach" valuing representativeness, responsiveness, and accountability to the citizenry through elected officials and emphasizing pluralist organizational structure; and the "legal approach" that promotes procedural due process, individual rights, and equity/fairness through the use of courtlike adversarial procedures. This book's executivist vision of the state emphasizing Weberian bureaucracy that is responsive to the president can be seen as a combination of Rosenbloom's managerial and political approaches except for the pluralist government structure emphasized in the latter approach, whereas the judicialist vision closely matches his legal approach. Among these approaches, he sees the biggest gap between the legal approach and the other two, arguing

42 Blachly and Oatman, *Federal Regulatory Action and Control*, 3–7; Also, the extreme judicialists and judicialists correspond respectively to what Morton Horwitz calls "legalist" and "scientific" approaches to administrative law. Horwitz, *Transformation*, 220–235.

43 Max Weber, *From Max Weber: Essays in Sociology*, trans. and ed. H. H. Gerth and C. Wright Mills (New York: Routledge, 2009), 214. Lewis Meriam, "An Analysis of the Problem," in Meriam and Schmeckebier, *Reorganization*, 79. Cf. Schiller, "American Regulatory Exception." Also see Max Weber, *The Theory of Social and Economic Organization*, trans. A. M. Henderson and Talcott Parsons (New York: Oxford University Press, 1947), 337.

that they are almost antithetical. The legal approach, according to Rosenbloom, is intended to "afford maximum protection of the rights of private parties," and it "militates against efficiency, economy, managerial effectiveness, representativeness, responsiveness, and political accountability" pursued by other approaches.[44]

Such contradistinction between the two visions of the state makes the judicialist vision worth close attention. Where does the difference come from? The two visions are at odds with each other in many ways, including the preferred degrees of institutional autonomy and hierarchy. But at the heart of the clash between them is a tradeoff between two core values: efficiency and fairness. As has repeatedly been pointed out, the academic discipline of public administration has emphasized efficiency as the primary value to be pursued by administrative agencies. In his 1887 essay, "The Study of Administration," pioneering the academic study of public administration, Woodrow Wilson identified efficiency, economy, and effectiveness as the three pillars of public administration.[45] In the first textbook on the subject in the United States published in 1926, Leonard D. White stated that the objective of public administration was "the most efficient utilization" of the resources available to agency officials. While the term *efficiency* has frequently been equated with efficacy and effectiveness, it has been understood as "the attainment of maximum values with limited means" or high input-output ratio. In *Administrative Behavior*, originally published in 1945, Herbert Simon stated that all rational behavior was determined by the criterion of efficiency, which was what " 'good' or 'correct' administrative behavior" was all about.[46]

Even though the importance of efficiency as a goal in public administration is beyond doubt, it may not be the only goal. In *The Administrative State* published a few years after Simon's classic, Dwight Waldo rejected the centrality of the value and argued that the way in which public administration could better serve democracy ought to be discussed. Students of public administration in different disciplines realize that efficiency is not its only goal and that hierarchical bureaucracy is not best equipped to realize all goals. In Jerry Mashaw's *Bureaucratic Justice*, the bureaucratic rationality model of administrative decision-making in pursuit of efficiency through hierarchical organization, similar to this book's executivist vision of the state, is one of the three "justice models" of public administration presented. Mashaw also offers a model of administrative policy making akin to Rosenbloom's legal approach based on autonomous, courtlike adjudication, which he calls the "moral judgment model" legitimized not by efficiency but by the fairness of decision-making.[47]

44 David H. Rosenbloom, "Public Administrative Theory and the Separation of Powers," *Public Administration Review* 43 (1983): 219–227. The quotes are from pp. 221 and 224.

45 Woodrow Wilson, "The Study of Administration," *Political Science Quarterly* 2 (1887): 197.

46 Leonard D. White, *Introduction to the Study of Public Administration* (New York: Macmillan, 1926), 2; Herbert Simon, *Administrative Behavior: A Study of Decision-Making Processes in Administrative Organizations*, 4th ed. (New York: Free Press, 1997), 45, 75, 257.

47 Dwight Waldo, *The Administrative State: A Study of the Political Theory of American Public Administration* (1948; repr., New York: Routledge, 2017), xiii, 19; Jerry L. Mashaw, *Bureaucratic Justice: Managing Social Security Disability Claims* (New Haven: Yale University Press,

Rosenbloom and Mashaw are far from alone in associating fairness with formal adjudication, which includes judicial court proceedings. At the core of the supremacy of law principle is the idea that only judicial courts could provide due process in application of law to individual cases, and in the common-law jurisdictions, the question of what constitutes due process in administrative adjudication has been discussed in relation to achieving fairness. According to Richard Stewart, "[t]he traditional core of administrative law" included "securing the rule of law and protecting liberty by ensuring that agencies follow fair and impartial decisional procedures."[48] Similarly, Bernard Schwartz notes that "It has been felt that fair procedure is one of the surest guarantees against the arbitrary exercise of regulatory power. Justice, in our view, goes hand in hand with judicial process." Outside the United States, "natural justice" is now used interchangeably with "procedural fairness." Also, Rebecca Brown emphasizes the close connection between procedural fairness and the separation of powers. The judicialization of the US administrative state, then, was a process in which administrative agencies systematically came to increasingly emphasize fairness as their goal in implementing public policy. Grisinger's work demonstrates how the politics of administrative law after the New Deal played out around the notion of fairness shares much with this book.[49]

Then what is fairness, or procedural fairness, to be precise, and what does it take to realize it in policy making? Impartiality to the parties in interest and correctness in fact finding are included in any description of fair decision-making. But there is more to it. Fair judgment goes beyond accurate application of ready-made policy to facts in question. As Mashaw argues, it involves a "value defining" aspect asking "who is to be preferred" given conflicting parties each with a set of rights and overall situation. Or, as Rosenbloom says, decision-making has more to do with intensive consideration of each case than the general cost-benefit analysis of what is good for the society. Fairness as understood here has not been valued only by lawyers and courts. Lewis Meriam argues that quasi-judicial regulation strongly requires "the evolution of sound doctrine from prolonged experience, mature deliberation, continuity and predictability of administrative action, protection from the possible passions, prejudices, and idiosyncrasies of a single

1983), Ch. 2. Also see Vincent Ostrom, *The Intellectual Crisis in American Public Administration*, 3rd ed. (Tuscaloosa: University of Alabama Press, 2008).

48 D. J. Galligan, *Due Process and Fair Procedures: A Study of Administrative Procedures* (New York: Oxford University Press, 1996); Giacinto della Cananea, *Due Process of Law Beyond the State* (New York: Oxford University Press, 2016), 20; Richard B. Stewart, "Administrative Law in the Twenty-First Century," *New York University Law Review* 78 (2003): 438.

49 Bernard Schwartz, *Professor and the Commissions*, 166; Cane, *Controlling Administrative Power*, 345; Martin Loughlin, "Procedural Fairness: A Study of the Crisis in Administrative Law Theory," *University of Toronto Law Journal* 28 (1978): 215–241; Rebecca L. Brown, "Separated Powers and Ordered Liberty," *University of Pennsylvania Law Review* 139 (1991): 1513–1566. Also see Philippe Nonet, *Administrative Justice: Advocacy and Change in a Government Agency* (New York: Russell Sage Foundation, 1969); Grisinger, *Unwieldy American State*, 5–6, 260–261.

individual, and the arbitration or reconciliation of conflicting interests" and that commissions are desirable for the purpose.[50]

As noted above, not all scholars were satisfied with measuring the performance of administrative agencies with the sole standard of efficiency. In fact, fairness has been considered a core goal of public administration since the birth of the discipline. Woodrow Wilson argued in the abovementioned essay that law must be administered not only with enlightenment and speed but with equity. Similarly, Frank Goodnow placed impartiality and efficiency as twin goals of administration in his classic *Politics and Administration*.[51] Later, the students in the New Public Administration tradition proposed social equity associated with "fairness, justice, and equality" as a core value in public administration. George Frederickson, a leader of the movement, offers it as a process value as opposed to efficiency as an outcome value that ought to be fulfilled for administrators to give due consideration to people's rights. Social equity is now considered a pillar of public administration after the three pillars that Wilson proposed back in 1887.[52]

Fairness is not just considered as important as efficiency in public administration; there is also a tradeoff between them. Put simply, making sure that a decision is both unbiased and does justice to all involved parties takes time and effort, which inevitably slows policy making and incurs additional cost. Even if Weber's modern legal-rational state is capable of attaining maximum efficiency, doing so for fairness at the same time is not possible. If Weber missed the tradeoff, it should not be surprising that participants in modern policy debates regarding administrative procedures have also done so. In creating the ACUS, President Kennedy stated that it was essential that administrative procedures "ensure maximum efficiency and fairness." Similarly, the Commission on Law and the Economy of the ABA stated in 1979 that regulatory procedures "must be made swifter and less expensive without sacrificing fairness" in its report proposing the dejudicialization of administrative process.[53]

50 Mashaw, *Bureaucratic Justice*, 29–30; Rosenbloom, "Public Administrative Theory and the Separation of Powers," 223; Meriam and Schmeckebier, *Reorganization*, 79.

51 See generally, Richard D. White, Jr., "More than an Analytical Tool: Examining the Ideological Role of Efficiency," *Public Productivity and Management Review* 23 (1999): 8–23; Woodrow Wilson, "Study of Administration," 198; Frank J. Goodnow, *Politics and Administration* (New York: Macmillan, 1900), 85, 91.

52 H. George Frederickson, *Social Equity and Public Administration: Origins, Developments, and Applications* (Armonk, NY: M. E. Sharpe, 2010), 53, 70; Rosenbloom, "Public Administration Theory," 51–55; James H. Svara and James R. Brunet, "Social Equity Is a Pillar of Public Administration," *Journal of Public Affairs Education* 11 (2005): 253–258. Also see Paul C. Light, *The Tides of Reform: Making Government Work, 1945–1995* (New Haven: Yale University Press, 1997), Ch. 2; David Osbourne and Ted Gaebler, *Reinventing Government: How the Entrepreneurial Spirit is Transforming the Public Sector* (Reading, MA: Addison-Wesley, 1993), xix, 185.

53 The tradeoff is usually traced back to Arthur Okun, *Equality and Efficiency: The Big Tradeoff* (Washington, DC: Brookings Institution, 1975); C. Stuart Greer, "Expanding the Judicial Power of the Administrative Law Judge to Establish Efficiency and Fairness in Administrative Adjudication," *University of Richmond Law Review* 103 (1992): 103–130; Giandomenico

It is this tradeoff between efficiency and fairness that makes the judicialist state vision a meaningful alternative to the Weberian, executivist one. As Joseph Chamberlain and others note, "Those elements of fair play and individual justice . . . are equally a purpose of government whatever may be their effect on regulatory efficiency." James Q. Wilson even argues that equity/fairness "is more important than efficiency in the management of many government agencies." But the two core values may not be treated in the same way everywhere. Because of the tradeoff, the same amount of effort in state building could result in a different balance between the state's efficiency and fairness. If that is the case, measuring the degree of state building only with the efficiency standard could be inappropriate. This is especially applicable to the United States, where the judicialist-executivist tug of war resulted in an extremely fairness-oriented, courtlike state. The judicialized US administrative state that looks like a "laggard" by the efficiency standard could then be a highly developed fairness-oriented state. State building must be measured two dimensionally, taking into account the efficiency-fairness tradeoff. From this perspective, the American state's inefficiency and inconsistency could be seen as the flip side of its orientation toward fairness.[54]

This argument on the direction of state building and the efficiency-fairness tradeoff comes with a few caveats. First, each of the two visions of the state could be supported by a variety of actors for different reasons. A supporter of the judicialist state may not be committed to procedural fairness, just as someone backing the executivist state could have reasons other than belief in efficiency in governance. With a powerful motivation to control policy implementation, presidents do not have to be mindful of agency efficiency to behave in an executivist manner. Members of Congress tended to be judicialist in their orientation toward the administrative state, and some were extremists in denial of the state. There is no doubt, however, that their preference derived not just from respect for the supremacy of law but other considerations, including wariness toward aggrandizement of presidential power and deference to the judiciary's support for IRCs.

Second, the fact that the American state is fairness oriented does not mean it is indifferent to efficiency. To the contrary, the strong judiciality of the US administrative state is an outcome of an effort to make the policy-making process

Majone, *Regulating Europe* (London: Routledge, 1996), 90; Paul R. Verkuil, "A Study of Informal Adjudication Procedures," *University of Chicago Law Review* 43 (1976): 739–796; Fuchs, "Fairness and Effectiveness"; Glen O. Robinson, "The Making of Administrative Policy: Another Look at Rulemaking and Adjudication and Administrative Procedural Reform," *University of Pennsylvania Law Review* 118 (1970): 485–539; Thomas K. McCraw, *Prophets of Regulation: Charles Francis Adams, Louis D. Brandeis, James M. Landis, Alfred E. Kahn* (Cambridge, MA: Belknap Press of Harvard University Press, 1984), 282–283, 302–303; Executive Order 10934, Apr. 13, 1961; Commission on Law and the Economy, *Federal Regulation*, 7.

54 Joseph P. Chamberlain, Noel T. Dowling, and Paul R. Hays, *The Judicial Function in Federal Administrative Agencies* (New York: Commonwealth Fund, 1942), 225; James Q. Wilson, *Bureaucracy: What Government Agencies Do and Why They Do It* (New York: Basic Books, 1989), 132.

more *efficient*. John Dickinson noted in 1927 that the advantages of administrative adjudication were in prompt implementation and flexible procedures. The same year, Joseph Eastman, a long-time member of the ICC, commented that the IRCs created to perform its duties "by impartial, judicial methods" could still attain "maximum economy and efficiency." Today, such statements may sound nonsensical. But the choice between the two goals of public administration is not a binary one. Even though judicialized IRCs were more fairness oriented in comparison to executive departments, those commissions were much more efficiency oriented than judicial courts that had been considered the default regulators until the late nineteenth century. This is why the courtlike administrative agencies flourished in the United States at the turn of the twentieth century, a time known for the predominance of efficiency as a goal in both politics and business.[55]

Third, just as the fairness-oriented American state does not ignore efficiency, it should not be assumed that other states, including Weberian ones, neglect fairness. Given the importance of fairness in public administration, there is no way those in charge of state building could take this lightly. The development of the administrative state, then, is not a blind pursuit of efficiency. Rather, the states more or less deviate from the path to efficiency, depending on their strength in orientation toward fairness. The American case stands out only because its unusually strong orientation toward fairness manifested in the readily observable form of judicialization. States that are considered highly Weberian, for instance Germany and France, may not be courtlike, but that certainly does not mean they ignore fairness; they are known for their legalism. To measure the degree of state building, then, one must rely not just on the scale of efficiency but take the efficiency-fairness spectrum into account.[56]

Having presented the analytical framework and the thesis of this study, an overview of the discussion to follow is in order. As noted above, the political battle fought by judicialists over the building of the courtlike administrative state with IRCs at its core took place on two fronts, one against extreme judicialists and the other against executivists. This is an important reason why regulatory agencies seemed to have developed in "eclectic confusion."[57]

55 Dickinson, *Administrative Justice*, 14–15; Joseph B. Eastman, "The Place of the Independent Commission," *Constitutional Review* 12 (1928): 99, 101.

56 Gyorgy Gajduschek argues that Weber's model of bureaucracy has been excessively associated with efficiency in the English-speaking world due to mistranslation. He shows that Weber was also attentive to the rationalized bureaucracy's strength in what he calls "uncertainty reduction," which minimizes arbitrariness and unpredictability in policy implementation, which in turn contributes to equitable treatment of citizens and realization of the rule of law. If this is the case, Weber cared greatly about fairness, too. Gyorgy Gajduschek, "Bureaucracy: Is It Efficient? Is It not? Is That the Question? Uncertainty Reduction: An Ignored Element of Bureaucratic Rationality," *Administration and Society* 34 (2003): esp. 718; John O. Haley, *Antitrust in Germany and Japan: The First Fifty Years, 1947–1998* (Seattle: University of Washington Press, 2001), 113–114.

57 Glen O. Robinson, *American Bureaucracy: Public Choice and Public Law* (Ann Arbor: University of Michigan Press, 1991), 12.

Of the two pillars of agency judiciality, the autonomy of IRCs from the three branches received much more political attention than courtlike procedures during the half century under study, owing much to the disagreement over the separation of powers principle. On the one hand, the executivists and extreme judicialists both opposed the judicialists' belief that IRCs ought to remain autonomous from the three constitutional branches out of consideration for the supremacy of law and separation of powers, although for very different reasons. Denying the legitimacy of administrative agencies with discretionary powers, extreme judicialists argued that they should be instructed by one of the three branches, if not abolished. The executivists' attack on agency autonomy was based on the notion that agencies must be subordinated to the president so that policy implementation would become consistent and accountable to the public. Interestingly, the two forces trying to pull administrative state building in different directions often ended up proposing the same solution: the presidential control of agencies. On the other hand, there was consensus among the three political forces with different views of the state on the importance of judicialized procedures. Over the half-century period, administrative procedures became a political issue only when extreme judicialists expressed dissatisfaction with the informality of agency hearings. Despite their emphasis on efficiency, the executivists almost never expressed doubt about the courtlike manner in which agencies handled their cases. Also, once the judicialization of the ICC's procedures was confirmed in the early twentieth century, the judiciary generally did not ask for further judicialization.

The institutional development of IRCs from the late nineteenth century resulting from such political battles consists of three phases. The first phase runs from the birth of the ICC to the early 1910s. In this period, the idea of courtlike public administration and the judicialist state emerged in the form of the ICC and came to enjoy widespread support. Those who developed the commission idea in Congress did so through the fight against extreme judicialists rejecting the legitimacy of regulatory adjudication by government bodies other than Article III courts. The institutional features of the ICC were intentionally made courtlike to rebut their argument that administrative adjudication would violate the supremacy of law. The courtlike commission created in 1887 was not just supported by a congressional majority; it also won the approval of the other two branches of the government. The presidents contributed to the judicialization of the ICC's operation by staffing the commission almost exclusively with lawyers. While the judiciary initially limited the scope of the ICC's jurisdiction, it soon became openly supportive of the commission's role as a courtlike adjudicator with expertise in railroad management. The ICC's self-identification was based on its judicial character. By the Progressive Era, the commission was widely considered a prototypical administrative agency with strong judiciality. This is why the ICC became the model of new government bodies such as the FRB and FTC created in the 1910s.

The trajectory of the IRCs' development, however, was not a linear one. In its second phase, from the Wilson administration to the mid-1920s, the presidents who had supported IRCs out of the need to install new regulations now began to challenge them. The irony here was that the commissions' setback had much to do with their popularity. As the number of IRCs steadily increased, the chief executives eager to realize their policy goals and executive departments in fear of losing their turf became more hostile to the creation of new commissions. The executivists first attempted to give the president limited authority to instruct new commissions and/or fill part or all of their memberships with cabinet officers. When this succeeded, they began demanding the assignment of new regulations to executive agencies. Congressional judicialists, let alone extreme ones, were certainly opposed to letting executive agencies adjudicate. While strongly believing in procedural fairness, they also came to fear that accumulation of IRCs could lead to fiscal inefficiency and irresponsibility. When it became clear that IRCs such as the ICC and FTC were too overburdened to accept additional responsibilities, Congress embraced, albeit reluctantly, the idea of authorizing executive agencies to conduct quasi-judicial adjudication. The judiciary not only acquiesced to this but further weakened IRCs through the Supreme Court decision in *Myers v. United States* in 1926, depriving members of all IRCs of protection from removal by the president.

The tide of administrative state building thus turned in favor of the executivists, and IRCs gradually lost ground. But the American state did not go straight down the path of dejudicialization. This was because the executivist challenge to the courtlike state was directed only at agency autonomy. Virtually no attempt was made to make agency procedures more informal from the outside. If anything, executive agencies vested with new regulatory authorities were often instructed by written law to follow IRCs' courtlike procedures. This meant that formal procedures, another pillar of judiciality, diffused into executive agencies. The executivists' indifference to agency procedures indicates that their attack on IRCs was not made out of a belief in efficient policy implementation. Still, had the executivist attack on them continued, IRCs could have become marginalized in the administrative state.

The IRCs, however, made a comeback over the next decade, marking the third phase of the administrative state judicialization and became fully established by the mid-1930s. The *Myers* decision robbing the IRCs of their autonomy proved a blessing in disguise to both the commissions and the judicialized state. Now free to fire any IRC commissioner, the presidents lowered their guard against the commissions and became indifferent to the institutional category of new regulators. As Congress still preferred commissions to executive agencies as regulators because of the former's procedural fairness, many powerful but nonautonomous commissions such as the Securities and Exchange Commission (SEC) and Federal Communications Commission (FCC) were created under the Franklin D. Roosevelt administration. But the nonindependent IRCs did not just grow in number. In 1935, the Supreme Court issued its decision in *Humphrey's Executor v. United States* which reversed *Myers* regarding the constitutional status of IRCs and reinstated members' immunity from discretionary presidential removal.

The decade-long truce between the executivists and judicialists over the course of administrative state building ended with *Humphrey's*. Determined to overcome the judicialized state, Roosevelt appointed the Brownlow Committee the next year. Giving paramount weight to achieving efficiency and accountability to the chief executive, the members and staff of the Committee sought a way to abolish IRCs through executive reorganization. In the end, however, they were unable to justify such reorganization, which would have entailed the loss of judiciality – and hence, fairness – of policy implementation and decided not to offer an organizational reform plan for IRCs. Although the Committee's final report included partial assimilation of IRCs into executive agencies at Roosevelt's insistence, the administration quietly dropped the plan in the face of fierce opposition from both inside and outside the federal government. The miserable failure of the executivist attack on IRCs confirmed that the commissions were now fully institutionalized and held a central position in the courtlike administrative state.

By demonstrating how the modern American administrative state was built around courtlike IRCs and became highly judicialized and fairness oriented, *Judicializing the Administrative State* makes a significant contribution not only to the study of the US administrative state building but also to two related fields of study. This book sets a new agenda for research on judicialization of politics, a topic that has received much attention from political scientists and legal scholars for several decades. Judicialization of politics, defined by an authority as "the reliance on courts and judicial means for addressing core moral predicaments, public policy questions, and political controversies" is widely observed around the globe. Robert Kagan, however, argues in his path-breaking work that American governance is distinctive in its strong adversarial legalism: that is, "policymaking, policy implementation, and dispute resolution by means of lawyer-dominated litigation." While the judiciary rightly occupies center stage in the study of the judicialization of politics, the analysis presented in this book shows that courts are not the only site of judicialization. It could take place by non-judicial government bodies behaving in a courtlike manner, as in the case of the judicialization of administrative agencies in the United States. The inattention to such a possibility is unfortunate, as adversarial legalism shares so much with administrative state judiciality.[58]

Most notably, Kagan's point that policy making based on adversarial legalism is both costly and leads to legal uncertainty corresponds closely with the inefficiency and inconsistency found in judicialized administrative policy making. In fact, Kagan himself admits that adjudications by ALJs have "adopted the forms of adversarial legalism" in the abovementioned work. Those scholars following Kagan's footsteps such as Farhang and Staszak have been looking into judicialized agencies and agencies that are promoting the use of the judiciary. Still, no work has explored the administrative state judicialization before World War II. This book makes a contribution to political science research on the

58 Ran Hirschl, "The Judicialization of Politics," in *The Oxford Handbook of Political Science*, ed. Robert E. Goodin (New York: Oxford University Press, 2011), 253; Robert A. Kagan, *Adversarial Legalism: The American Way of Law* (Cambridge, MA: Harvard University Press, 2001), 3.

judicialization of politics by expanding the scope of analysis both chronologically and thematically.[59]

This book also offers a comparative look at administrative state building, by taking into account the tradeoff between efficiency and fairness. State judiciality and procedural fairness are too important to remain below the radar screen of social scientists. Administrative state building cannot be fully captured in simple, one-dimensional terms of how advanced or backward the administrative state is with the single yardstick of efficiency. Both efficiency and fairness should be taken into account as related but separate dimensions of state building. This book argues that the study of the administrative state should be reconfigured to take fairness in public administration squarely into account. Bernard Silberman convincingly shows how the Weberian bureaucratic state could be organized differently under different political conditions. If the styles of state development could vary even when the goal is shared, it should come as no surprise when states have different orientations toward dual goals.[60]

It is in this context that an in-depth analysis of the seemingly exceptional case of the United States is meaningful to the research on comparative state building. The American administrative state comprising agencies taking after judicial courts is arguably as judicialized and fairness oriented as any state could be. The extreme judicialization of the American state not only enables close examination of what fairness-oriented state building could be like but also encourages the revision of the course of state building. The American state that has been treated as a "laggard" because of its un-Weberian characteristics is actually a highly developed fairness-oriented state.[61]

This book's double contribution to the literature on the judicialization of politics and administrative state building derives from the intermediate institutional nature of IRCs as administrative agencies modeled after judicial courts. As Robert Cushman pointed out in *The Independent Regulatory Commissions*, different actors can disagree over what kind of government body the commissions are and ought to be. Because IRCs are hybrid agencies, there is no way they could live up to everyone's expectations. As a result, extreme judicialists have viewed IRCs as pseudo-courts whose organizational forms and procedures do not satisfy the fairness standard of judicial courts, whereas executivists have looked down on the commissions as deformed agencies lacking in qualities essential to functional

59 Kagan, *Adversarial Legalism*, 9, 172; Farhang, *Litigation State*; Lynda G. Dodd, ed., *The Rights Revolution Revisited: Institutional Perspectives on the Private Enforcement of Civil Rights in the U.S.* (New York: Cambridge University Press, 2018); Staszak, *No Day in Court*; Robert Kagan, "Varieties of Bureaucratic Justice: Building on Mashaw's Typology," *Administrative Law from the Inside Out: Essays on Themes in the Work of Jerry L. Mashaw*, ed. Nicholas R. Parrillo (New York: Cambridge University Press, 2017), esp. 254.

60 Bernard S. Silberman, *Cages of Reason: The Rise of the Rational State in France, Japan, the United States, and Great Britain* (Chicago: University of Chicago Press, 1993).

61 On the comparative meaning of a narrative on an extreme "case," see Daniel Carpenter, *Reputation and Power: Organizational Image and Pharmaceutical Regulation at the FDA* (Princeton: Princeton University Press, 2010), 19–21.

bureaucracy such as efficiency and accountability. The situation is reminiscent of Aesop's fable in which a bat finds itself caught between warring beasts and birds. Unlike the bat in the story, however, IRCs were neither marginal nor unpopular as administrative agencies. Rather, they were mainstream agencies in the United States that laid the foundation of the modern administrative state because of their institutional hybridity. It is high time their contribution to state building was better understood.[62]

62 Cushman, *Independent Regulatory Commissions*, 417–418.

2 The judicial roots of the Interstate Commerce Commission

"The creation of national commissioners of railroads . . . involves a very important and delicate extension of administrative functions." The year 1887, which saw both the formation of the Interstate Commerce Commission and the publication of Woodrow Wilson's "The Study of Administration" – cited above – has been acknowledged as the starting point of the US administrative state and its research. In his classic work, Stephen Skowronek cited the rise of the ICC as a watershed in US state building. Many works on the subject published in or around 1987 acknowledged, if they did not celebrate, the centennial of the "founding of the administrative state" along with the bicentennial of the Constitutional Convention. The idea of the ICC, the first of the many administrative commissions in the United States, as an origin of the administrative state was one of the few points of agreement among students of history, law, and political science for most of the twentieth century.[1]

The state definitely had a difficult evolution in the United States. As is often suggested, this had much to do with the timing of state building relative to democratization. In Europe, where state bureaucratization was promoted by monarchs as their governing apparatus, the state had already taken firm root and was considered a given by the time ordinary citizens began to participate in political decision-making. In stark contrast, democracy stood in the way of state building in the United States. The authority to create administrative agencies of any kind rested primarily in a Congress responsive to the public. The notion of discretionary policy implementation using policy expertise by bureaucrats who were largely free of political control was hard to accept in such a political setting. Instead, the spoils system quickly developed early in the nineteenth century in

1 Wilson, "Study of Administration," 201; Lawrence M. Friedman, *A History of American Law*, 3rd ed. (New York: Touchstone, 2005), 329; Skowronek, *Building a New American State*; Richard J. Stillman, II, "The Constitutional Bicentennial and the Centennial of the American Administrative State," *Public Administration Review* 47 (1987): 4–8. Also see Ralph Clark Chandler, ed., *A Centennial History of the American Administrative State* (New York: Free Press, 1987); Geoffrey P. Miller, "Independent Agencies," *Supreme Court Review* 1986 (1986): 41–97; Larry S. Lutton, "History and American Public Administration," *Administration and Society* 31 (1999): 205–221.

tandem with the nationwide two-party system.[2] In addition, the United States after the War of 1812 was free from serious military threats and wars that could have jump-started the state. The Civil War certainly was an important exception. Although quick demobilization followed the termination of hostilities just as in other wars the United States had experienced, the size of the government did not return to its prewar level; at over 51,000, the number of paid federal civilian employees in 1871 was almost double the figure in 1851. But during most of what C. Van Woodward called the "era of free security" that lasted well into the twentieth century, the United States lacked strong motivation to innovate its government structure relative to its foreign affairs. The civil service reform movement that began shortly after the Civil War finally bore fruit in 1883 in the form of the Pendleton Act. The law passed only after the assassination of President James Garfield in 1881, however. It took another half century for a large majority of federal officers to become subject to the merit system introduced by the statute.[3]

The constitutional structure on which American democracy was based also hindered state building. While any bureaucracy could be accused of not doing something well enough, the American case is different in that the bureaucracy has undergone existential crises, often threatening its very existence. A central topic of the political debate over the legitimacy of bureaucracy has been its use of the three constitutional powers listed in the US Constitution. The document lacks reference to administrative agencies other than the provision in Article II, Sec. 2, on the role of executive department heads as advisors to the president. Those politicians, lawyers, and academics adhering to the strict constructionist view of the Constitution have denounced the quasi-judicial and quasi-legislative functions performed by agencies as usurpation not just of authorities reserved exclusively for the legislative and judicial branches of government but the separation of powers that prohibits the use of multiple powers by a government body. As James Madison declared in *The Federalist Papers*, No. 47, the "accumulation of all powers, legislative, executive, and judiciary, in the same hands . . . may justly be pronounced the very definition of tyranny."[4]

2 Skowronek, *Building a New American State*; Martin Shefter, *Political Parties and the State: The American Historical Experience* (Princeton: Princeton University Press, 1994); Goodnow, *Politics and Administration*, 98–100; Leonard D. White, *The Jacksonians: A Study in Administrative History, 1829–1861* (New York: Macmillan, 1954); Joel H. Silbey, *The American Political Nation, 1838–1893* (Palo Alto: Stanford University Press, 1991).

3 US Bureau of the Census, *Historical Statistics of the United States, Colonial Times to 1970, Bicentennial Edition* (Washington, DC: Government Printing Office, 1975), Pt. 2, 1102–1103; C. Vann Woodward, "The Age of Reinterpretation," *American Historical Review* 66 (1960): 3; Skowronek, *Building a New American State*; Ari Hoogenboom, *Outlawing the Spoils: A History of the Civil Service Reform Movement, 1865–1883* (Urbana: University of Illinois Press, 1961).

4 Freedman, *Crisis and Legitimacy*, esp. Ch. 1; James Madison, Alexander Hamilton, and John Jay, *The Federalist Papers* (1788; repr., New York: Penguin Books, 1987), 303; Anthony M. Bertelli and Laurence E. Lynn, Jr., *Madison's Managers: Public Administration and the Constitution* (Baltimore: Johns Hopkins University Press, 2006), Ch. 4.

While there had long been a scholarly consensus that the United States lacked a state before the twentieth century, the past generation has seen numerous challenges to that view. It has been demonstrated that not only did the federal bureaucracy develop in the nation's first hundred years but that agencies also often took the initiative in designing and implementing public policies. Synthesizing that research, Brian Balogh argues that the statelessness that pervaded early America did not derive from the absence of the state. It was only that much of the work done by the federal government remained "out of sight" of many contemporaries. There now is a widespread agreement that the administrative state has always been with the United States in some substantive form.[5]

Such shift in the accepted view on US state building had a side effect. The origins of the ICC, once a popular subject of study, quickly fell out of vogue, now that the commission's status as the first administrative agency became questionable. There is little doubt that the trivialization of the ICC and other ACs contributed to scholars' departure from the research topic.

But even if the 1887 Act to Regulate Commerce did not signal the birth of the US administrative state, the legislation still was a turning point in the American state's mode of operation.[6] It created a new type of regulatory agency charged with overseeing the nation's largest industry. The agency and its work turned out to be so important that scholars agreed for a long time that that was the beginning of the administrative state. If this was the case, why did the ICC take the form it did, later to be followed by many agencies? The origins of the ICC have arguably been scrutinized more than those of any other US agency, but for two reasons this question has gone unanswered. First, interested in elucidating what caused the emergence of the administrative state, the plethora of works on the origins of the 1887 act have focused on identifying the political forces primarily responsible for the railroad legislation but neglected the institutional form of the regulatory policy.[7] Another reason for such dismissal was a strong agreement, at

5 Brian Balogh, *A Government Out of Sight: The Mystery of National Authority in Nineteenth-Century America* (New York: Cambridge University Press, 2009); Stephen J. Rockwell, *Indian Affairs and the Administrative State in the Nineteenth Century* (New York: Cambridge University Press, 2010).

6 Following scholarly convention, the statute will hereafter be referred to as the "Interstate Commerce Act."

7 Morris P. Fiorina, "Legislator Uncertainty, Legislative Control, and the Delegation of Legislative Power," *Journal of Law, Economics, and Organization* 2 (1986): 32–51; Morris P. Fiorina, "Legislative Choice of Regulatory Forms: Legal Process or Administrative Process?" *Public Choice* 39 (1982): 33–66; Solon Buck, *The Granger Movement: A Study of Agricultural Organization and Its Political, Economic, and Social Manifestations, 1870–1880* (Cambridge, MA: Harvard University Press, 1913); Lee Benson, *Merchants, Farmers, and Railroads: Railroad Regulation and New York Politics, 1850–1887* (Cambridge, MA: Harvard University Press, 1955); Gerald D. Nash, "Origins of the Interstate Commerce Act of 1887," *Pennsylvania History* 24 (1957): 181–190; Gabriel Kolko, *Railroads and Regulation, 1877–1916* (New York: W. W. Norton, 1965); Ari Hoogenboom and Olive Hoogenboom, *A History of the ICC: From Panacea to Palliative* (New York: W. W. Norton, 1976); Gerald Berk, *Alternative Tracks: The Constitution of American Industrial Order, 1865–1917* (Baltimore: Johns Hopkins

least since Robert Cushman's classic, that the ICC was modeled upon existing railroad commissions. Cushman, however, only surmises that both state and British railroad commissions affected the legislative process of the 1887 act, without substantiating his assertion. More recent inquiries by Samuel DeCanio and Jed Shugerman both take for granted that state commissions were the primary model of the ICC, citing the strong influence of Charles Francis Adams Jr., who championed the commission idea in the railroad policy debate. Lacking an in-depth analysis of the legislative process, however, their evidence remains circumstantial.[8]

This chapter demonstrates how the ICC became a courtlike administrative agency, undermining the notion of the IRCs' institutional peculiarity in state building. Its goal is twofold. First, it offers a fresh interpretation of the origins of the ICC's institutional form. It shows that the widely held view tracing the agency's institutional roots in preexisting railroad commissions is unfounded. Although the blueprint of the commission initially proposed to Congress was indeed based on state-level railroad regulators, the promoters of the ICC later redesigned it in the wake of strong criticism from the extreme judicialists advocating judicial regulation, with judicial courts as its model. What was at work was not simple path dependence from existing commissions assumed by earlier works but creative syncretism. The drafters of the Interstate Commerce Act crossed institutional boundaries and combined the elements of an administrative commission and courts to create a new, highly judicialized administrative agency.

Second, this chapter demonstrates that the ICC indeed acted in a courtlike manner after its installation and paved the way for the diffusion of its judicial DNA to other parts of the administrative state. As Jerry Mashaw shows, some pre-ICC agencies such as the Patent Office and the Land Office had conducted courtlike adjudications. But in those cases, judicialization remained within each agency and attracted little outside attention. In contrast, the institutional features of the new agency were subjected to intense debate in the legislative process of the 1887 act. After its enactment, the president and judiciary promoted the judicialization of the ICC by appointing lawyers as its members and encouraging the adoption of courtlike procedures in reviewing its decisions. By the early twentieth century, the courtlike ICC was considered a model, archetypal administrative agency.[9]

University Press, 1994); Sanders, *Roots of Reform*, 179–195; Edward A. Purcell, Jr., "Ideas and Interests: Businessmen and the Interstate Commerce Act," *Journal of American History* 54 (1967): 561–578; James, *Presidents, Parties, and the State.*

8 Cushman, *Independent Regulatory Commissions*, 34–36; Breger and Edles, *Independent Agencies*, 23; William R. Childs, *The Texas Railroad Commission: Understanding Regulation in America to the Mid-Twentieth Century* (College Station: Texas A&M University Press, 2005), 28; Jed Handelsman Shugerman, "The Dependent Origins of Independent Agencies: The Interstate Commerce Commission, the Tenure of Office Act, and the Rise of Modern Campaign Finance," *Journal of Law and Politics* 31 (2015): 139–186; Samuel DeCanio, *Democracy and the Origins of the American Regulatory State* (New Haven: Yale University Press, 2015).

9 Mashaw, *Creating the Administrative Constitution*, 310.

While this book shares the new consensus that the American administrative state was born well in advance of the ICC, it also contends that the fact that the ICC and other commissions long considered marginal have yet played a central role in regulation must be squarely addressed to comprehend their lasting influence on the American state. This chapter argues that it was the ICC's status as the foundation of the modern, judicialized administrative state that led people to see the commission as the beginning of the state for such a long time. The courtlike ICC provided an institutional template of an administrative agency at once constitutional and effective, setting the stage for the politics of administrative state institutionalization in the twentieth century. The ICC and other commissions remained representative agencies in the administrative state in which being quasi-judicial, not Weberian, was the norm, at least until the dominant mode of administrative policy making shifted from adjudication to rulemaking in the mid-century.[10]

The judicialization of the ICC during the legislative process and in its early years was made with concern about procedural fairness in policy implementation based on consideration for the supremacy of law and separation of powers presented in the previous chapter. At the same time, the ICC, later criticized for its inefficiency in comparison with executive departments, was proposed as an *efficient* alternative to regulation by judicial courts. This is why the extreme judicialists in Congress countered by pointing out its lack of features guaranteeing equitable treatment of private parties. The clash between efficiency and fairness, a strong motif of modern US administrative state building, was already at work, and triggered the creative syncretism that engendered the judicialist vision of the state that took the form of the ICC.

The rapid construction of railroads in the United States from the mid-nineteenth century gave rise to intense competition among lines, which led to price discrimination such as rebates and drawbacks to large-scale shippers. In addition, a railroad company operating in many regions often tried to compensate for extremely low freight charges in highly competitive sectors by charging more in the sectors in which competition was less severe or nonexistent. Consequently, there were occasional cases in which the charge for hauling goods over a part of a line was higher than the cost of a longer haul along another segment of the same line. While such a situation was frustrating to shippers, carriers were no happier than their customers. Since railroad construction required an enormous initial capital outlay, waging a "rate war" often entailed the risk of bankruptcy. Hoping to avoid this, railroads attempted to form "pools," regional associations in which a uniform rate system was required and monitored. Most of these arrangements, however, broke down because of violations and failure to attract enough lines to ensure their implementation.[11]

10 Richard E. Levy and Sidney A. Shapiro, "Administrative Procedure and the Decline of the Trial," *University of Kansas Law Review* 51 (2003): 473–508.

11 Hoogenboom and Hoogenboom, *History of the ICC*.

To solve the "railroad problem," from the 1870s, several states began creating railroad commissions. Some states tried to eliminate rate discrimination by authorizing the commission to fix a new rate while others gave their commissions the power to investigate and expose discriminatory behaviors of carriers. In 1886, fifteen states had "strong" commissions with rate-setting power and ten states with "weak" ones without it, the latter type pioneered in Massachusetts under Charles Francis Adams Jr.'s leadership.[12] But as the number of lines crossing state borders increased, fears mounted that the regulation of such lines was beyond the constitutional reach of state governments. By the late 1870s, there was a national consensus about the necessity of federal regulation. Rep. John Reagan (D-TX) proposed in every Congress from 1878 a bill that listed forms of rate discrimination to be penalized by courts. In the Senate, Shelby M. Cullom (R-IL) began submitting regulation bills establishing a national commission to counter unjust rate discrimination immediately after joining the chamber in 1883, the same year the Pendleton Act introducing the merit system to the federal civil service was enacted.[13] Intensive debate on these bills in the Forty-Eighth and Forty-Ninth Congresses culminated in the adoption of the Interstate Commerce Act.[14]

The commission Cullom proposed in the Forty-Eighth Congress was loosely modeled on state-level railroad commissions, especially the one in his home state of Illinois. The ICC was to consist of five commissioners appointed to staggered six-year terms. The agency was to collect information on railroad management and was authorized to inspect the books of railroad companies, from which the commission could request the submission of annual reports. Unlike the "weak" commissions, the commission was charged with investigating individual cases of rate discrimination either upon the filing of complaints or on its own initiative. At the same time, it lacked, unlike the "strong" commissions including that of Illinois, the power to set a new rate and to enforce its decisions. Still, the *Chicago Tribune* described the commission as "the adoption substantially of the system that has been practiced . . . by the Railroad Commission of Illinois." Such a comment was only natural when Cullom, the Speaker of Illinois' lower house at the time of the state commission's installment, had also overseen the early workings of the commission as governor.[15]

It is worth noting that Cullom's ICC already bore some similarities to judicial courts. The commission was to conduct investigative hearings and was assigned

12 Frederick C. Clark, "State Railroad Commissions and How They May Be Made Effective," *Publications of the American Economic Association* 6 (1891): 11–110.

13 There were two commission bills by Cullom in the Forty-Eighth Congress, S. 848 and S. 2112. All further references in this chapter are to the more polished S. 2112.

14 Childs, *Texas Railroad Commission*, 36–37.

15 *Chicago Tribune* (hereafter *CT*), Apr. 2, 1884; Shelby M. Cullom, *Fifty Years of Public Service: Personal Recollections of Shelby M. Cullom* (1911; repr., New York: Da Capo Press, 1969), 306; Skowronek, *Building a New American State*, 146; William J. Novak, "The Public Utility Idea and the Origins of Modern Business Regulation," in *Corporations and American Democracy*, ed. Naomi R. Lamoreaux and William J. Novak (Cambridge, MA: Harvard University Press, 2017), 163–165.

powers commonly associated with courts, such as summoning witnesses and subpoenaing information. Such resemblance to courts was even more pronounced in another bill proposing a railroad commission. Drafted by Rep. John Stewart (R-VT) and brought to the House floor by the Committee on Interstate Commerce, the bill (H.R. 5461) was almost identical to the Cullom bill in its key aspects including those on the ICC. Stewart admitted that the provisions on the commission's powers were "drawn in conformity and analogy with the English practice," in a reference to the English Railway Commission established in 1873. But there was a crucial difference between Stewart's ICC and its English model. Although an administrative agency assigned both investigative and adjudicative functions, the English commission could rule with finality and was widely perceived as a *de facto* railroad court.[16]

While virtually overlooked in the literature on the origins of the Interstate Commerce Act, the debate in the Forty-Eighth Congress on these commission bills and the Reagan bill (which replaced the Stewart bill) was crucial in paving the way for the judicialization of the ICC, which Cullom described as a "kind of board of arbitration" to engage in "the adjudication of complaints by arbitration."[17] The proposed commission's similarity to a court and its matchup against judicial control prescribed in the Reagan bill made comparison with a court the focus of the debate. The opponents of the ICC brought up charges against it such as the possible capture by railroad interests and the absurdity of a five-member commission regulating a continent-wide business. But in both chambers, much time was spent on how the authority and capacity of the ICC should be understood in terms of a judicial court, especially whether the commission was going to exercise judicial power and whether the proposed powers were enough to enable the ICC to regulate railroads.[18]

On the question of the nature of the commission's power, the Reaganites, believing that it included judicial power, criticized the supposed unconstitutionality of the commission bill.[19] In his section-by-section parsing of the Cullom bill, Sen. Augustus Garland (D-AR) remarked that it was going to "make the commission a court to try the question of extortion and to assess damages for it," as its hearing was tantamount to "a judicial proceeding." In his view, the commission was "clothed with all the essential features as well as all the paraphernalia

16 *Congressional Record*, 48th Cong., 2nd sess. (1884), HR, 165, 194–195; Henry Parris, *Government and the Railways in Nineteenth-Century Britain* (London: Routledge & Kegan Paul, 1965); Marshall E. Dimock, *British Public Utilities and National Development* (London: G. Allen & Unwin, 1933), 70–72; Chantal Stebbings, *Legal Foundations of Tribunals in Nineteenth-Century England* (Cambridge: Cambridge University Press, 2006), 180–181.

17 *Congressional Record*, 48th Cong., 2nd sess. (1884), S, 328–330. A newspaper noted that the Cullom bill's ICC was "really a court to try certain specified railroad offences." *CT*, Feb. 4, 1885.

18 *Congressional Record*, 48th Cong., 2nd sess. (1884), S, 31, 200–201.

19 The term "Reaganites" was used in the 1880s to refer to Reagan and his allies both inside and outside Congress. See *Austin Weekly Statesman*, Jan. 13, 1887; *Statist*, Jan. 22, 1887, 92.

of a court."[20] Sen. Thomas Bayard (D-DE) commented more generally that a "government by commission" had a strong implication of "an unwarranted delegation of discretion." Such support for regulation by the judiciary on the part of the commission's opponents, almost invariably Democratic, might seem like a straightforward expression of their characteristic antistatism. But curiously, judicial courts had a strong reputation for being unfavorably inclined toward shippers such as farmers and merchants, important Democratic constituents. Legal historians have shown that federal courts, which came to monopolize the handling of railroad-related litigations, were known to be friends of big business, especially railroads. It was not surprising when, by early 1884, all Supreme Court justices and a large majority of lower-court judges were Republican.[21]

Why, then, did anticommission lawmakers see courts as the only legitimate regulator of railroads? There were two reasons. First, the Reaganites' perception of the complexity of the railroad market and the difficulty of its regulation differed markedly from that of the proponents of the ICC, who perceived that policy expertise was indispensable to railroad regulation. In his speech introducing his bill to the House, Reagan argued that Congress need not even regulate railroads; he was merely attempting to prohibit them from doing the things everyone knew ought not to be done, which he believed required no help from any expert commission.[22] The commission's advocates denounced this outlook as simplistic and portrayed the Reagan bill as little more than a codification of highly ambiguous common-law rules on common carriers. The Reaganites countered that all that was necessary was to "declare what is right and enforce it; declare what is wrong and prohibit it" through the courts. In their mind, the ideological orientation of the judiciary should hardly affect the outcome of litigations as long as the provisions in the statute were clear cut.[23]

Second, and more importantly, the dominant constitutional theory limited the power to regulate railroad rates to the judicial courts. The Supreme Court had set the scope of non-judicial adjudication in *Murray's Lessee v. Hoboken Land & Improvement Co*, handed down in 1856.[24] The decision was grounded on the separation of powers and the supremacy of law. According to the Court, cases

20 *Congressional Record*, 48th Cong., 2nd sess. (1885), S, 1568.

21 *Congressional Record*, 48th Cong., 2nd sess. (1885), S, 516; Philip L. Merkel, "The Origins of an Expanded Federal Court Jurisdiction: Railroad Development and the Ascendancy of the Federal Judiciary," *Business History Review* 58 (1984): 336–358; Tony Allan Freyer, *Forums of Order: The Federal Courts and Business in American History* (Greenwich, CT: JAI Press, 1979); Howard Gillman, "How Political Parties Can Use the Courts to Advance Their Agendas: Federal Courts in the United States, 1875–1891," *American Political Science Review* 96 (2002): 511–524.

22 *Congressional Record*, 48th Cong., 2nd sess. (1884), HR, 31. Also see Sanders, *Roots of Reform*, 189.

23 *Congressional Record*, 48th Cong., 2nd sess. (1884), HR, 195; James, *Presidents, Parties, and the State*, 42–43; DeCanio, *Democracy and the Origins of the American Regulatory State*, 182–183.

24 59 U.S. 272 (1856). The Supreme Court later admitted agency adjudication of private rights in *Crowell v. Benson*, 285 U.S. 22 (1932).

on "private rights" regarding "the common law, or in equity, or in admiralty" had to be ruled on by Article III courts. Since railroads were governed by the common-law rule of common carriers, allowing a new regulatory body to judge railroad rate disputes was a constitutional impossibility in the 1880s. Members of Congress, many of them lawyers, understood this well. The Court, however, did not prohibit administrative adjudication. Agencies could hear cases involving "public rights," people's rights involving the government such as those on patent and tax. Dealing with such rights, the major agencies taken up by Mashaw's work could adjudicate en masse without raising judges' eyebrows. Well aware of the distinction between the two types of rights, the legislators did not discuss these agencies as the ICC's precedent. This meant that promoters of an AC had to overcome opposition from extreme judicialists, especially Reaganites, and persuade a majority of lawmakers by presenting an institutional scheme that would not violate the two principles.[25]

To the Reaganites' charges that the proposed commission would infringe on judicial power, Cullom had a simple answer: the commissioners were not going to exercise any "absolute power." The commission could not "dispose of any question finally" to be submitted to them for consideration. This was why he labeled what was to be conferred to the commission "a quasi power of arbitration." In the end, courts would rule on any controversies "in case either party" chose to "take the controversy to the courts." This way, the commission did not have "any absolute power whatever so far as the finality of any finding that they may make" was concerned. Sen. Benjamin Harrison (R-OH) joined Cullom by commenting that the commission's powers were "simply supervisory" and that although it was authorized to administer oaths, that did not necessarily make the commission a court because congressional committees also exercised the same power.[26]

Cullom expected the ICC, armed with policy expertise, to tackle the "railroad problem" more efficiently than judicial courts even without the power to make a final decision. He believed that administrative adjudication had the advantage of rendering "recourse to the tedious processes of the courts unnecessary." At the same time, Cullom, an experienced lawyer, shared the critics' strong attachment to procedural fairness in policy implementation deriving from the separation of powers and the supremacy of law. This is why he quickly added that judicial proceedings must be selected if they were "considered to the advantage of either party in interest."[27] While his answer made perfect constitutional

25 Mashaw, *Creating the Administrative Constitution*, Ch. 14. In the Forty-Ninth Congress, however, Sen. John Morgan (D-AL) attacked the Cullom bill stating that the ICC would take away the power "for the settlement of the private rights" from the judiciary. *Congressional Record*, 49th Cong., 2nd sess. (1887), S, 399. On the historical development of the public rights jurisprudence, see Gordon G. Young, "Public Rights and the Federal Judicial Power: From *Murray's Lessee* through *Crowell* to *Schor*," *Buffalo Law Review* 35 (1986): 765–869.

26 *Congressional Record*, 48th Cong., 2nd sess. (1885), S, 517, 808, 1152.

27 *Congressional Record*, 48th Cong., 2nd sess. (1884), S, 330.

sense, conceding the powerlessness of the proposed commission had the effect of inviting its opponents to interrogate the capacity of the commission: what good can it do with such limited authority? Both houses frequently raised the question, and the answer was usually "not much, if any." Aside from its smallness, a point frequently raised, the proposed ICC had two related deficiencies. First, there was nothing it could do to penalize a noncompliant carrier other than request the district attorney to file suit. Second, the commission's report neither bound the attorney's action on the matter nor guaranteed the use of the commission's findings as evidence during court proceedings. As a Reaganite suggested, a shipper who had submitted a complaint to the ICC could, after spending more than a month with the commission, end up landing "in the court (a place where we had a right to go in the first instance) for an investigation of the case *de novo*."[28]

The proponents of the commission found themselves in a double bind. The proposed ICC could not be simultaneously effective and fit into the constitutional structure, at least according to its adversaries. If it were to have judicial power, it might be effective but unconstitutional – and vice versa. The tension between public administration's efficiency and fairness was already casting its shadow on the legislative process. After criticizing the duties of the commission listed in the Senate bill as "very vague and indefinite," Sen. Samuel Maxey (D-TX) aptly summarized the situation:

> One of the grand characteristics of a court is that it can hear and determine. Is this [the commission] a court? Is it designed to be a court? If so, undoubtedly the Senate bill is unconstitutional, because judges of the courts of the United States must hold their office during good behavior, and these commissioners do not hold their office during good behavior, but for a term of years. Are they invested with judicial powers? Then where have you the authority to invest a commission outside of a court with judicial powers? No such authority exists . . . It is admitted that the commissioners can not adjudge between the parties, because that would make them a court beyond all peradventure, but these facts are sent up, as gathered, as memoranda to the United States district attorney for him to prepare an indictment . . . to bring the railroad company complained of before the court. Then, after all this has been done, what next do you do? . . . So I can not see for the life of me what is the object of this commission.[29]

Interestingly, the railroad commissions that had inspired the drafters of the commission bills offered little help. State-level commissions did not just have powers different from the proposed ICC but had much less trouble acting like courts because of their institutional similarities to them. As John Dickinson points out, state-level judges

28 *Congressional Record*, 48th Cong., 2nd sess. (1884), S, 132. Also see *Congressional Record*, 48th Cong., 2nd sess. (1885), S, 1197.
29 *Congressional Record*, 48th Cong., 2nd sess. (1885), S, 859.

are often appointed or elected for fixed terms, whereas the US Constitution requires Article III judges to occupy their offices during good behavior. The significant federal-state difference in the gap in autonomy between judges and administrators made it difficult to legitimize the ICC by referring to state-level railroad commissions. In contrast, reference to the English Railway Commission was frequent, with the Reaganites calling attention to the ICC's weakness, helping them discredit the proposed commission. The English commission possessed "all the powers and attributes of a court" and could "do everything that any other court can do," which made it "no such powerless thing" as the commission in the Cullom bill.[30]

By the time the two chambers concluded their debate on the reform bills, it was painfully obvious that the ICC's double bind was a serious one. Some legislators surmised that railroads supported the commission precisely because of its impotence. Reagan argued that what was proposed was "a commission which means nothing" and "not intended to mean anything."[31] The ICC advocates' counterargument that the authority of its commissioners and public opinion behind the commission would be sufficient to pressure railroads into complying with its decisions rang hollow. The Cullom bill nonetheless passed the Senate by a party-line vote. But in the House, the Stewart bill died a silent death when it was substituted by the Reagan bill, which passed. The attempt to organize a conference committee ended in failure.[32]

Despite the defeat of the commission bill, the debate in the Forty-Eighth Congress had a crucial impact on the course of railroad regulation. It made Cullom realize that to create the ICC, he needed to break the double bind by revamping the commission, giving due consideration to the procedural fairness of administrative railroad regulation. Such a purposeful thought triggered the creative syncretism that led to the adoption of the judicialized ICC.

Before the adjournment of the Forty-Eighth Congress, the Senate appointed the Select Committee on Interstate Commerce with Cullom as its chair, instructing it to devise a new railroad regulation. With fresh memories of the debate, the committee immediately went to work, determined to end the double bind that incapacitated the ICC. It first sent out circulars to those with stakes in railroad regulation and expertise in railroad management, such as state railroad commissioners and railroad managers, requesting information about, and their views on, existing and desirable regulation. The committee then invited them to testify at marathon hearings held over six months from May 1885. The new Cullom bill drafted at the end of the committee's work contained the ICC that took on more attributes of the judicial body.

The members of the select committee apparently first considered the possibility of giving judicial power to the ICC and making it a special railroad court. They

30 Dickinson, *Administrative Justice*, 76; *Congressional Record*, 48th Cong., 2nd sess. (1885), S, 884. Also see *Congressional Record*, 48th Cong., 2nd sess. (1884), HR, 188–192, 194–195.

31 *Congressional Record*, 48th Cong., 2nd sess. (1885), HR, 128, 527.

32 *Congressional Record*, 48th Cong., 2nd sess. (1885), S, 1205.

routinely asked witnesses whether the commission ought to have judicial power. But the Committee in the end decided against the idea, for two reasons. The first was the risk of making the ICC part of the federal judiciary. The witnesses who answered this question in the affirmative – and many did – were quickly reminded that ICC commissioners had to be given life tenure pursuant to Article III of the Constitution if the commission were to have judicial power. At that point, most had second thoughts, thinking that appointing someone for life to an untested institution was simply too risky, and the committee obviously shared this view. The second reason was that the ICC, different from the English commission, would have had to sacrifice much of its strength in exchange for judicial power. The Supreme Court had resisted the imposition of non-adjudicatory tasks to judicial courts out of consideration for the separation of powers. If it were to become part of the judiciary, the ICC would be able neither to conduct investigation nor to initiate a case on a complainant's behalf, and this seemed too much of a concession to the drafters.[33]

If the commission were not to receive judicial power, its effectiveness had to come through other means. The committee's hearings revolved around a new proposal: to make the ICC's findings prima facie evidence in judicial proceedings. The logic behind this proposal was that even if the commission could not enforce its decisions by itself, its findings should carry significant weight in court if the findings were considered prima facie correct, which would induce the parties to obey the commission's decisions. The idea, later enshrined in the act, released Cullom's committee from the double bind. Its members used every occasion in the hearings to test the soundness of this idea against witnesses, who invariably approved it. In introducing his new bill (S.1532) in the Forty-Ninth Congress, Cullom described the prima facie provision as "one of the most important features of the new bill."[34]

From where did this idea derive? Cullom would comment in the Senate that it came from John D. Kernan, chair of the New York Railroad Commission, who testified in the first hearing of his committee. This matches Scott James's finding that the new Cullom bill was based on the model bill Kernan offered to the select committee. James uses this connection between Kernan and the new commission bill as evidence of the political clout of "business mugwumps," of whom he was a constituent, and attributes it to the group's special position in the partisan balance of power. While this book does not contest James's view, it does not see that the Kernan bill was in any way foisted upon Cullom, at least as far as the ICC was concerned. Avoiding the ordeal the commission idea had undergone in the preceding Congress, James fails to grasp the congruence of views on the

33 Select Committee on Interstate Commerce, *Report of the Senate Select Committee on Interstate Commerce*, 49th Cong., 1st sess. (1886), S. Rep. 46, Pt. 2, 60–61, 107, 167, 267; Justin Crowe, *Building the Judiciary: Law, Courts, and the Politics of Institutional Development* (Princeton: Princeton University Press, 2012).

34 *Congressional Record*, 49th Cong., 1st sess., (1886), S, 3474.

ICC's power between the two men and the meaning of their proposal.[35] What had eluded notice is that Kernan had also grappled with the legal implications associated with the ICC's double bind. While he thought that no law was "better worthy of imitation than the English act," Kernan was well aware that US constitutional constraints hampered the duplication of the English railroad court, and the prima facie provision was devised to break through those constraints. It would, in Kernan's words, help the commission "aiding the courts in carrying out any law" on railroad regulation, and the resulting regulatory framework would come "as near to the English systems as our different conditions will permit." Kernan's intention here was to make the commission's power analogous to that of a judicial court.[36]

For his part, Cullom adopted Kernan's idea precisely because he came to believe it was a way to break the double bind. During Kernan's testimony in the hearings, Cullom inquired if he were suggesting the prima facie idea as an alternative to "giving the board itself any absolute power to settle disputes," that is, judicial power. Kernan answered in the affirmative. By the end of the hearings, Cullom was certain that this was the course to take. It was, to use Cullom's own words, "about as far as you could go without making it [the ICC] a tribunal in the nature of a court, appointed for life." Cullom made his own efforts to judicialize the ICC, which resulted in parts of his bill not being traceable to Kernan's. Whereas both the Cullom and Kernan bills allowed the commission to establish its own rules, the new Cullom bill instructed the commission to ensure that its forms and notices "conform, as nearly as may be, to those in use in the courts of the United States." This clause, later Section Seventeen of the Interstate Commerce Act, reflects its author's intent: to create an administrative agency that resembled a court as closely as possible.[37]

It should be evident that the institutional form of the remodeled ICC was anything but the result of path dependence from state-level commissions. The literature either assumes that the Cullom bills in the Forty-Eighth and Forty-Ninth Congresses were identical or treats the commission proposed in the latter Congress as if it were created from nothing, but neither was the case. Cullom was engaged in creative syncretism, in which he crafted an administrative commission with institutional features of judicial courts fully integrated in it. In its course, he made a conscious choice between the commission's efficiency and fairness. To legitimize adjudication by the ICC, Cullom decided to judicialize it even at the cost of its efficiency. At the same time, the proposed commission was still expected to function much more efficiently than judicial courts. This was how Cullom conceived the judicialist vision of the modern administrative state.

35 *Congressional Record*, 49th Cong., 2nd sess., (1887), S, 659. Kernan, a Democratic lawyer from Utica, had been appointed to the New York commission by Grover Cleveland. Benson, *Merchants, Farmers, and Railroads*, 188; James, *Presidents, Parties, and the State*, 43.

36 *Report of the Senate Select Committee*, Pt. 2, 19–20, 23.

37 *Report of the Senate Select Committee*, Pt. 2, 22, 981.

How was the revised bill treated in the Forty-Ninth Congress? With the Stewart bill no longer in the House, most of the debate on the commission took place in the Senate, to which the select committee submitted its bill, and it confirmed that Cullom had discovered a way out of the double bind. This was visible in the complete switch from the preceding Congress in how the lawmakers described the commission's powers. Instead of ridiculing it as weak, as they had done before, critics now accused the ICC of having *too much* power.[38] In contrast, the proponents, who had failed to highlight the strengths of the commission, now argued that its powers were far from excessive. This shift in the tone of the debate was manifest from the outset. Cullom stressed in his introduction of the bill that its provisions would not "abridge or alter the common-law remedies" already open to the shipper. The new regulatory apparatus should instead be considered "as in addition to such remedies," and no one was "obliged to appeal to the commission." Behind this statement was a sense of confidence that the proposed commission was effective and yet compromised neither the separation of powers nor the supremacy of law. When Sen. John Morgan (D-AL) offered an amendment explicitly barring the commissioners from exercising either legislative or judicial powers, Sen. Orville Platt (R-CT), a member of Cullom's committee, countered that such a provision was unnecessary since the bill had been "carefully drawn so as to avoid the exercise of judicial powers by these commissioners, so as to deprive it of any constitutional objection."[39]

What best illustrates the impact of the revisions of the Cullom bill was the presence of a senator who switched from opposition to the commission to support. Sen. Maxey, Reagan's fellow Texan who had belittled the commission's powers in the preceding Congress as "very vague and indefinite," now praised the new bill, especially its prima facie clause:

> Mr. President, when the bill reported by the Senator from Illinois [Cullom] in the Forty-Eighth Congress was before the Senate I opposed that bill for the reason which I thought satisfactory, that there was nothing whatever effective in that measure; because the evidence gathered by the commission under that bill could not be used in the courts or anywhere else; because . . . practically all the testimony would simply be a guide to the district attorney . . . But this bill is entirely different. This is a very great advance, in my judgment, upon the bill of the Forty-Eighth Congress. This bill does make the testimony taken by the commissioners prima facie evidence in proceedings in court, and to that extent it does start in motion something which will result in a judgment one way or the other.[40]

In the House, where the Cullom bill that had passed the Senate was subsequently replaced with the Reagan bill, the situation was much the same. After denigrating

38 *Congressional Record*, 49th Cong., 1st sess. (1886), S, 4307.
39 *Congressional Record*, 49th Cong., 1st sess. (1886), S, 3471, 4422.
40 *Congressional Record*, 49th Cong., 1st sess. (1886), S, 4225.

the proposed commission by pointing out its lack of rate-setting power (which no one had wished to give to the commission in the first place), Reagan now denounced the commission as despotic. While he thought that Americans had great respect for the judiciary, they were "not accustomed to the administration of the civil law through bureau orders." To this, the proponents of the Cullom bill countered that the commission system, having been tried both in the states and overseas, was a "system . . . of experience." They now argued it was the Reagan bill, containing "nothing to soften the inflexible strictness of the prohibition applied elsewhere," that was a "system of experiment," worthy of avoiding at all costs. Ironically, the pro-commission lawmakers could now call state-level commissions to their aid after the proposed commission had been judicialized.[41]

There was another notable change in the debate over the ICC; now the commission was not just being discussed in terms of a court but came to be understood as something very *similar* to one. This is evident in the floor debates after the conference committee had shaped a compromise bill retaining most of the commission-related provisions in the Cullom bill, including those above. After pointing out the constitutional difficulty of giving summary judicial powers to the commission, Sen. George Edmunds (R-VT) described the bill as coming "the nearest" to doing what they could do.[42] In the House, Charles O'Neil (R-PA) similarly remarked that the bill made the commission "almost a court" and its proceedings "almost similar to proceedings in courts." It was not just the supporters of the commission who thought it resembled a court. In one of his final attacks on the commission, Sen. Morgan denounced the commission for taking away the power "for the settlement of the private rights and the redress of wrongs of citizen[s]" from the judiciary. Later, he described the commission's proceedings as "a court proceeding ex parte." Other opponents referred to the commission's powers as "quasi-judicial" and "half judicial," reflecting the syncretic nature of the ICC. But despite all the associations they made with courts, they no longer claimed it was unconstitutional.[43]

While the Reaganites continued to attack the ICC, the compromise bill was a much better deal for them than it seemed on the surface. Most importantly, the bill inherited from the Reagan bill the prohibition of certain practices by carriers, including pooling. By this time, Reagan was reportedly willing to concede to the commission idea, as long as the long-haul/short-haul clause would survive. In addition, because relevant actors were free to bypass the ICC and take their cases directly to a court, the judiciary could theoretically fully implement the bill, just as the Reaganites wished. And even if complaints were to come before the commission, there still was a good chance that it would rule in favor of shippers. In

41 *Congressional Record*, 49th Cong., 1st sess. (1886), HR, 7289, 7296.

42 Rohr, *To Run a Constitution*, 96–97; *Congressional Record*, 49th Cong., 2nd sess. (1887), S, 646.

43 *Congressional Record*, 49th Cong., 2nd sess. (1887), HR, 786; *Congressional Record*, 49th Cong., 2nd sess. (1887), S, 399, 529, 639. Also see Hoffer, *To Enlarge the Machinery of Government*, 160; Rohr, *To Run a Constitution*, 96–97.

contrast to the Republican-dominated judiciary, Section Eleven of the act guaranteed the appointment of two or more Democrats to the commission. Further, since the high cost of litigation had deterred many shippers from suing carriers, the commission's role as an attorney for complainants could very well tilt the balance to the advantage of shippers.[44]

Two institutional features of the ICC have been of much interest to scholars today but went almost unnoticed throughout the legislative process of the commission bill in the two congresses, both pertaining to the autonomy of the commission. The first was the ICC's relation to the Department of Interior. Both the new Cullom bill and the final bill stipulated that the commission report to, and be funded by, the executive department, and historians have wondered whether the Congress's intent was to subjugate the ICC to the executive department, and ultimately to the president. Jed Shugerman sees the inclusion of the provision as an intentional move toward the commission's political accountability, comparing it to the enforcement by the independent judiciary prescribed in the Reagan bill. He also suggests a connection to the repeal of the Tenure of Office Act in 1886 resurrecting the president's power to discretionarily dismiss public officials.[45]

It is difficult to conclude that the decision to house the ICC in the Interior was made with the intention of giving the president control over the commission, however. The Reaganites in support of regulation by independent judiciary would have surely attacked it if they sensed any political aim behind the provision, even when the incumbent president was Grover Cleveland, a Democrat. But hardly any comment was made on the provision during the congressional debate from members of either political party. Also, the commission had already been tied to the Interior in the Cullom bill in the Forty-Eighth Congress, when the abolition of the Tenure of Office Act was still beyond the horizon. It makes more sense that the arrangement was made out of sheer need to fit the ICC somewhere in the US government structure. The Interior department, which at the time was "the Great Miscellany," a hodgepodge of agencies with a range of tasks, was a natural destination. The ICC was supposed to be autonomous from the chief executive. This also explains why the ICC left the department without fanfare in 1889.[46]

44 Transcript, *Galveston News*, Nov. 29, 1886, Folder "Transcripts – Newspaper Articles, 1877–1886, (9)," Box 2K331, John H. Reagan Papers, Dolph Briscoe Center for American History, University of Texas at Austin. Contrary to Scott James's view, Reagan's acceptance of the ICC may not have meant the jettisoning of his "core agrarian conviction" against regulation by agencies. James, *Presidents, Parties, and the State*, 102–103. In the Forty-Eighth Congress, some Reaganites had expressed their readiness to support a commission bill with provisions specifying the practices to be banned. *Congressional Record*, 48th Cong., 2nd sess. (1884), HR, 64; *Congressional Record*, 48th Cong., 2nd sess. (1885), S, 858.

45 Shugerman, "The Dependent Origins of Independent Agencies." Also see Calabresi and Yoo, *Unitary Executive*, 214.

46 Rohr, *To Run a Constitution*, 95; Leonard D. White, *The Republican Era: 1869–1901: A Study in Administrative History* (New York: Macmillan, 1958), 175.

The second institutional feature of interest to scholars was that Section Eleven of the final bill stipulated that the president could remove any commissioner for "inefficiency, neglect of duty, or malfeasance in office." This provision was left almost untouched throughout the two congresses. The Cullom bill of the Forty-Eighth Congress stated in its Section One that the commissioners could be removed for "incompetency or malfeasance in office," and the clause had already taken its final form by the time the revised bill was introduced to the next Congress. Citing Cushman, Calabresi and Yoo argue that the absence of clear expression on the side of lawmakers to delimit presidential removal power during the legislative process signifies their indifference to the constitutional implication of this part of the bill. Given the treatment of the ICC as a courtlike agency in the Forty-Ninth Congress by both advocates and opponents, however, it makes more sense to think that the legislators paid little attention to the provision simply because it corresponded to their image of autonomous judges.[47]

The 1886 *Wabash* Supreme Court decision forbidding states from regulating interstate lines necessitated the passage of a railroad regulation law in the Forty-Ninth Congress. The pressure from the decision and the nature of the compromise bill probably induced lawmakers to accept the bill. It passed the Senate on January 14, 1887, and the House followed suit a week later, both with a lopsided majority. President Cleveland signed it into law on February 4.

The ICC, initially modeled on existing railroad commissions, was thus transformed into a strongly courtlike agency by the time of its creation. The implementation of an act, however, does not always reflect lawmakers' intentions. To elucidate why the ICC turned out to be a "quasi-judicial" institution, it is worthwhile to look into its formation and early operations. This is particularly important as the 1887 act was silent on two of the commission's fundamental structural elements. First, the statute said nothing about the qualifications of the commissioners except that no more than a bare majority of them could come from the same political party and that no member could have a pecuniary interest in railroads. Second, as Section Seventeen of the act only instructed the commission to "conduct its proceedings in such manner as will best conduce to the proper dispatch of business and to the ends of justice," this meant that the members of the ICC were free to choose the balance between efficiency and fairness in fixing the commission's rules. Under these conditions, who the commissioners were going to be and how they would steer the ICC would have a tremendous impact on its character.[48]

The selection of commissioners attracted much attention even before the president signed the bill because of the importance of the railroad problem and the authority – and perhaps also the generous salary – they were to enjoy. Available evidence suggests that throughout the candidate selection process, which took more than a month, his eyes were firmly set on a particular category of

47 Calabresi and Yoo, *Unitary Executive*, 213–214.
48 *Wabash, St. Louis & Pacific Railway Company v. Illinois*, 118 U.S. 557 (1886).

professionals: the lawyers. This was most visible in the search for the commission's chair. Cleveland, himself a seasoned lawyer, sought advice from Benjamin H. Bristow, best known today as the Secretary of Treasury of the second Grant administration who later bolted the Republican Party in 1884 over the presidential nomination of James G. Blaine. It also should be noted, however, that Bristow was one of the leading American lawyers at the time. He had served as the first US solicitor general for two years from 1870 and then become the president of the American Bar Association later in the decade. Such a career made him one of the best people to consult in selecting talented lawyers of all political stripes. Bristow's recommendation to Cleveland was Walter Q. Gresham, an old friend from his home state of Kentucky, by then a federal circuit judge headquartered in Chicago.[49]

Although the biographers of Bristow and Gresham disagree on why Gresham's name eventually fell out of consideration, Cleveland turned to Thomas M. Cooley, who accepted the nomination. As the author of influential articles on the railroad problem and the receiver of the Wabash railway from late 1886 – the appointment was made by none other than Gresham – his expertise in the railroad problem was so well known by the mid-1880s that Cullom asked him to submit a statement on desirable reform to his select committee and later recommended him to Cleveland for the chairmanship of the ICC.[50] Cooley's name was occasionally mentioned in congressional debates on the commission bills as a strong candidate for the commissionership. It was doubtful, however, that Cooley's knowledge on the railroad issue alone brought to him the post. After all, this ex-chief justice of the Michigan Supreme Court, on which he had served for two decades from 1865, and dean of the University of Michigan Law School was a towering figure in law during the postbellum period. His treatises were required reading for lawyers. Cooley's prestige in the legal community made the difference.[51]

The search process strongly suggested that Cleveland focused on recruiting lawyers for the ICC. As it turned out, all five of the first nominations intended to give "the new law a good start by appointing men of the highest character and national repute who would command the confidence of the country" went to lawyers. Of the commissioners other than Cooley, Walter Bragg had been the chairman of the Alabama Railroad Commission, and Aldace F. Walker had had

49 Ross A. Webb, *Benjamin Helm Bristow, Border State Politician* (Lexington, KY: University Press of Kentucky, 1969), 296.

50 Charles W. Calhoun, *Gilded Age Cato: The Life of Walter Q. Gresham* (Lexington, KY: University Press of Kentucky, 1988), 90; Kolko, *Railroads and Regulation*, 47.

51 Thomas M. Cooley, *A Treatise on the Constitutional Limitations Which Rest Upon the Legislative Power of the States of the American Union*, 3rd ed. (Boston: Little, Brown, 1874); Thomas M. Cooley, *The General Principles of Constitutional Law in the United States of America* (Boston: Little, Brown, 1880); Alan Jones, "Thomas M. Cooley and the Interstate Commerce Commission: Continuity and Change in the Doctrine of Equal Rights," *Political Science Quarterly* 81 (1966): 602–627; Alan Jones, "Thomas M. Cooley and 'Laissez-Faire Constitutionalism': A Reconsideration," *Journal of American History* 53 (1967): 751–771.

extensive railroad experience, which made him instrumental in the creation of the railroad commission in Vermont. But the career of the other two, William Morrison and Augustus Schoonmaker, had no immediate connection to the industry.[52]

This preference for lawyers was not unique to Cleveland. In appointing the successor to Cooley in 1891, President Benjamin Harrison wrote him with a request for recommendations, lamenting that it was "very difficult to find a lawyer of the first eminence in active practice who would consent to accept" a commissionership, indicating that his pool of candidates was limited to lawyers. In fact, the pattern persisted for a generation. All except one of the commissioners appointed in the ICC's first twenty years turned out to be lawyers by training, although some of them, most notably Martin Knapp and Franklin K. Lane, also had extensive knowledge of the railroad business.[53]

It should then come as no surprise that the lawyer-filled commission's conduct of business resembled that of a court. Cooley, to whom other commissioners deferred during his four-year term as chair before resigning because of poor health, had the vision "to understand that proceedings before the Commission required simplicity and not complexity in procedure." He stated in the ICC's first annual report that the proceedings before the commission "should be made as informal as should be consistent with order and regularity."[54] The ICC, then, began its work amid an inherent tension between judicialization and the pursuit of efficiency. Just as the FTC continued to experience creative syncretism after its formation, as Gerald Berk has shown, the ICC still had much room for institutional evolution. And probably because there was no other precedent to follow, the procedural rules the commission adopted were made very similar to those of courts – its rules of conduct explicitly borrowed some provisions from the rules on court proceedings – although they were also kept very general, enabling flexible operation. In this way Cooley developed the notion of "administrative due process of law."[55]

While the ICC was long destined to handle the tradeoff between efficiency and fairness, the pendulum initially swung toward judicialization, although efficiency was not ignored. In its inaugural year, the commission repeatedly stated that it

52 Benjamin Helm Bristow to Walter Q. Gresham, Feb. 9, 1887, Box 34, Walter Q. Gresham Papers, Manuscript Division, Library of Congress.

53 Benjamin Harrison to Thomas M. Cooley, Oct. 29, 1891, Box 5, Thomas M. Cooley Papers, Bentley Historical Library, University of Michigan; Clarence A. Miller, "The Interstate Commerce Commissioners: The First Fifty Years: 1887–1937," *George Washington Law Review* 5 (1937): 580–700. Also see I. L. Sharfman, *The Interstate Commerce Commission: A Study in Administrative Procedure* (New York: Commonwealth Fund, 1937), 4:28.

54 Elmer A. Smith, "Practice and Procedure before the Interstate Commerce Commission," *George Washington Law Review* 5 (1937): 413. Also see Paul D. Carrington, "Law and Economics in the Creation of Federal Administrative Law: Thomas Cooley, Elder to the Republic," *Iowa Law Review* 83 (1998): 379; *First Annual Report of the Interstate Commerce Commission* (Washington, DC: Government Printing Office, 1887), 27–28.

55 Berk, *Making of Regulated Competition*; *First Annual Report of the Interstate Commerce Commission*, 130, 133; Henry Carter Adams, "A Decade of Federal Railway Regulation," *Atlantic Monthly*, Apr. 1898, 433–443; Carrington, "Law and Economics," 386.

would not decide "on abstract questions, nor on questions presented by ex parte statements of fact, or on questions of construction of the statute presented for its advice but without any controversy pending before it on complaint of violation of law."[56] This was a declaration that the commission would handle cases exactly like a court. The commission's behavior came to resemble that of a court in other respects. It began to publish its decisions from a legal publisher, just like courts, and occasionally used a federal courtroom when conducting hearings outside Washington, DC. In its 1888 report, the ICC proudly stated that "[p]ower, judicial in its nature," was conferred upon it.[57]

It should be clear that the ICC was not only designed to be a courtlike administrative body; it actually became highly judicialized and functioned as judicialist lawmakers had intended. Marver Bernstein and Paul Verkuil attribute the way the ICC came to emulate courts to Cooley's chairmanship. Verkuil intimates that things would have been different had Cooley not been appointed to the ICC. But even if Cooley had not been available, Cleveland would almost certainly have named a lawyer, albeit perhaps not of equal stature. It was Congress that had produced a judicialized commission, and the president was following its lead by assigning lawyers. A railroad magazine observed after the organization of the ICC that the commissioners realized that they constituted "a new court" and that they were to "lay the foundations of a new body of American law."[58]

The judiciary, however, did not readily allow the ICC to take the initiative in railroad regulation and instead severely narrowed the scope of its authority. In the 1896 decision of *Cincinnati, New Orleans and Texas Pacific v. ICC*, the Supreme Court prohibited the commission from fixing a new rate when it found the existing one inappropriate. This case, coupled with the *ICC v. Alabama Midland Railroad Company* decision in the following year nullifying the commission's interpretation of the long-haul/short-haul clause, led to Justice John Marshall Harlan's famous dissent that it went "far to make that commission a

56 William E. Forbath, "Politics, State Building, and the Courts, 1870–1920," in *The Cambridge History of Law in America*, vol. 2, *The Long Nineteenth Century (1789–1920)*, ed. Michael Grossberg and Christopher Tomlins (New York: Cambridge University Press, 2008), 671–672; Interstate Commerce Commission, *Reports and Decisions of the Interstate Commerce Commission of the United States, April 5th, 1887 to April 5th, 1888* (New York: L. K. Strouse, 1888), 8; the commission was flooded with letters asking all sorts of "what if" questions. See, for instance, Thomas M. Cooley to Henry Stephens and Co., May 17, 1887, vol. 1, General Letters, 1887–1942, Records of the Operating Division, Interstate Commerce Commission, Record Group 134, National Archives, College Park, MD; Thomas M. Cooley to George M. Jackson, May 21, 1887, vol. 1, General Letters, 1887–1942, RG134, NA-College Park.

57 *Second Annual Report of the Interstate Commerce Commission* (Washington, DC: Government Printing Office, 1888), 104; Leonard S. Goodman, "Getting Started: Organization, Procedure and Initial Business of the ICC in 1887," *Transportation Law Journal* 16 (1987): 7–34.

58 Bernstein, *Regulating Business*, 29, 34, 134; Paul R. Verkuil, "Purposes and Limits," 261, n. 17; *Railway and Corporation Law Journal*, June 25, 1887.

useless body." The early ICC was so toothless that the railroads hardly needed to capture it.[59]

These decisions may give the impression that the judiciary did not seriously treat the ICC as a tribunal. But in denying rate-setting power to the ICC, the Court explained that it was part of legislative, not judicial power. It never squarely prohibited the commission from exercising (quasi-)judicial power and actually offered much support to the ICC concerning its role as an adjudicator. First, the Court backed the commission when the prima facie provision came to suffer from carriers' withholding their evidence from the commission's proceedings, which greatly undermined its fact-finding role. The ICC first complained of such a situation in its 1891 report and recommended confining the hearings by courts "to the record of proceedings had before the Commission."[60] In the 1896 *Cincinnati* decision, the Court condemned the carriers' practice, arguing that courts should be resorted to only "when the Commission prefers to enforce the provisions of the statute by a direct proceeding in the court, or when the orders of the Commission have been disregarded." By 1907, the Court had full confidence in the judgment of the commission, which it characterized as "a tribunal appointed by law and informed by experience."[61]

Second, the judiciary, commonly very restrictive in dealing with agency procedures, came to regard the commission's procedure as simpler than their own but still similar enough to it to pass the due-process test. In turning down the rate-making power of the Minnesota railroad commission whose procedures involved "nothing which has the semblance of due process of law," the Supreme Court almost equated due process with the judicial process in 1890. But it gradually changed its attitude. In the *Brimson* case ruled in 1894, the Court decided in favor of the exercise of subpoena power by the ICC, noting that its proceedings were "judicial in form." By 1904, the Supreme Court noted that the ICC's largely investigative function "should not be hampered . . . by those narrow rules which prevail in trials at common law."[62] Five years later, in declaring that "strict rules of pleading should not be held applicable" to the ICC, the circuit court headquartered in New York added that it had "established rules of practice

59 162 U.S. 184 (1896); 168 U.S. 144 (1897), at 176; Hoogenboom and Hoogenboom, *History of the ICC*; James W. Ely, Jr., *Railroads and American Law* (Lawrence: University Press of Kansas, 2001), 93–96.

60 *Fifth Annual Report of the Interstate Commerce Commission* (Washington, DC: Government Printing Office, 1891), 18–20.

61 162 U.S. 184 (1896), at 196; *Illinois Central Railroad Co. et al. v. ICC*, 206 U.S. 441 (1907), at 454. Also see *ICC v. Union Pacific Railroad Co. et al.*, 222 U.S. 541 (1912). See generally, Martin Tollefson, "Judicial Review of the Decisions of the Interstate Commerce Commission," *George Washington Law Review* 5 (1937): 503–542.

62 *Chicago, Milwaukee & St. Paul Railway Company v. Minnesota*, 134 U.S. 418 (1890), at 457; Rohr, *To Run a Constitution*, 108; *ICC v. Brimson*, 154 U.S. 447 (1894), at 486; Judge Glock, "The Forgotten Visitorial Power: The Origins of Administrative Subpoenas and Modern Regulation," *Review of Banking and Financial Law* 37 (2017): 243–244; *ICC v. Baird*, 194 U.S. 25 (1904). Also see *ICC v. Louisville & Nashville Railroad Co.*, 227 U.S. 88 (1913).

analogous to those in courts." The Supreme Court also expressed its hope that the commission would exercise its powers "in the coldest neutrality." These statements indicated that the ICC had successfully struck a balance between efficiency and fairness with the judiciary.[63]

Such treatment of the ICC accorded perfectly with that of its creators. The commission was not a court and was expected to regulate more efficiently than a court. But at the same time, the ICC was strongly oriented toward procedural fairness, doing what courts used to do in a way highly similar to courts. The judicialization of the commission was not in any way accidental; in the policy makers' mind, an administrative agency had to be "quasi-judicial" to remain both constitutional and effective. Thus all three branches of the US government promoted the ICC to become, to use the term in frequent use by this time, an ***administrative tribunal***, described by an observer as "administrative authorities which . . . closely resemble courts of general jurisdiction."[64]

The judicialized ICC was not just welcomed by the three branches but also received wide public support. The popularity of the commission was shown in the ways in which it was empowered through additional legislation in the early twentieth century. Adopted in 1903, the Elkins Act authorized the commission to impose heavy fines on carriers offering rebates but also upon the shippers accepting them. This was expected to be an effective countermeasure against trusts on both shippers' and carriers' sides pressuring individual railroads into paying rebates. The Hepburn Act of 1906 was a turning point in strengthening the ICC in many important ways. It not only reinforced the anti-rebate provision but also granted the commission the power to set "just and reasonable" maximum rates. Moreover, the act expanded the commission's jurisdiction to infrastructures such as bridges and terminals. To cover additional workloads, the act increased the number of commissioners to seven and allowed them to hire examiners who would conduct formal hearings on their behalf, something the commissioners had been asking for at least since 1890. The examiners were also expected to weaken the prosecutor-judge combination. Most importantly, the act made the commission decisions self-enforcing. The two laws were enormously popular; the latter act passed the Senate with only three members voting against it.[65]

63 *New York Central & Harbor Railroad Co. et al. v. ICC*, 168 Fed. 131 (1909), at 138–39; *ICC v. Chicago, Rock Island and Pacific Railway Co.*, 218 U.S. 88 (1909), at 102; Smith, "Practice and Procedure before the Interstate Commerce Commission"; Ernst, *Tocqueville's Nightmare*, 38.

64 Harold M. Bowman, "American Administrative Tribunals," *Political Science Quarterly* 21 (1906): 612.

65 Ernst, *Tocqueville's Nightmare*, 27, 45. Sharfman, *Interstate Commerce Commission*, 1:35–52. By 1890, the ICC commissioners were complaining to Sen. Cullom that it already was a "physical impossibility" for them to attend hearings held in different parts of the country. William R. Morrison et al. to Shelby Cullom, April 24, 1890, vol. 5, General Letters, 1887–1942, RG134, NA-College Park; W. R. Morrison to J. Brooks, June 28, 1890, vol. 6, General Letters, 1887–1942, RG134, NA-College Park. For the statutes authorizing the

These laws gave teeth to the ICC, which added to the contemporaries' now-firm trust in the courtlike commission as a regulator, despite the widespread public support for efficiency in economic and social affairs. The popularity of the ACs in this period was shown in the manner in which presidents dealt with them. President Theodore Roosevelt aggressively championed the strengthening of the ICC as part of his Square Deal, which boosted public support for the 1903 and 1906 legislations. But he was hardly a genuine advocate of ACs. Later in 1908, he declared in the annual message to Congress that "all existing independent bureaus and commissions should be placed under the jurisdiction of appropriate executive departments."[66] Just as executivist as any later president, Roosevelt still had no choice but to back the ICC in order to pursue his policy program because of the strong support the commission enjoyed. The same could be said for President William Howard Taft, Roosevelt's hand-picked successor. He insisted on the inclusion of a special appellate-level court to review ICC-related cases in the Mann-Elkins Act of 1910, designed to extend the commission's authority to telephone, telegraph, and wireless companies. Such an imposition of a judicial court to oversee the ICC, as Sidney Milkis explains, derived from Taft's progressive conservatism. Unlike Roosevelt, who did not hesitate to pursue progressive goals with ACs, Taft stuck to achieving the same within more traditional constitutional mechanisms. Constructing the Commerce Court with expertise in railroads was the maximum concession he could make. Taft's belief that a special railroad court could regulate better than the ICC, based on strict adherence to the separation of powers, however, found few sympathizers, even among fellow Republicans. Once organized, the court began to strike down the commission's orders, only to have the Supreme Court reinstate most of them. Criticism quickly mounted from both sides of the political aisle and with the court's abolition in 1913.[67]

The findings of this chapter clearly indicate that the rise of the ICC was a critical juncture that set off the systemic judicialization of the US administrative state, thereby introducing procedural uniformity to public administration. Studies of the early American state in different disciplines have discovered that federal agencies

---

use of examiners until 1940, see Lloyd D. Musolf, *Federal Examiners and the Conflict of Law and Administration* (Baltimore: Johns Hopkins Press, 1953), 53.

66 Hoogenboom and Hoogenboom, *History of the ICC*, 43–52; Lewis L. Gould, *The Presidency of Theodore Roosevelt* (Lawrence: University Press of Kansas, 1991), 106, 156–164; Theodore Roosevelt, "Eighth Annual Message," December 8, 1908. Online by Gerhard Peters and John T. Woolley, American Presidency Project. www.presidency.ucsb.edu/node/206223

67 Sidney M. Milkis, "William Howard Taft and the Struggle for the Soul of the Constitution," in *Toward an American Conservatism: Constitutional Conservatism during the Progressive Era*, ed. Joseph Postell and Johnathan O'Neill (New York: Palgrave Macmillan, 2013), 63–93. Sharfman, *Interstate Commerce Commission*, 1:60–70. Also see Harrison, *New American State*, 82–83; Felix Frankfurter and James M. Landis, *The Business of the Supreme Court: A Study in the Federal Judicial System* (New York: Macmillan, 1928), 156–174; Lewis L. Gould, *The William Howard Taft Presidency* (Lawrence: University Press of Kansas, 2009), 97–98; George E. Dix, "The Death of the Commerce Court: A Study in Institutional Weakness," *American Journal of Legal History* 8 (1964): 238–260.

carried out manifold tasks in very different ways. In contrast, works on early twentieth-century public administration have stressed that there was an expectation that the manner in which agencies unsanctioned by the Constitution conducted adjudication would emulate court proceedings. As Morton Horwitz and others have shown, many of the political battles fought during the twentieth century around administrative agencies were over how judicialized their procedures ought to be in light of "court-centered conceptions of legitimacy." This chapter bridges the two strands of research by situating the emergence of the courtlike ICC in US administrative state building as a turning point in how the state operated.[68]

The notion of the ICC as the watershed in the mode of administrative state operation should be familiar to legal scholars. They have argued that various agencies, including executive departments, adopted courtlike procedures that had been developed by the ICC (and the FTC explicitly modeled after it) under the supervision of the judiciary. Provisions of many statutes requiring agencies to hold hearings were modeled after those governing the ICC. Formal adjudication was to be made a permanent and standard method of policy implementation with the enactment of the 1946 Administrative Procedure Act.[69]

The legal scholars emphasizing the impact of the ICC's judiciality on the administrative state, however, have failed to explain why the commission became judicialized in the first place. They have either stressed the overall influence lawyers have had in politics or pointed to the role played by the judiciary after the commission began its work. While the two factors certainly contributed to judicialization, the ICC came to adopt various courtlike features ***during*** the legislative process, and it was consideration for procedural fairness that drove the legislators toward the courtlike ICC. Administration may have won its place in the American polity "only on terms fixed by lawyers," but it took the rise of the courtlike ICC as a prototypical agency for them to start setting the administrative process "in the courtroom mold."[70]

68 Horwitz, *Transformation of American Law*, 222; Paul R. Verkuil, "Emerging Concept"; Stephen G. Breyer et al., *Administrative Law and Regulatory Policy: Problems, Text, and Cases*, 7th ed. (New York: Aspen Publishers, 2011), 18; Robert L. Rabin, "Federal Regulation"; Morton Keller, *Regulating a New Economy*; Ernst, "Morgan and the New Dealers"; Ernst, *Tocqueville's Nightmare*; Reuel Schiller, " 'Saint George and the Dragon': Courts and the Development of the Administrative State in Twentieth-Century America," *Journal of Policy History* 17 (2005): 110–124; Bertelli and Lynn, *Madison's Managers*; Grisinger, *Unwieldy American State*. Also see Joanna L. Grisinger, "Law and the Administrative State," in *A Companion to American Legal History*, ed. Sally E. Hadden and Alfred L. Brophy (Chichester, UK: Wiley-Blackwell, 2013), 367–386.

69 White, *Constitution and the New Deal*, Ch. 4; Henry J. Friendly, "Some Kind of Hearing," *University of Pennsylvania Law Review* 123 (1975): 1267–1317; Landis, *Administrative Process*; Carl McFarland, *Judicial Control of the Federal Trade Commission and the Interstate Commerce Commission, 1920–1930: A Comparative Study in the Relations of Courts to Administrative Commissions* (Cambridge, MA: Harvard University Press, 1933); Chamberlain, Dowling, and Hayes, *Judicial Function in Federal Administrative Agencies*.

70 Daniel R. Ernst, "Law and the State, 1920–2000: Institutional Growth and Structural Change," in *The Cambridge History of Law in America*, vol. 3, *The Twentieth Century and*

It is therefore quite difficult to overstate the role that the judicialization of the ICC documented in this chapter played in American administrative state building. To appreciate this, we need only to think of a counterfactual: how would the commission have been constructed if the first Cullom bill had somehow passed in the Forty-Eighth Congress? Although it already had several courtlike characteristics, the ICC in the bill was treated as an agency alien from courts in the Congress. If adopted as such, the commission could even have been constructed as an *anti*-courtlike agency, which could have severely delayed, if not prevented, the systemic judicialization of the administrative state. It was the bill's later revision, driven by creative syncretism, that triggered the infusion of judicial DNA into the US administrative state.

It should also be kept in mind, however, that the creation of an administrative agency in the form of ICC was primarily driven by the motivation to make policy implementation more efficient, rather than by judicial courts. This is why many lawyers would be frustrated by "administrative tribunals" despite their strong judiciality. It was symbolic that the provision in the 1887 act on the removal of ICC commissioners, which was to be copied by many enacting statutes of later ACs, included a member's inefficiency as a possible cause of dismissal; the courtlike commission's autonomy hinged on its efficiency. In 1906, Roscoe Pound, future dean of Harvard Law School, argued in a provocative paper read at an ABA meeting in St. Paul that administrative commissions were flourishing because of the public's dissatisfaction with the judiciary's organization and procedures, including "exagerations [sic] of the common-law contentious procedure." The paper was so controversial among powerful lawyers who believed in the supremacy of the judicial procedures that the bar association almost refused to publish it in its annual report. As such, the ICC and other US administrative agencies were destined to be subjected to an endless tug-of-war between the forces of efficiency and fairness forces for years to come.[71]

After (1920–), ed. Michael Grossberg and Christopher Tomlins (New York: Cambridge University Press, 2008), 2; Bernard Schwartz, "Administrative Law: The Third Century," 300.

71 Roscoe Pound, "The Causes of Popular Dissatisfaction with the Administration of Justice," *American Law Review* 40 (1906): 738; Horwitz, *Transformation of American Law*, 217. Also see Roscoe Pound, "Executive Justice," *American Law Register* 55 (1907): 139; Roscoe Pound, *The Spirit of the Common Law* (Francetown, NH: Marshall Jones Co., 1921), xii.

3 Creating the "Supreme Court of Finance"

"In the judgment of the present writer," an observer noted in a 1906 journal article on state and national administrative tribunals, "the interstate commerce commission [sic] is sufficiently peculiar to be placed in a category by itself." As discussed in the preceding chapter, the ICC had established its reputation as a powerful and reliable administrative tribunal by the early twentieth century. But as indicated in the above comment, that did not guarantee that the ICC would be the institutional model of subsequent regulations, let alone administrative agencies in general. In discussing antitrust reform, reformers at the time, including the National Consumer Federation and President Roosevelt, strongly pushed for legislation in which the ICC was to regulate corporations together with the Bureau of Corporations at the Department of Commerce and Labor, created in 1903. The Pure Food and Drug Act of 1906 gave the power to regulate food and drugs to the Department of Agriculture. The Secretary of Agriculture was to hold hearings in cases of possible violations of law. Because their procedures were not particularly judicialized, the federal district attorney was not obligated to make use of the evidence gathered in departmental hearings in criminal proceedings. The versatility and potential scope of the diffusion of the commission form of regulation must therefore be measured in a different manner.[1]

This chapter achieves that goal by examining the political process that led to the establishment of the Federal Reserve System in 1913 with special attention to the Federal Reserve Board and its institutional features. This case is significant not solely because the FRB is considered the second IRC. It constitutes a "hard case" in this study in two related ways. First, the FRB has very little in common with the ICC in both its policy role and institutional form among the ACs created in the early twentieth century. Instead of regulating an industry through

1 Bowman, "American Administrative Tribunals," 614–615; Martin J. Sklar, *The Corporate Reconstruction of American Capitalism, 1900–1916: The Market, the Law, and Politics* (New York: Cambridge University Press, 1988), Ch. 4; William Murphy, "Theodore Roosevelt and the Bureau of Corporation: Executive-Corporate and the Advancement of the Regulatory State," *American Nineteenth Century History* 14 (2013): 73–111; Lauffer T. Hayes and Frank J. Ruff, "The Administration of the Federal Food and Drugs Act," *Law and Contemporary Problems* 1 (1933): 27–28; Schiller, "'Saint George and the Dragon,'" 114–115.

adjudication, the board plays the role of manager of the reserve system. In categorizing the FRB as an IRC, Robert Cushman admitted that the board and the ICC "bore only a very superficial resemblance to each other" in "composition, duties, and procedure"; about the only things they shared were the multimember panel format and protection from presidential removal. Second, because the FRB would have little adjudicatory function, lawyers had little reason to push for its judicialization. If this kind of FRB was still legitimized through institutional association with the courtlike ICC, that would be a clear indication that the notion of courtlike agency was already pervasive enough to judicialize new regulation without intervention from lawyers and the judiciary in practically any policy domain.[2]

Asking how and why the FRB adopted its institutional features in relation to the ICC is also worthwhile in comprehending the origins of the entire reserve system. Due to the chronic volatility of the finance market, by the early twentieth century there was a consensus on the need for wholesale currency reform. Shortly before the plan to create the FRS was made public in early 1913, however, Americans had been reminded of how selfishly high-profile bankers behaved in the Panic of 1907, thanks to a thorough investigation by a House subcommittee chaired by Rep. Arsène Pujo (D-LA). In addition to their long-standing hatred of the central bank, Americans were concerned that the establishment of a central banking system would only strengthen those same bankers. Besides, the creation of a central banking system was by no means considered the only available option of reform. Setting a new standard of currency issuance enabling banks to adjust the money supply as needed also was a popular measure. If Americans were far from friendly to a central banking system in 1913, how could a massive system of a dozen regional reserve banks with a central board overseeing them still be established? This important question remains unanswered.[3]

By focusing on the FRB and its institutional connection to the judicialized ICC, this chapter explains how the board, and ultimately the entire FRS, could be legitimized by the Wilson administration, which initiated the legislation. Its central argument is that this feat was achieved by situating the FRB in the central banking system not as coordinator of the reserve banks but as their regulator. In so doing, the board's role was presented as analogous to that of the ICC overseeing the railroad business, which was itself associated with the Supreme Court of the United States as an impartial and nonpartisan panel of experts. The opponents of the government-controlled FRB ultimately failed to undermine the analogy raised by its proponents. It was such an act of creative syncretism on the side of the administration that it legitimatized the FRB, and the board's strong ties

2 Cushman, *Independent Regulatory Commissions*, 146; Breger and Edles, *Independent Agencies.*

3 On the historical background of the Federal Reserve Act, especially the development of the currency reform movement, see the following: Richard H. Timberlake, *Monetary Policy in the United States: An Intellectual and Institutional History* (Chicago: University of Chicago Press, 1993); Susan Hoffman, *Politics and Banking: Ideas, Public Policy, and the Creation of Financial Institutions* (Baltimore: Johns Hopkins University Press, 2001).

to the judicialized ICC and the Court exemplify how pervasive and popular the notion of regulation by ACs already was.

The Federal Reserve Act of 1913 has been hailed as landmark legislation fundamentally reconfiguring the American monetary infrastructure, which had been based on the National Banking System since the Civil War. Before the reform measure, the United States had experienced an economic panic every decade, usually attributable to the monetary system's inability to adjust the amount of currency circulating in the market. Strict reserve fund requirements for national banks and idle government money deposited to the independent treasury were chief causes of severe deflation. Secretaries of treasury occasionally conducted buying operations using the government funds, but these were at best extemporaneous and probably illegal. The Reserve Act installing the Federal Reserve System was prompted by the Wilson administration with the hope of remedying such a sorry situation.[4]

Despite the significance of the legislation and all the attention from scholars it has received, no satisfactory answer as to why the central banking system could be established at all and took the form it did has been provided. Economic historians who have produced most of the scholarship on the creation of the FRS have not dealt squarely with the question. They have invariably treated the establishment of the FRS in the context of the currency reform movement led by bankers and economists since the late nineteenth century. In their view, the reform culminated not in 1913 with the enactment of the Reserve Act, but the year before, when economic experts' view on desirable currency reform converged in the formation of a central banking system as they devised a plan under the direction of Sen. Nelson Aldrich (R-RI). For instance, works by James Livingston and Richard McCulley on the origins of the FRS relegate their discussion of the legislative process of the reserve act to an afterthought. Robert West devotes two chapters of his book to the adoption of the act but skips early 1913, the crucial months in which the Wilson administration shaped the FRS. Synthesizing a generation of literature, Elmus Wicker notes that the debate from 1912 was to "continue with only one issue in mind – what kind of central bank?" From such a perspective, the actual form the FRS took and how it was adopted seem peripheral. Wicker brushes off the heated debate that led to the government appointment of FRB members as "a political accident."[5]

4 Eugene N. White, " 'To Establish a More Effective Supervision of Banking': How the Birth of the Fed Altered Bank Supervision," in *The Origins, History, and Future of the Federal Reserve: A Return to Jekyll Island*, ed. Michael D. Bordo and William Roberds (New York: Cambridge University Press, 2013), 7–54.

5 James Livingston, *Origins of the Federal Reserve System: Money, Class, and Corporate Capitalism, 1890–1913* (Ithaca: Cornell University Press, 1986); Richard T. McCulley, *Banks and Politics during the Progressive Era: The Origins of the Federal Reserve System, 1897–1913* (New York: Garland, 1992); Robert Craig West, *Banking Reform and the Federal Reserve, 1863–1923* (Ithaca: Cornell University Press, 1974); Elmus Wicker, *The Great Debate on Banking Reform: Nelson Aldrich and the Origins of the Fed* (Columbus: Ohio State University Press, 2005), x, 91.

In contrast, political historians have been more attentive to the conditions that facilitated the creation of a central banking system. They have pointed out different ways in which those involved in the drafting of the bill endeavored to make the reserve system acceptable to the anti-banker public. Most notably, they have shown that Rep. Carter Glass (D-VA), the chief architect of the reserve bill, initially proposed multiple reserve banks instead of a single central bank so as not to give the impression that bankers would gain excess power over finance. Elizabeth Sanders and others also emphasize the role of Democratic populists in the drafting of the bill. It was, they agree, at the populists' insistence that the entire FRB ought to consist of presidential appointees. In stark contrast to Wicker, Sanders argues that there was "no straight line from the capitalist-led banking-reform movement of the early 1900s to the Federal Reserve Act of 1913."[6]

While her observation on the complexity of the institutional origins of the FRS makes much sense, the previous works fall short of fully elucidating why the central banking system became politically possible. This is because they have invariably failed to give due consideration to Americans' hatred of bankers and the central bank. To appreciate this point, one needs only to turn to the fate of the Aldrich plan proposed in 1912. In the aftermath of the Panic of 1907, Congress adopted the Aldrich-Vreeland Act of 1908 as a stopgap reform measure. In addition to authorizing the use of clearinghouse loan certificates bankers had relied on as de facto currency during economic panics, the act created the National Monetary Commission and instructed it to conduct research and construct a comprehensive reform plan. Four years later, the commission headed by Sen. Aldrich released a bill proposing the creation of a "National Reserve Association" to solve the problem of "inelasticity of currency." The association would consist of fifteen regional associations, each with regional national banks as their members, and a central board comprising leaders of the regional associations, representatives of various economic sectors, and presidential appointees. Aldrich, who preferred a central bank but also was sensitive to the prevailing anti-banker climate at the time, presented the reserve association as a group of clearinghouses. Contemporaries, however, easily saw through the disguise and recognized it as a central bank with regional branches and fiercely opposed it. The bill died a quiet death in the Senate Banking and Currency Committee.[7]

There is no doubt that the Aldrich plan was proposed in a difficult political environment. By the time it was submitted to the Senate, the chamber was controlled by the Democrats, leaving little chance for the enactment of a major

6 Michael Kazin, *A Godly Hero: The Life of William Jennings Bryan* (New York: Alfred A. Knopf, 2006); Sanders, *Roots of Reform*, 238, 257. Also see Sarah Binder and Mark Spindel, "Monetary Politics: Origins of the Federal Reserve," *Studies in American Political Development* 27 (2013): 2.

7 National Monetary Commission, *Report of the National Monetary Commission*, 62nd Cong., 2nd sess. (1912), S. Doc. 243; Nathaniel Wright Stephenson, *Nelson W. Aldrich: A Leader in American Politics* (New York: Charles Scribner's Sons, 1930); West, *Banking Reform*, 73; Henry Parker Willis, *The Federal Reserve System: Legislation, Organization and Operation* (New York: Ronald Press, 1923), 79.

Republican reform bill. In addition, Aldrich's strong connection to financiers and the business community gave the impression that his plan was intended to reinforce their clout. There nevertheless is a scholarly agreement that the plan itself was to blame for its failure. Since then, it became common knowledge that any reform plan even remotely resembling a central bank would be dead on arrival. This was especially true for the Democrats, who would be responsible for the reserve act. Later in 1912, the Democratic party flatly rejected "the so-called Aldrich bill or the establishment of a central bank" in their national platform while their Republican counterpart only vaguely stated that the party was "committed to the progressive development of our banking and currency systems."[8]

The institutional proximity between the Aldrich plan and FRS and the former's fate make the adoption of the latter all the more puzzling. It was no secret that the proposed FRS had much in common with the Aldrich plan; they were both central banking systems composed of regional reserve banks and a central board, each with similar functions. Paul Warburg, a partner in Kuhn, Loeb & Co., who significantly shaped the Aldrich plan and advised Glass in constructing his bill, later claimed authorship of the reserve act, believing that it was little more than a copy of the Aldrich plan. Similarly, economic historians have not taken the legislative process of the reserve act seriously, precisely because they, too, saw little difference between the two schemes of currency reform.[9]

But if anti-central bank sentiment was so strong among Americans, and the proposed FRS closely resembled the much-opposed Aldrich plan, why did the Wilson administration even bother to present it, and why was it successful? These important questions have been neglected by both economic and political historians, probably because of the unexplained acquiescence of the public, especially those behind the Democratic majority in Congress. Neither strong anti-central bank feelings nor the FRS's similarity with the Aldrich plan was widely expressed during the legislative process. So why didn't the dog bark?

This chapter demonstrates that the manner in which the Wilson administration presented the FRB's role in the proposed FRS was crucial in legitimizing the central banking system during the legislative process despite its similarity to the Aldrich plan. The Wilson administration managed to sell the FRS to the American public because it did not simply try to detach the FRS from the notion of the central bank as Aldrich had done. Instead, it associated the FRB with several respected government bodies. The administration legitimized the FRS by persuading the public that the politically appointed FRB would be regulating banks rather than becoming a central bank board dominated by bankers. In the process, the board was harnessed to the ICC and the Supreme Court in the expectation that it would become as successful as they already were.

8 Kirk H. Porter and Donald Bruce Robinson, comp., *National Party Platforms, 1840–1964* (Urbana: University of Illinois Press), 171, 185.

9 Gabriel Kolko, *The Triumph of Conservatism: A Reinterpretation of American History, 1900–1916* (1963; repr., Chicago: Quadrangle Books, 1967), 242–247.

Correlating a central banking institution to a railroad regulator and a judicial body may seem far fetched, if not bizarre. But the frequent references made to the Supreme Court and the ICC during the 1913 debate on the FRB, especially by the administration, have not gone entirely unnoticed. In explaining the lawmakers' preference on the FRS's role, Richard Timberlake notes that "most legislators wanted to see embodied in law . . . the Federal Reserve as a public utility" and cites contemporary references to both the Supreme Court and the ICC to illustrate this. He only implies that the legislators' preference for the Federal Reserve as a public utility led to their reference to the two institutions, however, suggesting that such statements were little more than rhetoric. In contrast, this chapter argues that the association of the FRB with the two institutions was consciously made to legitimize the central banking system and was quite effective. The ICC had established its reputation as the nation's representative administrative agency owing to the fact that it was modeled upon courts. It was this context that led Americans in the Progressive Era to perceive a new government body in terms of the ICC and the Supreme Court. The administration took advantage of this and presented the FRB as a courtlike regulator of the banking industry rather than as part of a central banking system.[10]

The fact that the FRB could be associated with both the ICC and the Court, then, not only explains why the FRS was created but also attests to the strong judiciality of the modern US administrative state. This chapter demonstrates this by revisiting the process of the planning and enactment of the FRS from Woodrow Wilson's victory in the 1912 presidential election, focusing on the political discourse on the organizational form of the FRB, which became the "storm center" of the legislation.[11]

After the demise of the Aldrich plan, the burden of constructing a new currency reform scheme was to be borne by Carter Glass, who in 1912 became the chair of a House Banking and Currency subcommittee set up for the task. He worked closely with the committee's expert, Henry Parker Willis, an editor of the *New York Journal of Commerce* and former economics professor at Washington and Lee University, to draft the new legislation. Strictly following the national Democratic platform of that year, Glass believed that the only way to avoid the mistakes of the Aldrich bill and create a central banking system acceptable to the public was to divide the country into regions and put each of them under charge of a reserve bank, whose control rested primarily in the hands of banks that subscribed to its capital. Under his plan, the banks were to have substantial autonomy, but the Comptroller of Currency was assigned the role of coordination among reserve banks.[12]

It was only natural, then, that Glass and Willis were taken aback when president-elect Wilson suggested in a December interview that they should add the

10 Timberlake, *Monetary Policy in the United States*, 225–226.

11 Banking and Currency Committee, *Banking and Currency*. 63rd Cong., 1st sess. (1913), S. Doc. 232, 2139.

12 West, *Banking Reform*, 92.

"capstone to be placed upon the structure." Why Wilson, who had advocated expert rule as a scholar but openly expressed discomfort with "a smug lot of experts to sit down behind closed doors in Washington and play Providence to me" during the presidential election campaign, made such a suggestion is a mystery. Although Glass replied that he would "cheerfully go . . . for some body of central *supervisory* control" [emphasis in original] without the attributes of a central bank, he thought that such an organization might be politically unsustainable, even if economically desirable. It would be "the point of danger," he wrote to Willis shortly after the meeting, "where the bombardment will be directed." Without revealing their true preference to Wilson, they set out to revise their plan to incorporate a body atop the reserve banks.[13]

The new plan, completed a month later, contained provisions for the creation of a Federal Reserve Board designated to supervise reserve banks. It was given such powers as instructing the reserve banks to rediscount the paper discounted by another reserve bank, setting the interest rates for rediscounting, inspecting the reserve banks, and removing reserve bank officers, all carried over to the Federal Reserve Act. The board was to be staffed with nine members: three representing regional reserve banks and six presidential appointees, including three ex-officio members, the Secretaries of Treasury and Agriculture, and the Comptroller of Currency. Delighted with the revision, Wilson encouraged Glass to move forward with it in their interview in February 1913. Glass had already begun testing the waters with his plan by holding subcommittee hearings. Carefully refraining from disclosing his own scheme, he still managed to draw from influential bankers and economists a favorable response to the basic elements of his idea.[14]

It should be noted that the membership of the FRB at this point included representatives of reserve banks just as the Aldrich plan did for its central board. Why Wilson approved such a body remains unknown, although it probably resulted from weighing several factors, including his own principles, the view of the party's radicals, and prospective performance of the monetary system, as Sanders suggests. The idea of political appointees and representatives of banks

13 Woodrow Wilson, *The New Freedom: A Call for the Emancipation of the Generous Energies of a People* (Garden City: Doubleday, Page and Co., 1921), 60; Henry Parker Willis to Carter Glass, Dec. 29, 1912, in *The Papers of Woodrow Wilson*, ed. Arthur S. Link (Princeton: Princeton University Press, 1966–1994) (hereafter *PWW*), 27:643–644; *PWW*, 25:78; Carter Glass to Henry Parker Willis, Jan. 3, 1913, Carter Glass Papers, Box 26, Albert and Shirly Small Special Collections Library, University of Virginia; Henry Parker Willis to Carter Glass, Dec. 31, 1912, in *PWW*, 27:650; Henry Parker Willis to Carter Glass, Jan. 2, 1913, Box 26, Glass Papers; West, *Banking Reform*, 105.

14 Willis, *Federal Reserve System*, 1531–1553; Carter Glass, *An Adventure in Constructive Finance* (1927; repr., New York: Arno Press, 1975), 91–92; Arthur S. Link, *Wilson: The New Freedom* (Princeton: Princeton University Press, 1956), 205–206; Carter Glass to Woodrow Wilson, Jan. 27, 1913, Box 65, Glass Papers. At this point, the board was positioned as the executive committee of the Federal Reserve Commission with a larger, but unspecified, number of members from the above three groups.

jointly steering a central board itself was nothing new. Among the several currency reform plans by University of Chicago economist J. Lawrence Laughlin, who also was chair of the executive committee of the National Citizens League, a leading currency reform movement organization, named "Plan D" included a proposal for a "treasury board" with a similar composition. Both Glass and Willis knew of this plan. It was very likely that the bankers would have backed this version of the FRB, but it was equally likely that the public would have balked, just as it had at the Aldrich plan.[15]

Because of the controversial character of the proposed central banking systems, the next few months would see near chaos within the administration, followed by a decisive turn in the makeup of the FRB toward full government control. The turmoil was set off by William Jennings Bryan who, in a May meeting with Wilson on the development of the bill, insisted that all members of the board be government appointees, in addition to having the new currency issued by the reserve banks be an obligation of the federal government rather than that of the reserve banks. Otherwise, as Bryan later stated, the currency reform bill would surely "arouse great opposition in the democratic [sic] party" and may even jeopardize the passage of the Underwood tariff bill being debated in the Senate. Sen. Robert L. Owen of Oklahoma, a Bryan Democrat who would be responsible for the bill in the Senate as the chair of its Banking and Currency Committee, expressed similar dissatisfaction with the Glass bill soon afterward, hinting that he would go so far as to draft his own bill, which he soon did. At this point, Secretary of the Treasury William G. McAdoo added fuel to the fire by proposing another plan drafted in the Treasury involving the creation of a government-owned central bank as a bureau of the department. [16]

By early June, Wilson had three bills to work on, each with its own shortcomings. Sticking to the Glass bill as it stood undoubtedly would cause dissension from Bryan Democrats and might endanger the whole currency reform, but Owen's bill was too immature to be a viable option. Even worse, the McAdoo plan came under severe criticism from both within the administration's inner circle and bankers and economists who had seen it. Perplexed, on June 11, Wilson consulted with Louis D. Brandeis, his most trusted economic advisor. Brandeis, according to the summary he later sent to the president, advised that "The American people will not be content to have the discretion necessarily involved vested in a Board composed wholly or in part of bankers; for their judgment may be biased by private interest or affiliation." He also commented that "[t]he conflict between the policies of the Administration and the desires of the financiers and of big business" was irreconcilable. This emphasis on the public

15 Sanders, *Roots of Reform*, 246–247; West, *Banking Reform*, 93; Henry Parker Willis to Carter Glass, Dec. 24, 1912, Box 26, Glass Papers.

16 William Jennings Bryan, "On the Currency Bill of June 1913," July 6, 1913, Box 29, William Jennings Bryan Papers, Manuscript Division, Library of Congress; *PWW*, 27:413–414; Dale N. Shook, *William G. McAdoo and the Development of National Economic Policy, 1913–1918* (New York: Garland Publishing, 1987), 103–108; Sanders, *Roots of Reform*, 248.

hatred of bankers convinced Wilson to advance a plan giving the government full control of the FRB.[17]

At a White House conference with Glass, McAdoo, and Owen, held on June 17, Wilson stated his intention to go with the Glass bill with modifications reflecting Bryan's requests. Glass, who had thought that the government would have too much voice over the proposed reserve system even without such revisions, was horrified by the "Bryanization" of the bill. He wrote to Wilson the next day asking for a reconsideration of "the advisability of modifying somewhat your view of bank representation" on the proposed board and suggested a compromise of making the president choose some of the board members from a list submitted by the reserve banks. Wilson did not bend, however, and Glass had no choice but to redraft the bill as instructed. All seven of the FRB's members, including the three ex-officio members as stated in the earlier version, were to be government appointees, although with the condition that at least one of the other four members must be a "person experienced in banking."[18]

The publication of the revised bill on June 19 signaled the currency reform's entrance into a new stage, as the bill's contents had been available only to administration insiders. The plan immediately came under close scrutiny, and the role and composition of the FRB became a focal point of the bill. Wilson himself mentioned this on June 23 in an address to a joint session of Congress, declaring that "the control of the system of banking and of issue which our new laws are to set up must be public, not private, must be vested in the Government itself, so that the banks may be the instruments, not the masters, of business and of individual enterprise and initiative." Wilson's decision to make the FRB an exclusively government-appointed board has been explained by the need to retain the support of Bryanites. While this in itself is accurate, the president's own statement and his discussion with Brandeis strongly suggest that Wilson also took into account the public's staunch opposition to bankers and central banks. As Glass feared, the inclusion of a central board had already made the FRS dangerously similar to the Aldrich plan. Had the FRB also admitted banker representation, there would have been no way for the administration to differentiate it from its unpopular predecessor. Elimination of representatives of reserve banks, then,

17 Link, *New Freedom*, 208–211; Louis D. Brandeis to Woodrow Wilson, June 14, 1913, *PWW*, 27:520–521. Brandeis was already involved in discussion with members of Congress on the creation of the FTC. For example, see Brandeis to Robert Marion LaFollette, May 27, 1913, in *Letters of Louis D. Brandeis*, vol. 3, *1913–1915: Progressive and Zionist*, ed. Melvin I. Urofsky and David W. Levy (New York: State University of New York Press, 1973), 100–102; Philippa Strum, *Louis D. Brandeis: Justice for the People* (Cambridge, MA: Harvard University Press, 1984), 171; McCraw, *Prophets*, 116; Melvin I. Urofsky, *Louis D. Brandeis: A Life* (New York: Schocken Books, 2009), Ch. 16.

18 Carter Glass to Woodrow Wilson, June 18, 1913, in *PWW*, 27:535; Hoffman, *Politics and Banking*, 124–126; Willis, *Federal Reserve System*, 1584. The provisions regarding the Federal Reserve Commission also were dropped for the sake of simplicity of the system's structure.

was necessary to making the FRS palatable not just to the populists but to the Democratic majority.[19]

For two reasons, however, such a consideration alone was distasteful to the public. First, the Aldrich plan and the FRS still had much in common; the difference in the central board's configuration may not be taken as crucial. The public needed to be convinced that the FRB would not become the bastion of bankers. Second, those who were knowledgeable enough to see the difference between the Aldrich plan and the FRS could have a different concern; the FRB without banker representation might be free from banker influence, but it might fail to carry out sound monetary policy due to lack of expertise. In addressing these diametrically opposite concerns, the administration needed to present a clear vision of the institutional nature of, and the role to be played by, the FRB. Such legitimization was to be accomplished by associating the FRB with institutions that bore little resemblance to it: the ICC and the Supreme Court.

On June 25, Wilson, with Glass, McAdoo, and Owen, discussed the reserve bill with representatives of the Currency Commission of the American Bankers' Association. In the conference, several important changes were made, adopting the elite bankers' suggestions. But when the bankers requested the addition of four members to the FRB, to be chosen by the president from a list submitted by reserve banks, Wilson replied, "Will one of you gentlemen tell me in what civilized country of the earth there are important government boards of control on which private interests are represented? Which of you gentlemen thinks the railroads should select members of the Interstate Commerce Commission?" A painful silence ensued, and all the bankers could win was a Federal Advisory Council composed of representatives of reserve banks.[20]

This episode, commonly cited in the narratives on the origins of the FRS, has been mentioned as evidence of Wilson's firm belief in government control of the FRB, if not of his lack of knowledge in financial policy. But none has paid attention to his second question about the ICC, which has its own significance. Immediately after the conference, the administration openly began to justify the FRB's form, especially its exclusive control by government, referring to the commission. For instance, Owen stated later that month that, "We think it no more reasonable to grant this demand [of banker representation on the FRB] to the bankers than it would be to authorize the railroads to have representation and exercise a part of the governing power of the Interstate Commerce Commission" and denied the possibility of the then-rumored expansion of the FRB's membership to take in representatives of reserve banks.[21] Something even more intriguing was underway at the Treasury. Assistant Treasury Secretary John Skelton Williams,

19 *PWW*, 27:522–525; *PWW*, 27:571–573.

20 Joseph P. Tumulty to William G. McAdoo, June 25, 1913, Box 102, W. G. McAdoo Papers, Manuscript Division, Library of Congress; Link, *New Freedom*, 217; Glass, *Adventure in Constructive Finance*, 116; *PWW*, 27:564, 27:567–568.

21 Kolko, *Triumph of Conservatism*, 232; *Wall Street Journal* (hereafter *WSJ*), June 28, 1913. Also see *WSJ*, June 25 and 27, 1913.

who had played a central role in the drafting of McAdoo's plan, suggested to him that there was an "interesting parallel" between the outcry against government intervention during the legislative process of the Interstate Commerce Act and the one they were facing with the Glass bill. Williams's memorandum to McAdoo accompanied many extracts from newspaper editorials in 1886 and 1887, and McAdoo scribbled on it enthusiastically, "Send other extracts please!" The timing of Owen's statement and Williams's report strongly suggests a connection to Wilson's remark in the conference a few days before.[22]

The core members on the administration's side deliberately began to associate the FRB with the ICC when justifying the former. Based on the advice from Williams, McAdoo replied to a letter suggesting the danger of the FRB becoming politically controlled that the fear was unfounded, stating that if one referred to "the debates on the Interstate Commerce Commission measure, when it was proposed, and to the views expressed by statesmen of that day," the person would "realize how foolish it is to take counsel of fear. What was said then about the Interstate Commerce Commission is now being said about the Federal Reserve Board. None of the disasters which we were solemnly warned would follow the creation of the Interstate Commerce law have been realized." In introducing his bill on the House floor, Glass emphasized that the board was to be "an altruistic institution, a part of Government itself, representing the American people, with powers such as no man would dare misuse," and as such, it would perform "no banking function." As he went on to defend government control of the board, he not only brought up Wilson's confrontation with the bankers but also the debates on the Interstate Commerce Act back in the 1880s to support his view that the proposed board would not constitute an encroachment on banking.[23]

The administration's effort to connect the FRB and the ICC was not concerted or systematic enough to be called a campaign, but those involved were undoubtedly aware of each other's utilization of the ICC as a role model for the FRB. What deserves note is that people hardly needed any reminder to think about the FRB in terms of the commission. For instance, at the press conference after Wilson's address to Congress, journalists asked if he regarded the "Federal Reserve Board in the same way that" he viewed the ICC "in reference to putting railroadmen" on the latter – and he gave an affirmative answer. Also, those outside the Treasury were making reference to the ICC in discussing the FRB with McAdoo, without any apparent cue from him.[24]

People inside and outside the government naturally linked the proposed FRB with the ICC; this was not the first time they thought of a new agency in terms of the railroad regulator. As will be discussed in the next chapter, the debate on whether to create an Interstate Trade Commission – later established as the

22 John Skelton Williams to William G. McAdoo, June 26, 1913, Box 102, McAdoo Papers.

23 Edmund D. Fisher to William G. McAdoo, July 11, 1913, Box 103, McAdoo Papers; William G. McAdoo to Edmund D. Fisher, July 13, 1913, Box 103, McAdoo Papers; *Congressional Record*, 63rd Cong., 1st sess. (1913), HR, 4644–4645.

24 *PWW*, 27:564; William Libbey to William G. McAdoo, June 24, 1913, Box 102, McAdoo Papers; Joseph H. O'Neil to William G. McAdoo, July 2, 1913, Box 102, McAdoo Papers.

Federal Trade Commission – in charge of antitrust policy was already underway, and it was common knowledge that the commission was modeled after the ICC, including its name. While the Aldrich plan was being gestated, Sen. Francis Newlands (D-NV), a future sponsor of the FTC Act, occasionally commented that the new central banking system should have an ICC-like banking commission that would regulate, not manage, regional reserve associations. This was practically identical to the Wilson administration's later description of the FRB.[25]

The same could be said for the FRB's link to the Supreme Court. In sharp contrast to the frequent references to the ICC, only Glass and Owen among those substantively involved in the drafting of the bill mentioned the Court in their justification of the FRB before congressional debates. This did not mean that the connection between the Court and the FRB went unnoticed, though. The idea to situate an institution akin to the Supreme Court at the center of the currency system had already been circulated among currency reformers. As early as 1907, J. Laurence Laughlin argued in the *Journal of Political Economy* for the establishment of a body "wholly free from politics, or outside influence – as much respected for character and integrity as the supreme court – which shall be able, in a great emergency to use government bonds or selected securities." It was then not surprising that those without connection to the administration began making occasional references to the Supreme Court after publication of the bill.[26]

The administration thus characterized the FRB not as part of a central banking system but as a regulator of reserve and national banks. In so doing, it associated the board with two government bodies whose members also were exclusively appointed by the president, implying that the FRB would be just as successful as these respected tribunals. But there was no guarantee that such a justification would be convincing to the American people, let alone help build public support for the proposed board. As it turned out, the debate on the FRB inside and outside Congress during the legislative process evolved around the interinstitutional connection. This is best demonstrated by observing the earnestness with which opponents of Glass's bill sought to deny the validity of the analogy.

Cries of opposition and proposals for revision immediately followed publication of the Glass bill in late June, and the FRB's form, a defining feature of the FRS, became a major target. Most of the criticisms originated from two camps with conflicting concerns. First, some agrarians feared the dominance of the "Money Trust" over the FRS. Some even argued that the proposed bill was nothing but

25 Sklar, *Corporate Reconstruction*; Francis G. Newlands to C. A. Luthnow, July 12, 1911, Folder 242, Box 25, Series 1, Francis Griffith Newlands Papers, Manuscripts and Archives, Yale University Library; Frances G. Newlands to J. Lawrence Laughlin, Aug. 21, 1911, Folder 247, Box 25, Series 1, Newlands Papers.

26 *WSJ*, July 30, 1913; *New York Times* (hereafter *NYT*), June 28, 1913; J. Laurence Laughlin, "Currency Reform," *Journal of Political Economy* 15 (1907): 609; Thomas Wilson, *The Power "to Coin" Money: The Exercise of Monetary Powers by the Congress* (Armonk, NY: M. E. Sharpe, 1992), 248–249, n. 1; *NYT*, June 23, 1913.

a bankers' ruse to install a central bank just like the Aldrich plan. These objections most notably took the form of amendments offered by agrarian Democrats in Congress to eliminate the possibility of banker control of the system. From July 8, during debates by the House banking committee, now with Glass as its chair, the committee's southern and western members offered a series of amendments including a revision to open the membership of the FRB to representatives of agriculture and labor, in addition to former US presidents. As illustrated by this amendment, however, agrarians had no objection to the proposed board becoming a government body as long as bankers did not capture it.[27]

It was the attack from the second group, the bankers, that posed the more serious threat to the government-controlled FRB, which economists believed would lead to low-quality monetary policy. While most academic economists refrained from publicly denouncing the board, the hostility of the bankers, fearing the loss of dominance over the money market, was not only more intense but also openly expressed. Those in charge of the nation's leading banks, mostly the top-tier banks in New York and Chicago, sensed that their privileged status was in jeopardy. Having been prescribed in the bill to subscribe to the capitals of the reserve banks, the bankers also felt entitled to representation on the FRB. Interest alone, however, cannot explain bankers' animus against the FRB, since those country bankers who supported the Glass bill with the expectation that it would end their subordination to powerful banks still expressed reservations about the board's configuration.[28] At the bottom of the bankers' uneasiness with the FRB was the gap between the role they wished the body at the apex of the nation's monetary system to play and the one that they expected from the Glass bill's provisions on the board. As illustrated in Glass's explanation on the House floor, the administration's understanding was that the FRB's job was to oversee the workings of the reserve banks rather than to take part in their day-to-day operations; it would intervene only in case of emergency. In contrast, from the perspective of most bankers believing that a single central bank was the most efficient and effective measure of currency reform, such an institutional arrangement of the FRS was deeply flawed. In their view, the board was going to have too much influence on, and involvement with, banks to pass as a regulatory body. Without banker representation, there was no way it could make decent monetary policy. It should either play a smaller role in the system or at least be run by someone who would know what to do with its power.[29]

The bankers' fierce opposition to the FRB is well documented in the literature. What has escaped notice is that such contentions very often took the form of

27 Link, *New Freedom*, 220.

28 Sanders, *Roots of Reform*, 248–249; Link, *New Freedom*, 224–225; The economists, however, did comment on currency reform measures in scholarly publications and their communications with politicians, including those who were involved in the drafting of the Glass bill. David Michael Grossman, "Professors and Public Service, 1885–1925: A Chapter in the Professionalization of the Social Sciences." (Ph.D. diss., Washington University, 1973), 122–124.

29 Cf., Livingston, *Origins of the Federal Reserve System*, 222.

objections to the justification of the FRB associating it with the Supreme Court and/or the ICC. James B. Forgan, president of the First National Bank of Chicago and one of the most outspoken critics of the bill, argued in late July, "It has been claimed that the Federal reserve board would be organized somewhat along the lines of the Supreme Court of the United States and that it would be kept as free from political influence. I fail to see any analogy between the organization of the two bodies, nor can I admit that they would be equally free from political influence." Other opponents of the Glass bill emulated his style of denouncing the alleged connection between the FRB and the two institutions.[30]

The bankers' denunciation of the FRB made with reference to the two institutions covered all major aspects of their complaint against the board. One important component was that the FRB would not just be regulating but actually managing the FRS. George M. Reynolds, former president of the American Bankers' Association, summarized this view when he stated that the government's supervision over banking and currency "should be purely regulatory and not of an administrative or controlling character." It was argued that the FRB would be different from these two institutions by actively pursuing its policy. James Forgan also contrasted the Supreme Court with the proposed board, focusing on its expected behavioral style. Whereas the "duties and functions of the Supreme Court are deliberative in deciding controversies brought before it," the board's duties were "administrative with full power of initiative." When a comparison with the ICC was made, it often highlighted the differences between the two organs in the amount of regulatory power and the nature of the industry subjected to regulation.[31]

A few days after the publication of the Glass bill, the American Bankers' Association's currency commission stated that it conferred excessive supervisory power to the board. Instead, the commission was ready to accept a "board with powers analogous to those of the Interstate Commerce Commission, which exercised effective supervision over the railroads, but does not actually operate them." Along the same line, the *Wall Street Journal* praised the ICC for sound regulation and then argued that such government intervention beyond "mere supervision" was in the public interest only because "quasi-public organizations" like railroads and telephone companies ought to be strictly regulated. To extend regulation to a "corporation of no public character, as, for instance, a bank," was "open to the gravest objection."[32]

Explicit comparison of the FRB with the two institutions pointed out the board's institutional deficiencies. Two of them were frequently raised to illustrate the inappropriateness of government control of the board. The first was the danger of politicization. In contrast to Supreme Court justices who were appointed for life, for instance, the members of the FRB could be "removable at any time by

30 *WSJ*, July 23, 1913.
31 *WSJ*, July 11, 1913; *WSJ*, July 23, 1913. Also see George M. Reynolds to Carter Glass, July 7, 1913, Box 16, Glass Papers; *CT*, Aug. 11, 1913.
32 *WSJ*, June 25, 1913; *WSJ*, Aug. 8, 1913.

the President and the members are appointed for eight years at most, with nothing to prevent their removal at any time should the President request it."[33] Even when collated with the ICC, whose members also were appointed for a fixed term, the problem with the FRB was obvious; the board's composition of three ex-officio members from the cabinet and four members with staggered terms of eight years implied that every new president could nominate a majority of the members by the second year in office and that by the end of a two-term presidency, all members would be the administration's nominees. John V. Farwell, president of the National Citizens League, commented that while the Aldrich bill had been condemned for insufficient restraint on private control, the Glass bill went "to the extreme of political control" and suggested that the middle road of "close government supervision" should be pursued.[34]

Second, what seemed even more problematic to the bill's opponents was the FRB's prospective lack of expertise in banking, and here the contrast with the Supreme Court was frequently employed. A New Jersey banker advised Glass that the bill's effect would be akin to "what would result if a new Supreme Court was organized and all the members of the bench except perhaps one were laymen, not lawyers as at present," and many shared the view. Forgan was more straightforward when he remarked that the "Justices of the Supreme Court are selected with due regard to their professional eminence. The members of the Federal reserve board with one exception need not have either previous experience in, or knowledge of, the banking business, the destinies of which are to be placed in their hands."[35]

The bankers' attack on the proposed FRB in itself was nothing surprising and has been documented by previous research. Given their preference for a central bank under their control, the members of the government-controlled board that seemed to direct a system whose reserve was dispersed into twelve or more regional banks was nothing short of anathema. "Having no banks represented on the Federal Reserve Board," the *Wall Street Journal* lamented, represented "the politician's idea that knowledge is prejudice and ignorance is innocence."[36] In stark contrast, the way they expressed hostility toward the board through its comparison with the two institutions has received little attention. It is difficult, however, to dismiss the interinstitutional association made to criticize the FRB simply as a form of rhetoric when it was done so systematically. The following statement by a Missouri banker cogently represents the bankers' manner of discussion:

33 *WSJ*, June 23, 1913. Different from the ICC and most other ACs later created, the Glass bill (and the final act) simply prescribed that an FRB member could be removed "for cause." There were those who suggested that the members of the FRB should be given life appointment, with the Supreme Court in mind. John N. Rhoades to Carter Glass, Nov. 11, 1913, Box 26, Glass Papers.

34 *CT*, July 3, 1913; *NYT*, July 4, 1913.

35 Robert D. Kent to Carter Glass, July 8, 1913, Box 37, Glass Papers; *WSJ*, June 23, 1913. Also see Robert D. Kent to William G. McAdoo, Oct. 18, 1913, Box 106, McAdoo Papers.

36 *WSJ*, June 21, 1913.

It is cited that the Supreme Court is appointed by the President. The situation is quite different, as will be seen from the following:

1 The supreme [court] judges are appointed for life, to pass upon legal questions only, and in practically all cases they have precedent after precedent to guide them in their interpretation of the law. They review the acts of the lower courts, and take months and sometimes years to render a decision.
2 The men selected have been trained for a specific profession and, through force of circumstances, no President ever has appointed an obscure or inexperienced lawyer to the Supreme Bench.
3 They are appointed for life and thus not subject to the whims of ever-changing political power. In the minds of the people they hold the highest position in the world.
4 There is no analogy between a political appointment on the reserve board and the selection of a member of the Supreme Bench.

The Interstate Commerce Commission is cited, which is an admission of weakness in the position taken by the framers of the bill, as –

5 The Interstate Commerce Commission regulates and corrects abuses. They are given no opportunity to divert the assets of a railroad company from their ownership.
6 They cannot divert the assets of one railroad to help out another railroad in financial distress; nor can they appoint railroad managers.[37]

The bankers' frequent adoption of such a style of argument is significant. The sheer fact that the bill's opponents frequently referred to the Supreme Court and ICC suggests how popular the association of the two institutions with the FRB already was at the time. The notion was so prevalent that the bankers felt compelled to counter it, and they probably ended up actually spreading the idea. It is also worth noting that the Court and the commission were utilized almost interchangeably in the bankers' discussion, reflecting the institutional proximity between the two institutions in their minds. Also, in attacking the analogy, they were not just trying to argue that it was meaningless and unworthy of attention. In many cases, the bankers attempted to turn the table by explaining the incompatibility of the board and the two institutions in detail, often inserting their wish that the proposed board actually had shared certain characteristics of the Court or the ICC. They thus actively sought to undermine the legitimacy that the association with the two respected institutions might bring to the FRB. Pointing out the administrative character of the board and the danger of its politicization,

37 Cited by Rep. Leonidas C. Dyer (R-MO), *Congressional Record*, 63rd Cong., 1st sess. (1913), HR, 4680; West, *Banking Reform*, 117–120.

the critics tried to show that it was not going to become another nonpartisan regulatory body like the Court or the ICC that decides the cases brought before it. By emphasizing the possible exclusion of experts – meaning bankers – from the board, they argued that it would lack the competence to control the money market.

To the proponents of the bill, this meant that simple appeal to the interinstitutional association would not be persuasive in itself. They had to engage and overcome the objections of the opponents. The importance of counteroffensive becomes more evident when the claims made by the bill's opponents in Congress are examined.

The Glass bill was reported to the House floor on September 9, 1913, and the debate opened the next day. In a long caucus meeting the Democratic majority had decided that it would allow only members of the banking and currency committee to offer amendments to the bill. The unity of the party has often been attributed to the strong party discipline in the Congress of the day and Bryan's successful persuasion of the radicals into acceptance of the bill. But it would have been impossible for the bill to garner such support had the FRS been considered a central bank, as the Aldrich plan a year earlier suggested. The administration's repackaging of the banking system as a set of reserve banks and its regulator was crucial in gaining the backing of the Democratic majority.[38]

The Republicans, many of them supporters of the Aldrich bill, came out in strong opposition and closely followed the bankers' lead. Of the three aspects of the FRB that the bankers found most problematic, they were particularly intent on pointing out its excessive amount of power and the dangers of politicization, often linking the two. Many such statements denouncing the FRB mentioned the Supreme Court and the ICC, just as those of the bankers did. According to Republican lawmakers, the power to be vested in the FRB was unrivalled by both central banks overseas and other government bodies in the United States. When all of its authorities prescribed in the bill were put together, they would make the FRB "the greatest central banking institution in the world, with 12 branches." This was because the "whole working machinery of the 12 reserve banks, including the president and 6 out of 9 directors and all of the officials" were going to be under its control, and hence the "real directors of these 12 reserve banks are the 7 men" on the FRB. With plenary powers to manage the finance market and no authority to review its decisions, "No other board, official, or ruler ever was clothed with such authority."[39] In proposing an amendment giving minority representation on the board to the reserve banks, Rep. Martin Madden (R-IL) argued that whereas the ICC was given only regulatory power over railroads, the FRB was not just going to "direct but to control and regulate every phase of the

38 Rixey Smith and Norman Beasley, *Carter Glass: A Biography* (New York: Longmans, Green and Co., 1939), 121–124; West, *Banking Reform*, 113–114; Sanders, *Roots of Reform*, 251; Link, *New Freedom*, 222; Kazin, *Godly Hero*, 225–226. On the Democrats' use of caucus as a tool of party discipline in Congress, see James, *Presidents, Parties, and the State*, 141–143.

39 *Congressional Record*, 63rd Cong., 1st sess. (1913), HR, 5042, 4908.

management of the Federal reserve banks, down to the smallest item." This is why some Republican lawmakers sneered that the Glass bill was "none other than the much-discussed 'Aldrich plan' in disguise" or that it even was "much more centralized, autocratic, and tyrannical than the Aldrich plan."[40]

Given its enormous power, the danger of allowing political appointees to rule the FRB seemed ever more imminent to the Republican opposition. This was especially true when every new president could name its majority by the second year in office, and this point was actually raised by a Democratic legislator. The Glass bill was going to make the FRB a "political football" or "a political prize that has never been equated in the history of the country."[41] This implied, the Republicans thought, that "the control of the banking business of the country would be one of the prizes to be fought for in each presidential election." Since the composition of the FRB would change with the administration, a time would come when an "administration could so strengthen itself that neither the [monetary] policy nor the administration would change." Comparison with the Supreme Court and the ICC again seemed effective. To the supporters of the bill arguing that the FRB was similar to the ICC in its makeup, a Republican questioned if they were "willing now to change the method of the appointment of the members of the Interstate Commerce Commission and have each incoming administration appoint a majority of them." He then went on to ask if they were "willing to change the method of appointing the judges of the Supreme Court and let each President that comes into office appoint a majority of that court."[42]

The House Republicans' warnings about the FRB echoed those of the bankers regarding its power and the danger of politicization, including the frequent comparison to the Supreme Court and the ICC. In stark contrast to the bankers, however, the lawmakers refrained from criticizing the board for its prospective lack of expertise. Doing so would have undoubtedly given the suicidal impression that they wanted to put bankers on the board despite the public's hatred of the "Money Trust."[43] Although the Republican charges against the board were by no means easy to deal with, the Republicans' reluctance to raise the expertise issue, the Achilles' heel of the legitimization of the FRB with the interinstitutional association, gave proponents of the bill a critical advantage. Moreover, Glass's argument that the "real peril" was not in exclusion of bankers from the FRB but in having too many of them may have had a significant effect. According to him, the Secretary of Treasury and the Comptroller of Currency would almost always have experience in banking, aside from another presidential appointee who was to be a banker.[44]

40 *Congressional Record*, 63rd Cong., 1st sess. (1913), HR, 4924, 5026, 4810.

41 *Congressional Record*, 63rd Cong., 1st sess. (1913), HR, 4868, 5037.

42 *Congressional Record*, 63rd Cong., 1st sess. (1913), HR, 4896, 4871.

43 There were only two such instances throughout the House debate, and it is doubtful that they were taken seriously. *Congressional Record*, 63rd Cong., 1st sess. (1913), HR, 4852, 4705.

44 *Congressional Record*, 63rd Cong., 1st sess. (1913), HR, 4645. Also see *Congressional Record*, 63rd Cong., 1st sess. (1913), HR, 5035–5036.

How did the bill's supporters respond to the Republican charges to the FRB, and how did it retain its form? As stated above, the House Democrats decided in their caucus meeting to limit amendments to the Glass bill to those proposed by the members of the Banking and Currency Committee. Given the party's majority status, many took the bill's passage in the chamber as a fait accompli. Faced with the opponents' effort to undermine the legitimacy of the FRB, however, supporters of the bill hit back. In arguing for government control of the board and the power vested in it, the Democrats pursued two strategies. First, they insisted that any alternative to the FRB as prescribed in the Glass bill would give bankers additional control over the financial market and denounced it as outrageous. Second, when supporting the FRB, they repeatedly asserted that the board was not a bank but an overseer of both reserve and national banks. It was in this context the association with the Supreme Court and the ICC was used to show the board's authenticity as a US government body.

The confidence among the Democrats in government control of the FRB came at least in part from the strong rejection of its alternative, banker representation. Rep. Alben Barkley (D-KY) summarized the feelings shared by his fellow partisans when he said that "if it be suggested that the members of this Federal reserve board ought to be appointed by the banks themselves, as some of them desire . . . I desire to say that that appears to be the most preposterous proposal that I have heard upon this floor since I became a Member of this House. The thought of such a thing is abhorrent to all the traditions of the Democratic Party, and the consummation of such an idea would prove subversive of the liberties of the people." After all, as Rep. Edward Saunders (D-VA) noted, the "fundamental conception of the pending measure" was a "banking system free from the dominating control of that mysterious but real power, known as the Money Trust."[45]

This strategy seemed particularly effective in countering the argument that the FRB had too much power and was in fact a central bank in disguise. Rep. William Borland (D-MO) stated flatly that "the control of credits and money" must be turned over either "to the banker or the United States and their representatives" and argued that the publicity of the government-controlled FRB would prevent it from corruption. In this respect, the board was "simply a board of public officials similar to the Interstate Commerce Commission" or any other administrative agency. The Democrats also justified the FRB's power by comparing it with that of the ICC.[46] Rep. Michael Phelan (D-MA) emphasized that the FRB was not a bank but "a Government board, having a general supervision and control over the whole system." In his view, bankers were to be highly autonomous in their control of national and reserve banks. The FRB, as a "supervisory board," whose purpose was to "serve the public and not the banks," should accordingly

45 *Congressional Record*, 63rd Cong., 1st sess. (1913), HR, 4789. Also see *Congressional Record*, 63rd Cong., 1st sess. (1913), App., HR, 315, 330; West, *Banking Reform*, 87.

46 *Congressional Record*, 63rd Cong., 1st sess. (1913), HR, 4731; *Congressional Record*, 63rd Cong., 1st sess. (1913), HR, 5019, 5026.

be appointed by the president, "who represents the public interests of the whole Nation."[47]

Not all Democrats in Congress were in full support of the bill, however, and a few were openly critical. Rep. Oscar Callaway (D-TX) questioned the wisdom of government interference in the banking business, and Rep. Barkley replied that the ICC had also been objected to at its creation with a claim that "the Government was interfering with private business and to that extent was 'going into' such business." But, he continued, "no intelligent person would now advocate abolishing that commission, which has done such good service in protecting the people from the rapacity and greed of the railroads." According to Barkley, bankers opposed the creation of the FRB for the same reason. Such comparisons with the situation in which the ICC was established were often made to assuage public fears of the FRB's abuse of power.[48]

The discussion on the possible politicization of the FRB followed the same line. Rep. James Graham (D-IL) emphasized that the "members of the Supreme Court of the United States and members of the Interstate Commerce Commission are chosen in the same way" the Glass bill prescribed the method of appointment to the board. "[W]hile some may claim that partisan politics [has] at times been manifest in Supreme Court action," he noted, it should be admitted that neither the court nor the ICC was "fairly open to the charge of being under partisan control or of being a political body." He then went on to argue that only some among bankers would dare to support banker representation on the FRB. As suggested above, the Democrats, especially the populists, did not shrink from openly supporting the political appointment of board members. According to Rep. Finly Gray (D-IN), "all the public institutions of benevolence, all the charities that soothe and heal and bless," including the ICC, were "administered under political control." In fact, political control meant "the rule of the people, and it has terrors only for those who are afraid and recoil from the rule of the people." Many also stated the importance of trusting the president to make the right choice in picking the board members.[49]

The Glass bill passed the House on September 18, 1913, by a vote of 287 to 85, with only three Democrats defecting and thirty-three Republicans and Progressives in support. Although the explanation of the passage of the entire bill is outside the scope of this chapter, its proponents seemed to gain advantage from the association between the FRB and the Supreme Court and the ICC. The connection between the FRB and the two institutions worked best regarding the issue of politicization as the court and the ICC were models ideal in guaranteeing that the FRB would stay above politics. Luckily for the Democrats, the issue of expertise, which could have worked against the board when the

47 *Congressional Record*, 63rd Cong., 1st sess. (1913), HR, 4673; Timberlake, *Monetary Policy in the United States*, 223.

48 *Congressional Record*, 63rd Cong., 1st sess. (1913), HR, 4790, 4854.

49 *Congressional Record*, 63rd Cong., 1st sess. (1913), HR, 4843, 5038.

comparison was made with the other two institutions, was hardly raised in the House debates.[50]

The House floor proceedings turned out to be the first and last congressional showdown between the supporters and opponents of a government-controlled FRB. This did not mean that the bill's passage in the Senate was guaranteed, however. In fact, the opposition from several Democratic members of the Senate Banking and Currency Committee led to lengthy hearings that resulted in a substitute bill that almost killed the Glass bill. But at the same time, the center of gravity of the discussion on the FRB's organizational form shifted from the appropriateness of government control to the kind of government control to be exercised by the board.

The Senate committee began its hearings on the Glass bill in early September 1913, and the bankers were quick to make their views known. In a grand meeting in late August with the currency commission of the American Bankers' Association, the bankers had adopted a report that demanded, among other things, minority representation on the FRB and restricting some of the board's powers, including the authority to force a reserve bank to rediscount the paper of another. The bankers who testified at the Senate committee hearings freely reiterated their opposition to the bill and made a point of requesting minority representation. James Forgan argued for their "ownership" of the reserve banks and contended that they were entitled to the management of the FRB; Sol Wexler of Whitney-Central National Bank of New Orleans stressed the importance of expertise and noted that having men trained in banking selected by reserve banks was "sine qua non to the success" of the board.[51]

At the same time, the tide was turning. A. Barton Hepburn, chair of the banker association's currency commission, remarked at the Senate hearing that he was neither afraid of "political control" nor of "incompetent control" under the provisions of the Glass bill. Also, most nonbanker economists were ready to accept the government-controlled FRB, if only as a political inevitability. Harvard economists Oliver M. W. Sprague and Charles A. Conant respectively expressed indifference to the method of selecting the board's members and faith in the president to nominate competent individuals. Samuel Untermeyer, who had led the "Money Trust" investigation for the Pujo committee, expressed uneasiness about the politicization issue. But when asked what check there could be if the politically controlled FRB acted out of favoritism, he countered, "what check is there against the United States Supreme Court, or against the Interstate Commerce

50 However, an amendment to make no more than two of the four non-ex-officio members of the FRB could come from the same political party was adopted, responding (but not fully) to the claim that every incoming president could name the majority of the FRB. This provision was removed in the conference committee, as a new president became unable to appoint a majority of the board because of the removal of the Secretary of Agriculture from the board and the addition of a new provision giving five non-ex-officio members the term of ten years.

51 Link, *New Freedom*, 226; *CT*, Aug. 24, Sep. 7, 1913; *Banking and Currency*, 32, 40, 43, 59. Also see *Banking and Currency*, 256.

Commission, or against any public body in any part of the world[?]"[52] As illustrated by this statement, the Court and the ICC were frequently mentioned in the hearings, especially among the committee members, regardless of their attitude toward the Glass bill. Sen. Atlee Pomerene (D-OH), who sided with the administration, expressed his stance that the president should be trusted to make appropriate appointments just as with the Supreme Court and the ICC. He also pointed out that the ICC was respected despite not being composed exclusively of those with experience in the railroad business. The way of thinking about the FRB in terms of the two institutions thus clearly carried over to the Senate.[53]

In mid-October, committee Democrats were about to reach an agreement in support of the Glass bill. They were, however, split again by a legislative bombshell, known as the Vanderlip Plan. The new measure presented on October 23 by Frank Vanderlip, the president of the National City Bank of New York, would create a central bank within the government and under its control. He explained his move as a response to a request from committee members to construct an alternative to the Glass bill. It was widely believed, however, that his true intention was to kill it. While the administration eventually managed to win over six of seven Democratic committee members, Gilbert Hitchcock (D-NE) joined five Republican members in support of a substitute bill based on Vanderlip's plan. Now deadlocked, the committee reported both the slightly modified Glass bill (the Owen substitute) and the Hitchcock proposal to the Senate floor without indicating a preference. The biggest difference between the two committee bills was in the provisions on the organization and control of the FRS. Hitchcock's bill also had an FRB, but it would have a much tighter rein over the reserve banks than the Glass bill. There even was a clause giving the board the authority to appoint a majority of the directors of each reserve bank. This power was linked to another radical provision stipulating the sale of the stock of the reserve banks to the public; subscription by national banks was given only a secondary position.[54]

In contrast to the House, where no hearings were held after the bills' submission and many members therefore lacked the knowledge to discuss the details of the currency issue, senators had ample time and opportunities to study them during the hearings. They engaged in a heated debate on the floor for more than a month. But behind the tension between the two sides, the bills on table had one important thing in common: the FRB was to be fully controlled by the government. In addition, Hitchcock saw to the removal of the Secretary of Agriculture

52 *CT*, Oct. 16, 1913; *Banking and Currency*, 362, 525, 1393; Samuel Untermeyer to William G. McAdoo, May 6, 1913 (copy), Box 100, McAdoo Papers. Also see *WSJ*, July 28, 1913. Conant used to favor banker representation on the board, but became satisfied with the Glass bill when the Federal Advisory Council was adopted. Charles A. Conant to Albert S. Burleson, July 11, 1913, Box 103, McAdoo Papers; Charles A. Conant to Carter Glass, Aug. 1, 1913, Box 20, Glass Papers.

53 *Banking and Currency*, 1044, 1223–1224.

54 *Banking and Currency*, 2911–2967; *CT*, Oct. 27, 28, 1913; Edward M. House to William G. McAdoo, Oct. 25, 1913, Box 107, McAdoo Papers; Link, *New Freedom*, 232–235; West, *Banking Reform*, 128–130.

and the Comptroller of Currency from the board, making the treasury secretary the sole ex-officio member working with six other members in the Owen substitute and eight in the case of the Hitchcock bill. The latter also influenced the former in adopting another feature, carried over to the Federal Reserve Act: the FRB was given the power not just to suspend but to remove any officer or director of the reserve banks. In this way, the board was given full veto power over the reserve banks. In the words of Sen. James Reed (D-MO), this power would make the board "the supreme court of finance."[55]

This matchup opened a new horizon to the debate on the FRB, which as a whole worked in favor of the friends of the Owen substitute in three ways. First, the position in the Owen-Glass bill regarding the board's power shifted radically. Whereas it had been denounced in the House for creating a de facto central bank, it now was criticized by the advocates of the Hitchcock proposal, including many Republicans, for not giving enough authority to the FRB.[56] Now, the supporters of the Owen substitute could criticize such Republicans for their inconsistency and opportunism. Second, the two bills in the Senate were almost identical in the risk of politicization. The Hitchcock bill lessened the risk by increasing the total number of board members while reducing the number of ex-officio members from the Glass bill. This was true, but when compared to the FRB in the Owen substitute, which also had only one ex-officio member, the difference was a matter of degree, not of kind. As a result, no one was complaining about the FRB's possible politicization.[57]

Third, by allowing the FRB to appoint a majority of reserve bank directors, the Hitchcock proposal was even more vulnerable to the charge of slighting bankers and their expertise than the Owen substitute. This recasting of the terms of the debate completely freed the latter's supporters from the accusation that they were not taking expertise seriously. The Senate debate was far from silent on this issue, however. The supporters of both bills repeatedly argued that the members of the FRB would have the requisite banking knowledge and experience. Both sides did this, often utilizing the association of the board with the Supreme Court and the ICC. Sen. John Weeks (R-MA), arguing in support of the Hitchcock proposal, noted that its framers intended that "only those who are experienced in commercial and banking affairs shall be given places on these boards." They should be "men as representative and of general recognized capacity in the business world as are appointees to the Supreme Court in the legal world." In support of the Owen substitute, Sen. John Shafroth (D-CO) remarked that experienced bankers were not just eligible but that some actually deserved to be appointed.[58] Here,

55 *Congressional Record*, 63rd Cong., 2nd sess. (1913), S, 174.
56 *Congressional Record*, 63rd Cong., 2nd sess. (1913), S, 980.
57 *Congressional Record*, 63rd Cong., 2nd sess. (1913), S, 279.
58 *Congressional Record*, 63rd Cong., 2nd sess. (1913), S, 279; *Congressional Record*, 63rd Cong., 1st sess. (1913), S, 6025.

a near consensus on government control of the FRB emerged in Sen. Claude Swanson's (D-VA) argument:

> The President of the United States names the judges of the Supreme Court, who are supreme in the determination of life, liberty, and the rights of property. Has this trust in any way been violated? No. The President of the United States names the members of the Interstate Commerce Commission, who fix transportation rates for communities, cities, and sections and thus largely control the development of this country. Has this trust been violated? No. The members of the Federal reserve board when appointed by the President must be confirmed by the Senate. Can not the Senate be trusted to see that those selected are men of character and capacity, worthy to discharge the duties imposed upon them in this bill?[59]

Behind such a development toward agreement in the Senate was a rising sense of urgency among the public for currency reform and for acceptance of the Glass bill on the side of the bankers. The administration's friends worked to gain support from both the public and bankers by discussing currency reform at numerous venues. The best known of these was the dinner at the Economic Club of New York on November 10, at which Glass delivered an address along with other notables, including Vanderlip, the club's president. He justified government control of the FRB by recalling how he himself came to support it when Wilson associated the board with the ICC in his June conference with bankers, and the speech was widely praised. At a banquet of the Association of Commerce later that month, he appealed again to the bankers by stating that his concern was seeing too many of them being appointed to the FRB, rather than the opposite. Bryan joined the campaign to defend the Glass bill, and in a speech he denounced banker representation on the FRB: "What would you think of a railroad that said: 'We must control the Interstate Commerce Commission, that controls us in the railroad business'?"[60]

The Owen substitute passed the Senate on December 19 by a vote of fifty-four to thirty-four, shortly after the Hitchcock proposal had been voted down. Every Democrat, even Hitchcock, supported the bill in the end. The conference committee met the next day and adopted most of the features of the House bill as they worked out a compromise. As for the FRB, the committee dropped the Secretary of Agriculture from the House bill's ex-officio list and increased the minimum number of non-ex-officio members with banking experience from one to two, thus making minor concessions to bankers over politicization and expertise. The House approved the committee report on December 22. The Senate

59 *Congressional Record*, 63rd Cong., 2nd sess. (1913), S, 431.

60 *NYT*, Nov. 11 and 21, 1913; *CT*, Nov. 29, 1913; Walter I. McCoy to Carter Glass, Dec. 26, Box 67, Glass Papers; Smith and Beasley, *Carter Glass*, 129–132; *NYT*, Oct. 18, 1913.

concurred the following day, and Wilson immediately signed the bill into law, making it his own Christmas present.[61]

This chapter has answered the question why the FRS, very similar to the detested Aldrich plan from the previous year, could still turn out to be successful. The "Bryanization" of the reserve bill, especially the modification to make the FRB part of the government, certainly contributed to this. But given the strong antibanker sentiment of the time, it alone cannot explain the different fates of the two currency reform plans. It was the characterization of the FRB as a regulator of banks through the association with the ICC and the Supreme Court, offered by the Wilson administration, that held the key to the legitimization of the FRS. Declaring his support for the conference committee bill, Rep. Irvine Lenroot (R-WI), a progressive Republican, stated that he had come to believe that the FRB in the bill would establish public control over finance similar to that "exercised over the interstate commerce of the country through the Interstate Commerce Commission."[62]

The installation of the FRB is exceptional among the creation of ACs taken up in this book in that the policy in question and the government body that was to administer it had little connection to the judiciary. The FRB would have practically no adjudication function; it was to manage, rather than regulate, the central banking system. The legislative process of the Federal Reserve Act still makes a fascinating case of the judicialization of the administrative state precisely because of the absence of the shadow of courts and lawyers. The fact that the FRB was likened to the Supreme Court without involvement from lawyers as a profession is a clear indication that the administrative state judicialization was not monopolized by lawyers. Rather, it was a political process involving a large variety of actors. In addition, if a central banking board with little resemblance to railroad regulation or the judiciary could still be legitimatized by bringing up the ICC and the Supreme Court, there should be no difficulty in justifying the creation of ICC-like ACs for other regulatory policies. This chapter has shown that the ICC was quite ready to serve as an institutional model to subsequent regulations, further diffusing its judicial DNA. This is what happened over the next fifteen years, although ACs were to confront powerful challengers along the way.

61 West, *Banking Reform*, 131–133; Allan H. Meltzer, *A History of the Federal Reserve*, vol. 1, *1913–1951* (Chicago: University of Chicago Press, 2003), 19, n. 1.

62 *Congressional Record*, 63rd Cong., 2nd sess. (1913), S, 1442.

4 Retrenching administrative commissions, expanding state judiciality

"Of course, I feel that is almost like constituting a whole Supreme Court," President Wilson commented in January 1914, replying to a press question on the task of appointing the FRB's inaugural members. It was "almost equal in importance" to nominating the entire Court, he added. The legislative process of the Federal Reserve Act documented in the previous chapter confirmed that, by the Progressive Era, the ICC had already established a reputation as a prestigious courtlike tribunal. The words of the president who had initiated the fight for the FRB by comparing it to the ICC indicated that the United States already had a tradition of judicialized ACs. It may seem natural that the "movement" to create ICC-modeled ACs reached its peak under Wilson.[1]

Wilson did not promote the FRB and other ACs out of sheer respect for their judiciality, however. He advocated their creation primarily to win the support of judicialist members of Congress. In doing so, he also made proposals that would enlarge presidential influence on the ACs to be created. Although the commissions established in the first three decades of the twentieth century were modeled after the ICC, their autonomy from the chief executive was somewhat restrained. In contrast to the creative syncretism during the creation and development of the ICC that worked to judicialize the commission, the new ACs became dejudicialized in favor of the presidents. It should be recalled that the Wilson administration modified the ICC model in establishing the FRB by creating ex-officio memberships, thereby securing presidential influence over the board. With the help of executive departments jealous of ACs, Wilson and his successors attempted to either obtain partial control over new commissions or assign new regulatory authorities to executive departments. The executivists' project turned out quite successful, thanks to acquiescent lawmakers who came to believe that producing new ACs was fiscally irresponsible despite their continued belief in procedural fairness. The executivist turn of ACs would culminate in a Supreme Court decision depriving all AC members of autonomy from the president.

The antitrust reform resulting in the creation of the FTC in 1914 was a clear illustration that the diffusion of the ICC model of government control that had

1 *PWW*, 29:138; Cushman, *Independent Regulatory Commissions*, 146.

begun with the FRB would continue into other policy domains. The effort to devise a reform plan to counter unfair business activities had been long in the making. The Sherman Act of 1890 prohibiting contracts and combinations "in restraint of trade or commerce" had been administered through investigation and legal action by the Department of Justice against possible violators. But the department's commitment to prosecution, which ultimately hinged upon the president's attitude, was sporadic at best. Even when cases reached the courtroom, there seemed to be little consistency in judicial opinions due to the vagueness of the statutory provisions. This frustrated both the business community wishing to determine what kind of activity did and did not fall within the law, and the public demanding harsh punishment for monopolists. In 1903, the Bureau of Corporations was installed in the Department of Commerce and Labor with an eye on what constituted unfair trade activities, although only with the nonregulatory task of analyzing corporate behavior.[2]

Such general discontent with the status quo coalesced in the plan for an expert, full-time enforcer of antitrust law in the form of an AC. Around 1910, promoters of progressive reform from both political parties, most importantly those gathered in the National Civic Federation, came to support the adoption of an AC with the ICC as its model. Andrew Carnegie described it as an "industrial Supreme Court" to replace the Bureau of Corporations. The reformers rallied to Theodore Roosevelt who also backed the ICC model. Their movement gained momentum in 1911 when the Supreme Court handed down the decision in the *Standard Oil* case. The notorious ruling declared that whether corporate contracts and combinations unlawfully restrained trade had to be determined in light of their effects. This meant that the legality of business combinations had to be decided on a case-by-case basis by judges with no expertise in antitrust matters. Any remaining hope for a more predictable antitrust policy was lost with the ruling.[3]

Later that year, Sen. Newlands drafted, with the aid of ICC staffers, a trust reform bill containing an Interstate Trade Commission (ITC). The commission was described as a "semi-judicial body" whose work was to be "quite analogous" to that of the ICC.[4] In his view, "there should be a commission rather than one executive official [for antitrust regulation], because there are powers of judgment and powers of discretion to be exercised. The organization should be quasi-judicial in character . . . Such work must be done by a board or commission . . . independent of executive authority . . ." The Democratic lawmaker was not alone

2 William Letwin, *Law and Economic Policy in America: The Evolution of the Sherman Antitrust Act* (Chicago: University of Chicago Press, 1965).

3 Carnegie quoted in James Weinstein, *The Corporate Ideal in the Liberal State, 1900–1918* (Boston: Beacon Press, 1968), 82; Sklar, *Corporate Reconstruction*, 204–220, 249–250, and 282; *Standard Oil Co. of New Jersey v. United States*, 221 U.S. 1 (1911).

4 Franklin K. Lane to Francis G. Newlands, June 8, 1911, Folder 238, Box 25, Series 1, Newlands Papers; "Press Notice Regarding Newlands Trade-Commission Bill," n.d., Folder 616, Box 60, Series 2, Newlands Papers; Sklar, *Corporate Reconstruction*, 302–303, 309–323.

in thinking of antitrust reform in judicialist terms. During the 1912 presidential election campaign, the Republican and Progressive national platforms also proposed the establishment of an AC. The former stated that there was "much that may be committed to a Federal trade commission, thus placing in the hands of an administrative board many of the functions now necessarily exercised by the courts," insisting that it would "promote promptness in the administration of the law and avoid delays and technicalities incident to court procedure." Efficiency and fairness were thus both taken seriously as had been the case with the establishment of the ICC.[5]

Despite the broad swath of support for the AC, it was far from certain that antitrust reform would follow the ICC model at the beginning of the Wilson administration. The authority of the new commission would be fiercely debated in the legislative process of the FTC Act, and the wisdom of giving it quasi-judicial power became the flash point. This was partly because Wilson was still uneasy with the idea of regulation by experts when Congress turned to antitrust legislation in early 1914. He was willing to give an AC no more than investigative and publicity powers to aid the chief executive, not much more than those held by the Bureau of Corporations. Faithfully reflecting Wilson's preference expressed in the message to Congress in January, the House passed a bill containing an ITC, a sunshine commission, by voice vote on June 5.[6]

By this time, however, Wilson's view on the antitrust commission was rapidly changing. The Democratic antitrust legislation package, of which the House's Covington commission bill was a part, came under widespread criticism for the excessive rigidity of its provisions regarding the clarification and enforcement of the Sherman Act. Louis Brandeis, inspired by the ICC's railroad regulation with which he was familiar but hesitant to accept the progressive proposal of an ICC-like regulatory commission, asked his friend George Rublee to devise a reform plan including an AC that would, to use Gerald Berk's expression, "cultivate" competition through cooperation with the business community. By early June, both Wilson and Brandeis were convinced by Rublee's scheme that included an AC with the power to issue orders to stop those engaging in "unfair methods of competition." The AC was quickly written into Section Five of the Senate bill (and the final act), which was introduced to the floor shortly after the passage of the House bill.[7]

In the Senate, the ITC became a quasi-judicial agency. The legislation was far from a done deal upon its proposal, and as Berk has demonstrated, the proposed

5 Committee on Interstate Commerce, *Hearing[s] before the Committee on Interstate Commerce, United State Senate, Sixty-second Congress, pursuant to S. Res. 98, a resolution directing the Committee on Interstate Commerce to investigate and report desirable changes in the laws regulating and controlling corporations, persons, and firms, engaged in interstate commerce*, 62nd Cong. (1912), 1:11; Porter and Johnson, comp., *National Party Platforms*, 184.

6 *PWW*, 29:153–158; James, *Presidents, Parties, and the State*, 170–176; Alvis, Bailey, and Taylor, *Removal Power*, 152–154.

7 Berk, *Regulated Competition*, 94–101, 122–124.

commission had different meaning to each political force engaged in the debate. But as far as the institutional form of the proposed commission was concerned, one thing was clear: it was going to be modeled after the ICC. This was especially true when Sen. Newlands, who had long been pushing for "an impartial quasi judicial tribunal" similar to the ICC which he thought had "become a tribunal second in importance only next to the Supreme Court of the land," enthusiastically steered the legislation as the chair of the Committee on Interstate Commerce.[8] His colleagues discussed the new commission in terms of the ICC and judicial courts. Sen. George Norris (R-NE), for instance, predicted that the commission was "going to be somewhat similar to a court, or to the Interstate Commerce Commission." As already mentioned, the name of the proposed ITC was taken from the ICC – it would be changed later to avoid confusion. In contrast to the legislation of the Federal Reserve Act, even opponents of the commission did not dispute the adequacy of the ICC as an organizational model.[9]

After the Senate passage of the bill in September 1914, the House acquiesced to the Senate version, and the Federal Trade Commission Act was enacted later that month. It created the FTC armed with strong regulatory powers including the authority to issue "cease and desist" orders to unfair methods of competition. As Berk shows, the legislators and the president agreed to keep the commission's role intentionally ambiguous, allowing it to undergo further creative syncretism.[10] Still, as Felix Frankfurter commented in 1915, "the Interstate Commerce Act and the experience of its enforcement have, *mutatis mutandis*, served as the basis for far-reaching regulation of interstate industrial business embodied in the Federal Trade Commission Act . . ." The FTC Act allows the commission members to sign subpoenas and confers both the commissions' members and examiners the judge-like power "to administer oaths and affirmations, examine witnesses, and receive evidence" in Section Nine, and formal hearings became a pillar of the commissions' activities.[11]

8 Berk, *Regulated Competition*, 102–106; Cushman, *Independent Regulatory Commissions*, 188; *Congressional Record*, 62nd Cong., 1st sess. (1911), S, 1226; James, *Presidents, Parties, and the State*, 188.

9 *Congressional Record*, 63rd Cong., 2nd sess. (1914), S, 11598.

10 Berk, *Regulated Competition*, 107–109. Alvis, Bailey, and Taylor, *Removal Power*, 157–159. For the procedures of the early FTC, see John Leland Mechem, "Procedure and Practice before the Federal Trade Commission," *Michigan Law Review* 21 (1922): 125–159.

11 Felix Frankfurter, *A Selection of Cases under the Interstate Commerce Act* (Cambridge, MA: Harvard University Press, 1915), vii. In the same passage, Frankfurter also noted that the 1887 act also served as a model for state-level regulatory policies, which by this time involved many courtlike ACs. National Civic Federation, Department on Regulation of Interstate and Municipal Utilities, *Commission Regulation of Public Utilities: A Compilation and Analysis of Laws of Forty-Three States and of the Federal Government for the Regulation by Central Commissions of Railroads and Other Public Utilities* (New York: National Civic Federation, 1913), esp. Ch. 14; W. Stull Holt, *The Federal Trade Commission: Its History, Activities, and Organization* (New York: D. Appleton and Co., 1922), 17–23; George C. Henderson, *The Federal Trade Commission: A Study in Administrative Law and Procedure* (New Haven: Yale University Press, 1924).

The legislation of the FTC Act signifies the centrality of ACs in the fairness-oriented state and the validity of the model of administrative state building proposed in this study. The FTC modeled after the ICC was meant to be a strongly judicialized agency. But at the same time, the new commission was presented as a more efficient alternative to the judiciary that had been administering the Sherman Act with the help of the Department of Justice. In the Senate committee hearing, Newlands defended the AC by asking if it was better to wait for the courts to "go through their slow processes" and expect them eventually to create order in antitrust policy or to organize an AC that would tackle the abuses "through continuous supervision."[12] During the legislative process of the FTC Act, he even entertained the idea of creating a "Federal Commerce Commission" to be in charge of economic regulation and then placing the FTC under it along with the ICC and FRB. In his view, the three ACs held a common policy goal and organizational form. Newlands' commitment to ACs undoubtedly was stronger than that of many of his colleagues; Sen. John Sharp Williams (D-MS), strongly opposed to the proposed ITC, privately groused that Newlands could not "imagine any sort of legislation without a commission." But there also was no doubt that the ACs were quickly forming a category of government bodies in the minds of political elites.[13]

Lawyers were the least likely group to back policy making by such agencies. But some prominent lawyers began to acknowledge their contribution to the advancement of efficiency in governance. In his presidential address to the ABA in 1916, Elihu Root discussed how the American bar could better contribute to "the permanent higher efficiency" of the nation. After criticizing the excess supply of lawyers, Root presented a long list of symptoms of the sorry situation of the bar, including how "the efficiency of our courts is reduced, their rate of progress retarded, the expense increased, their procedure muddled and involved by an appreciable proportion of untrained and incompetent practitioners." One of the solutions he proposed was to accept administration of law by ACs, both federal and state. He described the shift toward policy execution by agencies as "inevitable." In Root's view, what was required was a new system of law governing regulatory agencies. He was thus in open support of both the efficiency and expertise of courtlike ACs. In the nascent field of administrative law, scholars would study administrative agencies in the firm belief that the agencies were, and ought to be, courtlike. In 1915, Felix Frankfurter published a casebook on the Interstate Commerce Act containing decisions of both judicial courts and the ICC, thinking that they were together creating "one of the most vital branches of the law."[14]

12 Committee on Interstate Commerce, *Federal Trade Commission*, 63rd Cong., 2nd sess. (1914), S. Rep. 597, 22.

13 "Additional Section. Sec. 11," 1914, Folder 621, Box 60, Series 2, Newlands Papers; John Sharp Williams to Robert R. Reed, Jan. 21, 1914, Box 3, John Sharp Williams Papers, Manuscript Division, Library of Congress.

14 Elihu Root, "Public Service by the Bar," *Annual Report of the American Bar Association* (1916): 356, 361, 368–369; Chase, *American Law School*; Felix Frankfurter, *Selection of*

Just as the ACs came to be accepted as courtlike agencies, attempts were already being made to prevent them from adopting strong judiciality. The earliest challenges to ACs came from the Wilson administration. The attacks took the form of proposals intended to weaken new ACs' autonomy from the president in different ways. First, as was the case with the ex-officio members of the FRB, the president tried to gain control over new ACs by making some or all commission membership ex-officio ones accountable to him.[15] Second, the chief executive sought to gain influence over new ACs by conferring upon himself the authority to instruct commissions for certain functions. For instance, the FTC Act gave the president the power to direct the FTC "to investigate and report the facts relating to any alleged violations of the antitrust Acts by any corporation." Such a power could easily be used to affect the commission's agenda. But the appropriateness of the particular provision was not debated during the legislative process, probably because the authority had no immediate connection to adjudication and was also to be given to the two houses of Congress.[16]

The Wilson administration's effort to undermine commission autonomy was ironic, as the president had been a leading proponent of the politics-administration dichotomy. Early scholars of public administration such as Wilson and Francis Goodnow preached the importance of keeping politics and public administration distant from each other. In "The Study of Administration," Wilson stated that "administration lies outside the proper sphere of *politics*. Administrative questions are not political questions" [emphasis in original]. Public policy could be best administered by expert agencies free from outside political influence, and such a separation was achievable. Shielding ACs from executive influence would have clearly reinforced the dichotomy Wilson advocated. The commissions came to be seen as the embodiment of the widely supported dichotomy and became an added reason for the commissions' strong popularity among judicialist lawmakers.[17]

Why, then, did Wilson attempt to encroach on ACs? While there is a line of research on how Wilson shifted from a legislature-centered view of the government to an executive-centered one at odds with the autonomy of agencies, his interference in the ACs could be explained simply as an ambition to control

---

Cases, vii; G. Edward White, *Intervention and Detachment: Essays in Legal History and Jurisprudence* (New York: Oxford University Press, 1994), esp. Pt. 2.

15 The FTC Act's Section Two exempted the secretary, clerks to commissioners, the attorneys, and special experts and examiners from the classified civil service, expanding the scope of presidential control of the FTC. See Joseph Postell, *Bureaucracy in America: The Administrative State's Challenge to Constitutional Government* (Columbia: University of Missouri Press, 2017), 203.

16 Cushman, *Independent Regulatory Commissions*, 222–223.

17 Patrick Overeem, *The Politics-Administration Dichotomy: Toward a Constitutional Perspective*, 2nd ed. (Boca Raton, FL: CRC Press, 2012); Ronald J. Pestritto, "The Progressive Origins of the Administrative State: Wilson, Goodnow, and Landis," *Social Philosophy and Policy* 24 (2007): 16–54; Goodnow, *Politics and Administration*; Wilson, "Study of Administration," 210.

policy implementation. Wilson was the first president to repeatedly face the creation of ACs. It was not surprising that he would want to secure as much influence as possible over important regulations, even if it risked resistance from Congress. With the aid of executive departments, Wilson and his successors sought to avoid the creation of autonomous ACs, resulting in an executivist-oriented creative syncretism of commissions.[18]

The legislation of the Merchant Marine Act of 1916 is a case in point. The American shipping industry had been on the decline since the late nineteenth century. By 1910, less than 10 percent of US foreign trade was carried out by American vessels. The outbreak of World War I in 1914 and the obstruction of transatlantic trade by the belligerents made the revival of the US merchant marine an urgent matter. The Wilson administration proposed the creation of a shipping board designated not only to invest in corporations that would purchase and operate commercial fleets but also to regulate maritime traffic just as the ICC had done for land transportation. The administration proposed a bill (H.R. 18518) to the Sixty-Third Congress in August 1914, through Rep. Joshua Alexander (D-MO), chair of the House Committee on Merchant Marine and Fisheries. The board prescribed in the bill would comprise three ex-officio members, the Postmaster General with the Secretaries of Treasury and Commerce, whose departments had close connection to the duties of the proposed agency. The composition of the board reflected the president's determination to control maritime policy. In addition, the board was to request permission from, or act under the direction of, the president in purchasing and managing of the vessels. Congress, however, never took up the bill.[19]

Alexander submitted a similar bill (H.R. 10500) to the next Congress. While there was a consensus on the importance of the merchant marine and the need for a government body for its promotion, both the institutional features of the proposed board and its enormous power including possible government ownership of vessels were closely scrutinized in the House. The promoters of the bill justified the shipping board's regulatory power over "the common carrier by water," arguing that it was only a subset of what the ICC already exercised ashore, mentioning the extensive overlap between the bill and the Interstate Commerce Act.[20]

The appointment of cabinet officers as ex-officio members became the focus of debate regarding the board's form. There were two types of criticism against the ex-officio membership provision: one based on the fear of excessive presidential influence on the board and the other deriving from apprehension about

18 Overeem, *Politics-Administration Dichotomy*, 53–61; Pestritto, "Progressive Origins," 37–43.

19 Richard Sicotte, "Economic Crisis and Political Response: The Political Economy of the Shipping Act of 1916," *Journal of Economy History* 59 (1999): 861–884; Andrew Gibson and Arthur Donovan, *The Abandoned Ocean: A History of United States Maritime Policy* (Columbia: University of South Carolina Press, 2000); Cushman, *Independent Regulatory Commissions*, 231.

20 *Congressional Record*, 64th Cong., 1st sess. (1916), HR, 8081, 12345.

the board's possible loss of judiciality. From the debate on the FRB's ex-officio membership, there was no way a new regulatory board composed entirely of cabinet members could be easily accepted. Anticipating opposition, Rep. Alexander revised his bill so that the board now had five members, two ex-officio ones and three political appointees protected from presidential removal. Despite this precaution, opposition remained formidable. In the House committee hearings, representatives of the US Chamber of Commerce that stood to benefit greatly from the legislation stated a preference for a "non-partisan board," noting that the business organization "did not favor having the officials of the Government a party to that board, in ex-officio positions." Alexander retreated by submitting a substitute bill (H.R. 15455) for a seven-member board, now with five independent members. This new bill was brought to the House floor, where it failed to satisfy many representatives. Critics argued that the appointment of cabinet secretaries accountable to the president would politicize the board, making it vulnerable to interference from business.[21] Unlike the FRB, whose members could come from any political party, the Alexander bill prescribed that no more than three out of five independent members of the US Shipping Board (USSB) could come from the same party. It was thought that such an arrangement would enable the two ex-officio members to hold the board's casting vote. The bill's opponents also feared that presidential influence and the danger of politicization would become more pronounced later into an administration, with the increase of the number of independent members appointed by the president.[22]

The ex-officio provision in the shipping board bill was found problematic also in relation to the board's quasi-judicial functions, which were absent in the case of the FRB. The cabinet officers' presence in the USSB's formal hearings was thought not only to undermine the autonomy of adjudication but also to violate the fundamental common-law principle of "one who decides must hear," as they would surely be too preoccupied with departmental affairs to attend lengthy board hearings. Immediately after Rep. Alexander's introduction of the bill, Rep. James Mann (R-IL) pointed out the danger of "political, partisan appointments" to a regulatory agency, casting doubt on the wisdom of letting ex-officio members "vote on a proposition where they did not hear the arguments." One Democrat concurred, reminding them that "in all judicial bodies, those who do not participate in hearing of arguments always refuse to take part in a decision." Such arguments were so convincing that Alexander himself switched sides and began to oppose the ex-officio idea.[23]

The members of the House thus vigorously attacked presidential encroachment on the shipping board. Although the board was to be assigned a multitude of tasks including the purchase and management of ships, the lawmakers still saw that it was supposed to "act largely as a court" and would not let politics

21 House Committee on the Merchant Marine and Fisheries, *Creating a Shipping Board, a Naval Auxiliary, and a Merchant Marine*, 64th Cong., 1st sess. (1916), 10; *Congressional Record*, 64th Cong., 1st sess. (1916), HR, 8285.

22 *Congressional Record*, 64th Cong., 1st sess. (1916), HR, 8261.

23 *Congressional Record*, 64th Cong., 1st sess. (1916), HR, 8278–80.

interfere with its operation.[24] A comment defending the ex-officio membership referring to the cabinet members' policy expertise was met with strong criticism that department secretaries' lack of time to familiarize themselves with the board's work would cancel out the benefits of their expertise, that is, if they had any.[25] In contrast to the strong opposition to the ex-officio membership on the shipping board, the provisions allowing the president to instruct and authorize the board regarding fleet organization attracted little attention. This probably had to do with the urgency of the matter and the fact that the board's role did not involve adjudication. Opponents attacked the federal government's meddling with the shipping business itself, not presidential interference with the board.[26]

Although the ex-officio provision survived the House, the unpopularity of cabinet members' involvement in formal adjudication became abundantly clear in the debate. Upon receiving the House bill, the Senate Committee on Commerce casually eliminated the ex-officio memberships and made the USSB autonomous from the president, stating in its report that the duties of the cabinet members "would probably preclude from giving the requisite time to the duties of the board in the discharge of its several functions, especially those with regulation, supervision, and control of water carriers."[27] Few if any senators expressed regret. Sen. Wesley Jones (R-WA) praised the committee's Democratic majority for the amendment, arguing that the shipping board "ought to be one entirely free from politic; as free as it possibly can be."[28] After the passage of the amended bill in the Senate, the House, including Rep. Alexander, happily concurred with it, and the Merchant Marine Act was signed into law in September 1916.[29]

While Congress was at least partly successful in rejecting the presidential encroachment on the US Shipping Board, there was no guarantee that such would also be the case in the future. This was because skepticism on the wisdom of creating an additional AC for every new regulation was beginning to be heard. This arose from the concern that doing so would both be too financially costly and make the government bloated. During the debate on the shipping board bill, Rep. William Green (R-IA) stated:

> [T]his bill is like the other administration measures that have been put through Congress since the present occupant of the White House controlled the situation . . . The result has been that we are loaded down by new boards

24 Comment by Representative Rufus Hardy (D-TX). *Congressional Record*, 64th Cong., 1st sess. (1916), HR, 8282.

25 *Congressional Record*, 64th Cong., 1st sess. (1916), HR, 8280–8281.

26 Comment by Rep. Woodson Oglesby (D-NY). *Congressional Record*, 64th Cong., 1st sess. (1916), HR, 8261.

27 *Congressional Record*, 64th Cong., 1st sess. (1916), HR, 8259, 8278, 8283; Committee on Commerce, *Creating a Shipping Board, a Naval Auxiliary, a Merchant Marine, and Regulating Carriers by Water Engaged in the Foreign and Interstate Commerce of the United States*, 64th Cong., 1st sess. (1916), S. Rep. 689, 2.

28 *Congressional Record*, 64th Cong., 1st sess. (1916), S, 12447. Also see S, 12576 for a similar argument.

29 *Congressional Record*, 64th Cong., 1st sess. (1916), HR, 13366.

> and commissions, secretaries, departments, and hordes of new officeholders, with Government expenses constantly rising higher and higher in the millions until with an empty Treasury . . . These hopes [aroused by the Wilson administration] have been disappointed and the promises have been unfulfilled. Nothing has resulted but the ever-increasing bill of expenses and ever-increasing multitude of officeholders. The result will be the same with this bill – a new commission, practically a new department, more officeholders, more expense, and nothing else. [Applause on the Republican side.][30]

While Green's argument was obviously partisan, the fear of aggrandizement of government and additional financial cost that new ACs would incur was not. The House committee had at first considered assigning maritime regulation to the ICC but abandoned the idea upon realizing that the commission was overburdened. At that point, "the conclusion was forced upon the committee that the advisable thing to do was to create a new board or commission." The Senate was also concerned that the accumulation of ACs could lead to big government. While no direct objection to the AC idea itself was raised, the chamber cut the salary of the board members by 25 percent from the original $10,000 to reduce the financial cost. It was also rumored that the senators would attempt to do the same for existing ACs.[31]

The above effort to downsize the government reflected the strong social mood for efficiency. The Progressive Era saw what historian Samuel Haber calls an "efficiency craze" or a "secular Great Awakening." The term "efficiency" was used in all sorts of contexts, and often equated with goodness.[32] The enthusiasm was sparked by Frederick W. Taylor's 1911 book, *The Principles of Scientific Management*. Originally presented as a method of industrial management, Taylor's scientific management, better known as "Taylorism," linked productivity with morality and was considered applicable to almost any social setting. It instantly gained popularity, and progressive leaders such as Brandeis, Croly, and Walter Lippman remained committed to it even after its impact waned with the beginning of World War I. Scientific management enabled progressives to reconcile the potential tension between policy expertise and democracy through the former's contribution to the latter by promoting efficiency. Contrasting ACs, or

30 *Congressional Record*, 64th Cong., 1st sess. (1916), HR, 8341. This was not the first time the accumulation of ACs was attacked in Congress. During the legislative process of the FTC Act, Sen. Charles Thomas (D-CO) stated that "[w]e are rapidly becoming a government by commission or by bureau, or by both," which in his view was not the "good, old Anglo-Saxon method of administering justice which recognizes the right of every person . . . to have his day in court," and opposed the creation of the FTC. *Congressional Record*, 63rd Cong., 2nd sess. (1914), S, 11182.

31 *Congressional Record*, 64th Cong., 1st sess. (1916), HR, 8095; *NYT*, Aug. 22 and Sep. 6, 1916.

32 Samuel Haber, *Efficiency and Uplift: Scientific Management in the Progressive Era, 1890–1920* (Chicago: University of Chicago Press, 1964), ix–x. Also see Thomas C. Leonard, *Illiberal Reformers: Race, Eugenics and American Economics in the Progressive Era* (Princeton: Princeton University Press, 2016), Ch. 4.

"administrative courts," with judicial courts, Croly praised them in his 1914 work as a "convenient means of consolidating the divided activities of the government for certain practical social purposes" in carrying out new social programs. The support for ACs by such strong advocates of efficiency signified that America's fairness-oriented administrative state judicialization was an outgrowth of the motivation to make governance more efficient.[33]

While much of efficiency-oriented government reform during this period was made at state and local levels, the president and Congress also promoted it. In fact, the president had begun taking the initiative well before the publication of Taylor's book. Having been US Civil Service Commissioner and governor of New York, Theodore Roosevelt had had ample administrative experience before assuming the presidency and publicly preached the gospel of efficiency.[34] As president, he organized the Commission on Department Methods, an advisory committee known as the Keep Commission, in 1905. It offered recommendations for improvement of various aspects of department business such as budget and personnel management, with a particular eye on efficiency, but in Congress they fell on deaf ears. President Taft inherited Roosevelt's commitment to administrative reform and created the Committee on Economy and Efficiency in 1910, this time with congressional approval. Although one of its recommendations led to the creation of the consolidated federal budget, the committee's proposals gained little interest from Congress under the Taft administration. The subsequent presidential effort for executive reorganization into the 1920s would also pursue economy and efficiency.[35]

Despite their apparent lack of sympathy for presidential efforts at administrative reform, the lawmakers were themselves not immune from the "efficiency craze." In 1912, Congress passed an appropriations act directing the Civil Service Commission to establish a uniform efficiency rating system for all agencies; the Division of Efficiency was created in the commission for the task. In 1916, the division was transformed into the Bureau of Efficiency reporting directly to

33 Haber, *Efficiency and Uplift*, 20, 74, and Chs. 5–6; Herbert Croly, *Progressive Democracy* (New York: Macmillan, 1914), 364; Earlier, Croly had warned that it would be a great error to believe that ACs such as the ICC would "discipline the big corporations severely without injuring their efficiency." While Croly had no illusion about regulatory policy and ACs, he still believed that the commissions would "perform a useful public service" and suggested that antitrust regulation should be conducted by an AC once the Sherman Act was repealed. Herbert Croly, *The Promise of American Life* (1909; repr., New York: Capricorn Books, 1964), 113, 363–364.

34 Theodore Roosevelt, *An Autobiography* (New York: Charles Scribner's Sons, 1926); Arnold, *Remaking the Presidency*, 25–38.

35 Peri E. Arnold, *Making the Managerial Presidency: Comprehensive Reorganization Planning, 1905–1996*, 2nd ed. (Lawrence: University of Kansas Press, 1998), 23–28, 37–49; Harold T. Pinkett, "The Keep Commission, 1905–1909: A Rooseveltian Effort for Administrative Reform," *Journal of American History* 52 (1965): 297–312; Haber, *Efficiency and Uplift*, 113; Jonathan Kahn, *Budgeting Democracy: State Building and Citizenship in America, 1890–1928* (Ithaca: Cornell University Press, 1997), Ch. 7.

the president.[36] Later, the Taft Commission's proposal on the federal budget finally saw the legislative light of day as the Budget and Accounting Act in 1921 that organized the Bureau of the Budget and the General Accounting Office. They were to work toward "securing greater economy and efficiency in the conduct of public service," respectively, as the nation's budget supervisor and independent auditor. The congressional enthusiasm for efficiency also derived from serious fiscal concerns after World War I. During the war, the number of paid civilian employees more than doubled from four hundred thousand in 1916, and remained above five hundred thousand throughout the 1920s. The total federal debt in 1921 was close to $24 million, more than eight times the figure in 1917. The lawmakers' growing wariness toward additional ACs, combined with the president's executivist ambition, led to encroachment of executive departments on ACs that continued beyond Wilson's presidency.[37]

The executivist creative syncretism soon resulted in a major change in ACs' institutional features in the waterways regulation. Since the late nineteenth century, regulation and conservation of inland streams had been a headache to government officials. It was hard enough to reconcile different usages of streams such as navigation, irrigation, and power generation, but coordinating regulation by federal and state agencies focusing on different waterways usage was a nightmare. Since the Theodore Roosevelt administration, presidents had sought to clear up such regulatory disarray by integrating the waterways management scattered across many executive departments. In 1917, the Inland Waterways Commission was created for that purpose. President Wilson never appointed its members, however, as a new plan was already in preparation.[38]

The Departments of Interior, War, and Agriculture jointly proposed a comprehensive waterways regulation bill that entailed the creation of a new AC, the Federal Power Commission (FPC). At Wilson's request, the House created the special Water Power Committee tasked with considering the merits of the interdepartmental plan. The proposed FPC was not another ICC-like independent commission, though. Instead, it was as executivist as any commission could be. Just like the original administration plan of the USSB, the FPC would comprise

36 Mordecai Lee, *Institutionalizing Congress and the Presidency: The U.S. Bureau of Efficiency, 1916–1933* (College Station: Texas A&M Press, 2006); Haber, *Efficiency and Uplift*, 114.

37 Frederick C. Mosher, *The GAO: The Quest for Accountability in American Government* (Boulder: Westview Press, 1979), Chs. 1 and 2; Roger R. Trask, *The General Accounting Office, 1921–1966* (Washington, DC: Ross and Perry, 2001), Ch. 2; Arnold, *Managerial Presidency*, 53; US Bureau of the Census, *Historical Statistics*, 1102, 1104. For the war's impact on business regulation by ACs, see Marc Allen Eisner, *From Warfare State to Welfare State: World War I, Compensatory State Building, and the Limits of Modern Order* (University Park: Pennsylvania State University Press, 2000), Ch. 4.

38 Donald J. Pisani, "Water Planning in the Progressive Era: The Inland Waterways Commission Reconsidered," *Journal of Policy History* 18 (2006): 389–418; Donald J. Pisani, *Water and American Government: The Reclamation Bureau, National Water Policy, and the West, 1902–1935* (Berkeley: University of California Press, 2006), Ch. 8; Milton Conover, *The Federal Power Commission: Its History, Activities and Organization* (Baltimore: Johns Hopkins Press, 1923).

the secretaries of the three executive departments from which the bill originated. Responsible for overall waterways regulation, the FPC's policy role included the adjudication of disputes regarding electricity rates and usage of waterways.

The perception gap between the administration and Congress over the cabinet secretaries' involvement in regulation immediately surfaced. As soon as the House took up the administration bill, the Senate passed its own water power bill (S.1419). While cabinet officers were given important regulatory roles in this measure, it was still based on the judicialist view of the state; the ICC was to be responsible for formal adjudication. In contrast, proponents of the FPC in the administration displayed no hesitation in calling for an AC manned exclusively by cabinet members. According to Secretary of Agriculture David Houston, the creation of the FPC was nothing more than a convenient means to draw together department heads and bring about comprehensive regulation of inland waterways. The work of the commission was to be carried out utilizing the organizational resources of the three departments. Houston therefore could not care less about how such an institutional arrangement could disrupt the separation of powers principle. Asked in the House committee hearing if giving "executive heads legislative functions" through the FPC was "a good tendency in governmental affairs, remembering the strong convictions of the American people of keeping separate the three departments of government," Houston replied that he saw no impropriety in such an arrangement.[39] This view was shared by Secretary of Interior Franklin K. Lane, who had conceived the idea of the interdepartmental AC. When asked if it was not more appropriate for an ICC-like independent commission to undertake the regulation, Lane, a former ICC commissioner, answered that that was just a matter of policy choice.[40]

In stark contrast to the strong reaction against the executivist USSB plan only four years before, however, little opposition to the FPC plan was raised in Congress. In the House, criticism was heard from both parties. Rep. Albert Johnson (R-WA) complained that Congress would be meaningless if it acceded to the demand of executive departments and just "put on the rubber stamp of approval" to their proposal. Also, it was feared that the cabinet officers would not do their work. Their hands were already full, Rep. Benjamin Humphreys (D-MS) argued, and "they will and necessarily must detail somebody else in the various departments to perform their services."[41] Still, support for the bill, also bipartisan, was much more pronounced. It was based on the notion that the bill would bring about a consistent waterways policy with minimum impact on government size and structure. According to Rep. John Esch (R-WI), the creation of the FPC involved "no additional expenditure" and would render the dormant Waterways Commission unnecessary.[42] Rep. Richard Parker (R-NJ) also praised the departmental commission of cabinet officers already controlling water power as a

39 House Committee on Water Power, *Water Power*, 65th Cong., 2nd sess. (1919), 677, 696–7.
40 *Water Power*, 461–462.
41 *Congressional Record*, 65th Cong., 2nd sess. (1918), HR, 846–847, 9659.
42 *Congressional Record*, 65th Cong., 2nd sess. (1918), HR, 9663.

"practical, sensible way of obtaining a consistent administration." With such support, the administration bill passed the chamber with only minor changes, replacing the contents of the Senate bill.[43]

In the Senate, the objection to the departmental commission idea was a bit stronger. Sen. Albert Cummins (R-IA) and others complained that they had never seen a bill with so few constraints on government authority.[44] The bill, however, remained intact until its passage. In the conference committee discussing the two versions of the administration bill, the House version prevailed. While the bill was not enacted due to the inaction of the Senate, it was introduced in the next Congress as H.R. 3184. After debates similar in both contents and length from the preceding Congress, the Federal Water Power Act became law in June 1920.[45]

Why could the FPC with exclusive membership of cabinet members gain the approval of Congress? The intensive presidential lobbying to the House on an urgent policy matter undoubtedly contributed to the acceptance of the departmental bill. The Democratic party discipline in favor of the bill displayed on the House floor is testimony to this. But as shown above, many lawmakers were still reluctant to let executive secretaries exercise quasi-legislative and quasi-judicial powers through formal hearings. In their mind, judicialized ACs were much better suited for adjudication. Otherwise, the conference committee of the Sixty-Fifth Congress would not have inserted a provision requiring the FPC to follow the ICC's adjudication procedures. It was added at the request of Senate conferees who had unsuccessfully resisted the interdepartmental commission idea.[46] In the end, however, what Rep. Esch described as the lawmakers' "growing opposition to increasing commissions" prevailed. Although there was a consensus in favor of some kind of waterways regulation, opposition to creating a brand-new agency for the purpose was repeatedly heard in the two chambers during the legislative debate. The legislators came to see the FPC of cabinet members outsourcing its operations to their departments was, as Secretary Houston noted, "the direction of simplicity and efficiency."[47]

The outcome might have been different had there been viable alternatives to the utilization of executive agencies. Members of Congress would have certainly preferred assigning new regulations to existing ACs, especially the ICC and FTC, but they were clearly unavailable. This was most obvious for the ICC, which by this time regulated both land transportation and telecommunications. The assessment of the value of railroad property required by the Valuation Act of 1913 severely strained the commission. The federal government operated the

43 *Congressional Record*, 65th Cong., 2nd sess. (1918), HR, 9284.

44 *Congressional Record*, 65th Cong., 2nd sess. (1918), S, 10474

45 See, for instance, *Congressional Record*, 66th Cong., 1st sess. (1919), HR, 2018–2024.

46 Robert V. Remini, *The House: The History of the House of Representatives* (New York: HarperCollins, 2006), 280–281; Conference Committee, *Dams across Navigable Waters*, 65th Cong., 3rd sess. (1919), H. Rep. 1147, 11–12; *Congressional Record*, 65th Cong., 3rd sess. (1919), HR, 4637. Such a provision instructing agencies to emulate the procedures of the ICC became a common feature in regulatory statutes. Musolf, *Federal Examiners*, 52.

47 *Water Power*, 678, 696.

railroads during World War I but returned them to the ICC's jurisdiction by the Transportation Act of 1920, which expanded the commission's duties. The act also increased the number of commissioners from nine to eleven. In order to keep up with its workloads, the ICC began to use "Shortened Procedures," a sort of alternative dispute resolution process more informal than courtlike adjudication, with the consent of involved parties, starting in 1923. This evolved into informal "Modified Procedures" later came to be widely used as substitutes for formal proceedings. Similarly, the FTC developed in the 1920s the system of "Trade Practice Submittals," conferences at which the commission and the business community discussed and hammered out fair practice for each industry, expected to relieve the commission from dealing with numerous complaints through costly formal procedures.[48]

Once cabinet secretaries were able to adjudicate as members of an AC, making them conduct hearings in their own capacity was only one step away. Such a legislation was in fact already underway in the livestock marketing regulation. In its massive, six-volume report published in 1919 on the meatpacking industry, the FTC warned that the nation's largest meatpackers were on their way to monopolizing the entire food industry. By the early twentieth century, the meatpackers already had a decades-long history of oligopoly in their business. As portrayed in Upton Sinclair's *The Jungle* and in works by other muckrakers, stockyards and meatpacking facilities were accused of unsanitary working conditions. In response to the public outcry over the FTC report, Congress began regulating the industry. The anger against the meatpackers dominating the nation's food supply chain even led to a proposal that the government take ownership of the industry. But after the initial fervor subsided, the discussion shifted to how best to control it.[49]

In February 1920, the Senate Committee on Agriculture and Forestry reported a bill (S. 3944) creating a Federal Livestock Commission of three full-time, independent members. The proposed commission would inherit all the powers and duties regarding the regulation of the livestock business from the FTC, and was made subject to relevant provisions of the FTC Act in its operation. At the same time, the new commission was to assume the authority to collect and distribute information that the Department of Agriculture had collected on the livestock industry. Armed with such powers, the proposed AC was to undertake

48 Hoogenboom and Hoogenboom, *History of the ICC*, 81–97; Ely, *Railroads and American Law*, 227, 242–249; Gary J. Edles, "The ICC Hearing Process: A Cost-Benefit Approach to Administrative Agency Alternative Dispute Resolution," *Transportation Law Journal* 16 (1987): 99–105; Sharfman, *Interstate Commerce Commission*, 4:220–226; Henderson, *Federal Trade Commission*, Ch. 2; Berk, *Regulated Competition*, Ch. 5. The membership of the ICC had been increased from seven to nine in a 1917 legislation. 40 Stat. 270 (1917).

49 The commission's research was initiated in 1917 by President Wilson's order. Robert M. Aduddell and Louis P. Cain, "Public Policy toward 'The Greatest Trust in the World,'" *Business History Review* 55 (1981): 217–242; Henry Veeder, "The Federal Trade Commission and the Packers," *Illinois Law Review* 15 (1921): 485–503.

comprehensive oversight of the livestock markets, which the Senate committee considered public utilities.[50]

Proposition of a new AC was now a routine part of introducing a new regulation. Just as the USSB was positioned as a maritime counterpart to the ICC, the livestock commission was intended to be an offshoot of the FTC, taking over its duties on the livestock industry. As was the case with earlier ACs, the proposed commission was characterized as a court "[t]o all intents and purposes," according to Sen. John Kendrick (D-WY), who introduced the commission bill to the Senate. Echoing Sen. Cullom's justification of the ICC's power to adjudicate in the 1880s, he added that because those dissatisfied with the decisions made by the livestock commission were guaranteed the right to appeal to judicial courts, no one doing business honestly had any reason to be afraid of its regulation. Up to this point, the regulatory policy was discussed in familiar, judicialist terms.[51]

What had changed, however, was the intensity of opposition to a new AC. Although practically everyone favored additional regulation of livestock markets, proponents of the bill repeatedly wondered why existing agencies, especially the FTC, could not achieve this goal. From the critics' viewpoint, the proposed commission only seemed to inherit the job the FTC and Department of Agriculture had already been doing.[52] Behind such a view was the concern for the large cost of creating and maintaining ACs and the fear that they would accumulate endlessly. After pointing out how big and costly the ICC and FTC had become, Sen. Bert M. Fernald (R-ME) sarcastically commented, "[w]e have now too many bureaus and too many commissions . . . If a commission is good for the packing industry, why not for the shoe industry, the clothing industry, the cotton, the coal, the iron, and the steel industry?"[53] To such attacks, the bill's advocates responded by emphasizing both the scale of the livestock industry and how overworked the FTC already was. Sen. Asle Gronna (R-ND), the bill's sponsor, argued that the industry amounted "in volume . . . to more than the business of the railroads" regulated by the ICC.[54] But the proponents of the bill shared the critics' concern. Sen. William Kenyon (R-IA) argued that even though he himself did not "like to increase the number of commissions," there was just no choice but to create a new commission because of the FTC's institutional strain and importance of the subject matter.[55]

While the livestock commission bill did pass the Senate, it was clear that a new AC was becoming very hard to create, especially when its jurisdiction overlapped that of existing agencies. Upon receipt of the Senate bill, the House Committee

50 *Congressional Record*, 66th Cong. 2nd sess. (1920), S, 7403.

51 *Congressional Record*, 66th Cong. 2nd sess. (1920), S, 7406.

52 *Congressional Record*, 66th Cong. 2nd sess. (1920), S, 7461; *Congressional Record*, 66th Cong. 3rd sess. (1920–1921), S, 327, 1933, 1951.

53 *Congressional Record*, 66th Cong. 3rd sess. (1921), S, 1821–22, 1824.

54 *Congressional Record*, 66th Cong. 2nd sess. (1920), S, 7461.

55 *Congressional Record*, 66th Cong. 3rd sess. (1920), S, 83. Also see the statement by Sen. Gronna, *Congressional Record*, 66th Cong. 3rd sess. (1921), S, 1935.

on Agriculture held extensive hearings, after which it concluded that creation of a commission was inadvisable and "existing agencies may be utilized instead." It then removed the provisions on the livestock commission from the bill and gave the regulatory authority on stockyards to the ICC, which had been regulating cattle transportation. The Secretary of Agriculture also was assigned oversight of the industry.[56]

After the bill's failure to reach the floor, the House committee devised a new bill (H.R. 6320) in the next Congress, now giving "the Secretary of Agriculture complete inquisitorial, visitorial, supervisory, and regulatory power over the packers, stockyards, and all activities connected therewith." The brevity of floor debates in both houses on the appropriateness of endowing a cabinet member with full regulatory authority, including that of quasi-judicial adjudication, illustrated how much the lawmakers' attitude toward this issue had changed in a matter of a few years. In the House, Rep. Ross Collins (D-MS) opposed the provision allowing a party dissatisfied with the hearings by the Secretary of Agriculture to appeal to a circuit court, suggesting that that would effectively make the secretary a trial court. Believing that such blending of the three powers of the government could destroy the "very form of our Government," he argued that a commission must be created for regulation, which he "infinitely" preferred to departmental regulation.[57] Otherwise, no serious resistance to adjudication by the cabinet member was made. On the House floor, the debate emphasized how well prepared the department was in conducting meat inspection, with "men in every packer's plant in the United States."[58] During the discussion, it was confirmed that both the secretary and department officials would be authorized to preside over hearings.[59]

In the Senate, the legislators were only slightly less amenable to letting the Secretary of Agriculture adjudicate. But the Senate Agriculture and Forestry Committee saw the secretary as unfit for the regulation because he was appointed in a partisan manner and lacked the knowledge and time necessary to carry out the task. It strove to make the regulation as judicialist as possible. Knowing that creating a new AC was unattainable, the committee offered an amendment to the House bill, creating the post of "Federal Live Stock Commissioner" in the Department of Agriculture. The commissioner, whose appointment and removal were to be made in a manner similar to those of independent AC commissioners, would be in charge of the regulation. While the officer would be directed by the Secretary, all adjudication was to be conducted either by the commissioner or examiners of the department.[60] The commissioner idea, offered to appease the opponents of a new AC, however, failed to win their hearts. They refused to hire even a single commissioner, citing the cost. According to Sen. Thomas Sterling

56 Committee on Agriculture, *Federal Live Stock Commission*, 66th Cong., 3rd sess. (1921), House Rep. 1297, 9.
57 *Congressional Record*, 67th Cong. 1st sess. (1921), HR, 1799, 1917, 1919.
58 *Congressional Record*, 67th Cong. 1st sess. (1921), HR, 1811.
59 *Congressional Record*, 67th Cong. 1st sess. (1921), HR, 1800–1802.
60 *Congressional Record*, 67th Cong. 1st sess. (1921), S, 1921–1922, 2319–2320.

(R-SD), the Senate had been "denouncing the creation of new commissions time out of mind. We have done it both on the score of efficiency and on the score of economy in the public service, and yet here in this bill it [the commissioner idea] is proposed to violate needlessly the very things for which we have stood when denouncing the creation of so many Government commissions."[61] The efficiency-based hostility to ACs was now widespread. Sen. Bert Fernald (R-ME) commented, "You once establish a commission here and it is here to stay. It is never abolished. Nobody that comes here is ever sent home." The committee amendment was rejected, and the House bill was adopted. The conference committee agreed on a bill largely along the lines of the House version. It passed both houses with little additional debate, and the Packers and Stockyards Act was enacted in August 1921.[62]

The passage of the Packers Act was a turning point in the US administrative state judicialization. Conferring formal adjudication functions upon the Secretary of Agriculture was unthinkable from the hitherto dominant, judicialist view of the state that saw courtlike ACs as the only legitimate administrative adjudicators. Although cabinet secretaries had already been designated to conduct formal adjudication under the Water Power Act, the authority still technically derived from their capacity as members of the FPC. Commenting on the adoption of the Packers Act, Ernst Freund, an eminent administrative law scholar, noted that "We associate the new government control of business with administrative commissions. The commission form was intended to express the quasi-judicial spirit in which that control was to be exercised." Because an executive officer was "a political officer and instrument of public policy" who was expected to promote a certain political view rather than being an impartial umpire, Congress, in his view, must now be presumed to have changed its theory of regulation accordingly.[63]

While the loss of autonomy in adjudication was definitely a setback for state judicialization, the Packers Act had different implications for courtlike administrative procedures, another pillar of judiciality. The act instructed the Secretary of Agriculture in Sec. 203(d) to follow the procedures of the FTC in conducting quasi-judicial hearings, meaning that an AC's courtlike procedures were transplanted to an executive agency. While most hearings would be conducted by examiners, the act significantly judicialized the department. In addition, Congress passed legislation in 1925 empowering officers and agents of the Department of Agriculture to administer and take oaths, affirmations, and affidavits at the instruction of the secretary, effectively giving them powers similar to those of hearing examiners.[64]

61 *Congressional Record*, 67th Cong. 1st sess. (1921), S, 2625.

62 *Congressional Record*, 67th Cong. 1st sess. (1921), S, 2582; Conference Committee, *Meat-Packing Industry*, 67th Cong., 1st sess. (1921), House Rep. 324.

63 Ernst Freund, "Legislative Problems and Solutions," *American Bar Association Journal* 7 (1921): 657.

64 "An Act To empower certain officers, agents, or employees of the Department of Agriculture to administer and take oaths, affirmations, and affidavits in certain cases, and for other purposes," 43 Stat. 803.

The efficiency-fairness tradeoff regarding state judiciality thus hung in a delicate balance by the early 1920s. Many legislators now thought that procedural fairness would not justify the enormous cost of new ACs, particularly when there already was an agency with similar jurisdiction. At the same time, as indicated in the requirement of the judicialized FTC procedures for the hearings conducted by the Secretary of Agriculture, most legislators clearly still cherished judiciality in public administration.

Congress continued to rely on the hybrid regulatory scheme of making executive departments conduct courtlike regulatory proceedings. Only nine days after the enactment of the Packers Act, the Future Trading Act on the regulation of grain futures contracts became law. In the House, where the bill originated, regulatory authority was given to the Secretary of Agriculture alone, just as in the Packers Act. But in the Senate, an FPC-like commission of three executive officers, the Secretary of Commerce and Attorney General in addition to the agriculture secretary, was added. With the Secretary of Agriculture as chair, the commission was to conduct formal adjudication following the procedures of the ICC.[65] Similarly, the Air Commerce Act of 1926 placed the Secretary of Commerce in charge of the regulatory regime to ensure safety in civil air transportation. Its early legislative proposals included the creation of the Bureau of Aeronautics within the Commerce Department, with a commissioner appointed by the president in charge of administrative matters. In the final legislation, however, the secretary was vested with all regulatory authorities, although he was to be supported by a new assistant secretary. Also, the department officials were authorized to preside over formal hearings, and their proceedings to collect penalty was to "conform as nearly as may be to civil suits in admiralty."[66]

Executive departments were thus steadily empowered to conduct formal adjudication in the 1920s, but ACs did not become obsolete as a category of administrative agency. As illustrated in the provisions of the legislation requiring executive officers to adjudicate with the procedures of ACs, they were still considered superior to executive departments as adjudicators; executive agencies were given regulatory powers only because existing commissions were overburdened, and creating new ones was financially impractical. This meant that an AC would be a viable regulatory option under certain conditions. This was what happened with radio regulation.

After entering commercial application by the Italian inventor Guglielmo Marconi in the late nineteenth century, radio transmission technology quickly spread

65 Although the Supreme Court declared the law unconstitutional as a violation of the taxing power of Congress, the legislature immediately responded by enacting the Grain Futures Act later in 1922, which inherited its regulatory mechanism from the 1921 act. *Hill v. Wallace*, 259 U.S. 44 (1922).

66 S. 76, 68th Congress; Air Commerce Act, 44 Stat. 568. By another statute passed the same year, the examiners and officers at the Department's Bureau of Naturalization were authorized to take testimony, subpoena witnesses, and to administer oaths, in conducting preliminary hearings for US districts courts regarding naturalization petitions. 44 Stat. 709.

in the United States. As the number of radio stations and the capacity of their transmitters soared, airwave interference became a serious problem. In an early attempt to resolve the situation, Congress required in the Radio Act of 1912 that all radio stations and operators be licensed by the Department of Commerce and Labor. The statute, however, gave the department no regulatory authority to enforce compliance.[67] Still, order had been secured among the military and commercial broadcasters, schools, churches, and amateur radio enthusiasts. Responding to the desperate demand for radio traffic control from both operators and listeners, in 1922 Secretary of Commerce Herbert Hoover invited representatives of various groups of operators to the first radio conference. The conferees negotiated the allocation of bandwidths among different categories of stations at the meeting and then assigned the channels to the operators they represented. Popular with its participants, the conference met annually until 1925.[68]

Meanwhile, regulatory legislation did not make progress despite repeated encouragement from Hoover and the beneficiaries of radio communication. In 1921, Rep. Wallace White (R-VT) began proposing a radio bill giving extensive regulatory authority to the Secretary of Commerce. The secretary was to receive suggestions from an intradepartmental advisory committee including radio experts. The department's experience in radio policy made it a natural choice for the task. Although generally welcomed, the bill failed to advance, for several reasons. First, the almost dictatorial power the commerce secretary was to enjoy under its provisions aroused fears of abuse of power. Rapid innovation of radio technology and lawmakers' lack of expertise in it made the vesting of broad – or vague – powers inevitable. Even radio operators who were satisfied with Hoover's handling of the situation hesitated to back the adoption of such provisions; after all, there was no guarantee that his successors would be as knowledgeable and thoughtful as he was. Second, there was interdepartmental rivalry. Executive departments operating their own radio facilities such as Navy, War, and the post office, resisted regulation by Commerce by lobbying against the legislation. Third, there was sheer procrastination. Ironically, the success of Hoover's regulation through negotiation with stakeholders, a model of the "associative state" he believed in, gave lawmakers the impression that the legislation was not urgent.[69]

67 Marvin R. Bensman, *The Beginning of Broadcast Regulation in the Twentieth Century* (Jefferson, NC: McFarland & Co., 2000), 8–10.

68 Louise Benjamin, "Working It Out Together: Radio Policy from Hoover to the Radio Act of 1927," *Journal of Broadcasting and Electronic Media* 42 (1998): 221–236; Bensman, *Beginning of Broadcast Regulation*, 47–55, 80–87, 101–114, 140–148; Hugh R. Slotten, *Radio and Television Regulation: Broadcast Technology in the United States, 1920–1960* (Baltimore: Johns Hopkins University Press, 2000).

69 Bensman, *Beginning of Broadcast Regulation*, 35–36; Philip T. Rosen, *The Modern Stentors: Radio Broadcasters and the Federal Government, 1920–1934* (Westport, CT: Greenwood Press, 1980), 49–50; Wallace H. White to C.B. Graves, Jan. 8, 1924, Folder "Radio," Box 42, Wallace H. White Papers, Manuscript Division, Library of Congress; Ellis W. Hawley, "Herbert Hoover, the Commerce Secretariat, and the Vision of an 'Associative State,' 1921–1928," *Journal of American History* 61 (1974): 116–140; Gordon Lloyd and

The radio legislation that had already been stalled for several years took a sudden turn for the worse, however, and Hoover was largely responsible. Frustrated with Congress's foot-dragging, in December 1924 he sent White the draft of a short bill which would give him wholesale regulatory power, albeit temporary, and urged its swift passage. It read that "The wavelength of every radio transmitting station for which a license is now required by law, its power, emitted wave, the character of its apparatus, and the time of transmission, shall be fixed by the Secretary of Commerce as in his judgment and direction he shall deem expedient, and may be changed or modified from time to time in his discretion."[70] When the contents of Hoover's letter and the bill became public, a political uproar against his arrogance erupted. Later that year, the president of the National Association of Broadcasters castigated Hoover and recommended the creation of an ICC-like commission for radio regulation. The intensity of the reaction was partly due to the rumor that Hoover was entertaining presidential ambitions. It was feared that he would misuse his regulatory authority to advance his electoral prospects, perhaps even by introducing censorship. Newspapers began to refer to Hoover as "radio czar."[71]

Ironically, such attacks on Hoover helped generate interest in the kind of radio regulation that was badly needed to move the legislation forward. The Sixty-Ninth Congress, which convened the next year, became a battleground of executivists and judicialists, each backing their favorite radio bill.

Hoover's response to the fears directed at his potential abuse of power was an indication that the support for judicialized administrative adjudication still rested in the hands of political elites. At a House committee hearing on radio legislation in January 1926, he attempted to assuage the widespread anxiety over the excessive concentration of regulatory authority and offered a solution: a part-time intradepartmental committee of nine, which would adjudicate cases autonomously from the secretary, at his request. Hoover remarked that quasi-judicial functions were too grave to be borne by a single individual and that a collegial body was more appropriate.[72] It is worth noting that he was not improvising such a plan just to ward off criticism of the White bill, again submitted to the House. Back in 1924, a bill had been proposed in the Senate to transfer all powers and functions of the USSB to the Commerce Department. As a central figure in President Warren Harding's executive reorganization effort, Hoover expressed opposition to the idea, noting that while he thought the commission form was

---

David Davenport, "The Two Phases of Herbert Hoover's Constitutional Conservatism," in *Toward an American Conservatism*, ed. Postell and O'Neill, 237–238.

70 Herbert Hoover to Wallace H. White, Dec. 4, 1924, Folder "House of Representatives White, Wallace H., 1921–1928 & undated," Box 283, Commerce Series, Papers of Herbert Hoover, Herbert Hoover Presidential Library.

71 Rosen, *Modern Stentors*, 77–79; Kendrick A. Clements, *The Life of Herbert Hoover: Imperfect Visionary, 1918–1928* (New York: Palgrave Macmillan, 2010), 353; Bensman, *Beginning of Broadcast Regulation*, 117–119.

72 House Committee on the Merchant Marine and the Fisheries, *To Regulate Radio Communication*, 69th Cong., 1st sess. (1926), 14–15.

unsuited for efficient administration, it nonetheless was superior in carrying out quasi-judicial duties. He supported the conversion of the USSB to a more ICC-like AC specializing in adjudication.[73]

Hoover's intradepartmental committee proposal shifted the focus of radio legislation. Rep. White modified his bill to accommodate Hoover's "National Radio Commission" as its adjudicator. The bill, H.R. 9971, submitted in early March 1926, also prescribed for the secretary's advisory committee composed of representatives of radio operators. After an intensive debate, the House passed the bill later that month.[74] In the Senate, Sen. Clarence Dill (D-WA), then chairing the Committee on Interstate Commerce, offered a new bill containing provisions for the Radio Commission, an ICC-like AC, as an amendment to the White bill. Although Dill's earlier bill had given regulatory powers to the Secretary of Commerce, a fellow progressive, Sen. William Borah (R-ID), who himself had submitted the first AC bill for radio regulation (S. 3968), persuaded him to propose an AC. The bill was reported to the floor in May and passed the Senate the following July. The two chambers agreed to a conference to work out the difference between the two versions of the bill. Now, no matter which radio bill was to be adopted, formal hearings would be conducted by a multimember body.[75]

In the meantime, the collapse of the Hoover-led associative regulation was looming. In April 1926, the federal district court in Chicago ruled in favor of a radio station broadcasting outside its allocated bandwidth in *United States v. Zenith Radio Corporation*, declaring that the Department of Commerce lacked the authority to coerce stations into operating within specific wavelengths. Upon department consultation, Attorney General John Sargent stated his agreement with the court, denying the commerce department any discretion on the granting of licenses to radio stations as written in the 1912 act. Radio operators rushed to file applications, and conforming to the legal authorities, the department grudgingly began accepting whatever requests it received, beginning in July 1926. The department was now nothing more than a registry. Mayhem ensued, and cries of agony from operators and listeners filled the air. The complaints of airwave anarchy immediately reached the ears of lawmakers who had been busy arguing

73 Herbert Hoover to Sen. Wesley Jones, Feb. 12, 1924, Folder "Senate, Jones, Wesley L., 1924," Box 548, Commerce Series, Hoover Papers; Herbert Hoover to Walter F. Brown, Apr. 7, 1924, Folder "Reorganization of Government Depts. 1924," Box 514, Commerce Series, Hoover Papers; Clements, *Hoover*, 292–293; Arnold, *Managerial Presidency*, 64–65. Also see Herbert Hoover to Joseph H. Defrees, Jan. 26, 1922, Folder "Hoover, Herbert, Correspondence General 1920–1933," Box 11, Commerce Department File, Herbert Hoover Subject Collection, Hoover Institution.

74 Bensman, *Beginning of Broadcast Regulation*, 185–193; *Boston Globe*, Apr. 23, 1926; *CT*, May 2, 1926.

75 Kerry E. Irish, *Clarence C. Dill: The Life of a Western Politician* (Pullman, WA: Washington State University Press, 2000), 70–71; Donald G. Godfrey and Val E. Limburg, "The Rogue Elephant of Radio Legislation: Senator William E. Borah," *Journalism Quarterly* 67 (1990): 216; Also see S. 1754, 69th Congress.

over radio legislation. Now, the compromise between the two houses became ever more urgent.[76]

Even in the face of regulatory breakdown, the two opposing forces supporting different forms of regulation remained stubborn, which hindered interchamber negotiation. With Hoover's advice, President Calvin Coolidge issued a statement promoting the commerce department as regulator, denying the need for another AC.[77] In the end, the two houses reached a last-minute agreement early in 1927, and the compromise bill was finally enacted on February 23. The Radio Act established the Federal Radio Commission (FRC) as proposed in the Dill bill, but the commission was designated to be converted to the intradepartmental committee proposed in the White bill after one year; the idea was offered by Dill himself, who hoped that the FRC would extend its tenure by proving its usefulness. The legislative deal came so late in the Sixty-Ninth Congress that the bill to finance the new commission failed to pass before its adjournment. The FRC could still go to work immediately, thanks to Hoover, who graciously made his department's resources available to the commission's inaugural members.[78]

The intensity and confusion of the legislative battle for radio regulation indicated how difficult it had become to create an AC for new regulation. Because of the combined opposition from the executivist presidents, executive officers, and judicialist members of Congress who thought that fiscal efficiency should outweigh procedural fairness, a new AC was by this time at best at par with an existing executive department as an institutional option. Still, the establishment of the FRC signified the strength of the judicialist sentiment in Congress, even if the commission was scheduled to be reduced to an intradepartmental committee.

It was not just the congressional commitment to state judiciality that made the FRC happen, however. Also at work was another court ruling handed down in the midst of the legislative fight. The case of *Myers v. United States*, decided by the Supreme Court in October 1926, had no immediate connection to ACs. In 1917, President Wilson removed Frank Myers, a postmaster of the first class in Oregon, and Myers filed suit to secure the salary for the remainder of his four-year term. Because a provision in an 1876 law required advice and consent by the Senate for the *removal* of certain classes of postmasters, Myers argued, his dismissal was illegal and therefore void. In the lengthy majority opinion of the six-to-three decision, Chief Justice William Howard Taft pronounced the statute unconstitutional after meticulously reviewing the constitutional development regarding the president's removal power. He argued that the silence of the Constitution on the authority meant that the presidential executive power prescribed

76 Bensman, *Beginning of Broadcast Regulation*, 164–175; Clements, *Hoover*, 352.

77 "HR 9971 – Act for regulation of radio communication, etc.," Folder "Radio: Correspondence, Press Releases, Misc. 1926 Jan. – April," Box 490, Commerce Series, Hoover Papers; Rosen, *Modern Stentors*, 104.

78 Mark Goodman and Mark Gring, "The Ideological Fight over Creation of the Federal Radio Commission in 1927," *Journalism History* 26 (2000): 122; Bensman, *Beginning of Broadcast Regulation*, 200.

in Article II included an exclusive authority to dismiss any federal officer he had appointed. This was because "[t]he power of removal" was incidental to the power of appointment, not to the senatorial power of advising and consenting to appointment.[79] From this logic, members of ACs were also subject to the president's discretionary removal even if statutory provisions stated otherwise. In discussing the constitutional status of "executive officers and members of executive tribunals" with quasi-judicial duties, Taft went so far as to argue that even if the president could not "properly influence or control" their handling of particular cases, their outcomes could still be used as a reason for removal. Otherwise, he argued, the president did "not discharge his own constitutional duty of seeing that the laws be faithfully executed."[80]

The ruling was a major reinterpretation of a precedent. The 1903 *Shurtleff* decision concerning the removal of a general appraiser also stated that the president's act was valid even if there was a statutory provision that only allowed for-cause dismissal. But it was generally understood that the decision covered only federal offices without fixed tenure and was not applicable to members of ACs, who were set to serve only for a predetermined number of years. Some presidents, including Taft himself, suspected that *Shurtleff* gave them the power to remove AC commissioners at will, but they never ventured to act on such an assumption.[81] Taft now used *Myers* to buttress his view relative to the members of "many administrative boards" with fixed tenure who could be removed only for certain causes. Just as he had created the Commerce Court to check the ICC as president, he handed the reins of ACs to the president, in order to bring the US government closer to the tripartite constitutional system.[82]

The *Myers* decision capped the gradual dejudicialization of regulation that had been going on for more than a decade through the undermining of ACs' autonomy. In his fiery dissent to the decision, Justice Louis Brandeis defended the requirement of senatorial consent to the presidential removal of administrative officers in the 1876 statute as a necessary part of interbranch checks and balances, noting that the separation of powers was embedded in the Constitution "not to promote efficiency but to preclude the exercise of arbitrary power." By making all administrative agencies accountable to the president, the ruling further damaged the administrative state's judiciality and orientation toward fairness. Still, the decision had an immediate effect. Now that members of ACs could be fired at any time for any reason, shielding them from the president was meaningless. The

79 272 U.S. 52 (1926), at 122. On *Myers*, see Alvis, Bailey, and Taylor, *Removal Power*, Ch. 4.

80 272 U.S. 52 (1926), at 135.

81 *Shurtleff v. United States*, 189 U.S. 311 (1903); William J. Donovan and Ralstone R. Irvine, "The President's Power to Remove Members of Administrative Agencies," *Cornell Law Quarterly* 21 (1936): 215–248. Taft made the first presidential for-cause removal in 1912, firing two members of the Board of General Appraisers. Aditya Bamzai, "Taft, Frankfurter, and the First Presidential for-cause Removal," *University of Richmond Law Review* 52 (2018): 691–748.

82 272 U.S. 52 (1926), at 171; Milkis, "William Howard Taft," 88; Calabresi and Yoo, *Unitary Executive*, 248.

new Radio Act did not include the now-usual clause listing the possible causes of dismissal of commission members that had appeared in the Dill bill. Such would also be the case for subsequent ACs to be formed before *Myers* was overturned in 1935. The creation of the FRC, then, was not just the result of Congress's continued support for judicialized commissions but also of the presidential tolerance to them because of their institutional recession.[83]

The impact of *Myers* on radio policy did not end with the creation of the FRC. Instead of merging into the Department of Commerce after one year as prescribed in its organic act, the commission was given not just one but two one-year renewals after its original expiration date; Sen. Dill's prediction proved accurate. The FRC had strengthened its reputation not only by accumulating policy expertise but also by judicializing its procedures, which had been quite informal before it began facing lawsuits by radio operators frustrated by its decisions. This change in procedures worked in favor of the FRC, as most lawmakers at the time supported courtlike administrative adjudication. In addition, *Myers* had a significant impact on President Coolidge. Now that he could remove any member of the FRC, he could remain confident of its loyalty. The extension of the commission would not have been proposed without its wide popularity among radio operators, but it became possible only with the president's tolerance.[84]

The survival of the FRC therefore did not depend on who the president was. In December 1929, Hoover, now president, urged in his first annual message to Congress the conversion of the commission into "a permanent body from its temporary status." There was already a consensus for freeing the FRC from its insecure status, and the bill to indefinitely extend the commission's tenure swiftly became law before the year's end. Given his strenuous opposition to the creation of the FRC a few years before, Hoover's advocacy for a permanent FRC is difficult to explain without considering the impact of *Myers*.[85]

As it turned out, the FRC was not the only AC affected by the Supreme Court decision. In the same 1929 message to Congress, Hoover also suggested that the FPC have "full-time commissioners" instead of ex-officio cabinet members. During its first decade, the FPC languished under insufficient funding, personnel, and attention from its three commissioners lacking both expertise in energy policy and time to do commission work, all because the commission was a joint venture of three competing cabinet departments. But this miserable situation alone would not have led to the presidential proposal of a changeover to a commission of five full-time commissioners with its own budget and staff. The institutional effect of the *Myers* decision was common knowledge by this time. Although the Senate bill for FPC reform initially contained the customary provision delimiting

83 272 U.S. 52 (1926), at 293; Paul R. Verkuil, "Separation of Powers, the Rule of Law and the Idea of Independence," *William and Mary Law Review* 30 (1989): 303–304.

84 Rosen, *Modern Stentors*, 143; Herring, *Public Administration and the Public Interest*, 164.

85 Herbert Hoover, "Annual Message to Congress on the State of the Union," Dec. 3, 1929. Online by Gerhard Peters and John T. Woolley, The American Presidency Project, www.presidency.ucsb.edu/node/209213.

the president's power of removal, it was later struck because the president could now "remove any public official at any time."[86]

This chapter has demonstrated that the presidencies from Wilson to Hoover in which quasi-judicial ACs were thought to have thrived actually entailed a gradual recession of the commissions and their judiciality, punctuated by their loss of autonomy at the end. Many ACs were established to oversee a variety of industries during this period, but the trajectory of their institutional development was very different from what has been described as a "movement" to promote them. While it was commonplace to propose the creation of an AC in introducing a new regulation until the early 1920s, the political headwind against the ICC-like ACs made it increasingly difficult to create new independent commissions. The executivist creative syncretism led by the president and executive departments continued. It strengthened presidential influence on agencies in different ways, even producing an interdepartmental AC composed exclusively of executive officers. With the growth of fiscal anxiety in Congress, no major AC without connection to an executive department was established for an entire decade after the USSB until the FRC was created in 1927. Meanwhile, executive departments worked their way into adjudication, and won the quasi-judicial and quasi-legislative functions with the Packers and Stockyards Act. The departments were quite successful in their challenge to the separation of powers and the supremacy of law, which transformed the administrative state. The life extension of the FRC and the reorganization of the FPC took place only because the president no longer cared about the institutional type of agencies after *Myers*.[87]

At the same time, the period characterized by the setback of independent ACs and the advance of executive departments was not just that of simple dejudicialization of the administrative state. There is no doubt that the loss of agency autonomy completed by the *Myers* decision adversely affected state judiciality. But the situation was quite different regarding agency procedures. Practically no attack was made against ACs' courtlike procedures, which were inherited not just by new commissions but by executive agencies vested with regulatory authority. Such diffusion of ACs' judicial DNA to executive departments was an indicator that even those actors opposed to new commissions were in favor, or at least tolerant, of procedural fairness in the administrative process in principle. The ICC-like AC was still considered the best mechanism for adjudication, even when its creation was suppressed. This was the atmosphere in which John Dickinson wrote his renowned treatise on the reconciliation of administrative adjudication with the supremacy of law, published in 1927.[88]

86 Herring, *Public Administration and the Public Interest*, Ch. 9; Cushman, *Independent Regulatory Commissions*, 286; *Congressional Record*, 71st Cong., 2nd sess. (1929), HR, 10332.

87 Also, in the cases of ACs like the FPC for which the president could choose all their inaugural members, the chief executive could appoint some members who would outlast his term of office thanks to the long terms enjoyed by AC commissioners.

88 Dickinson, *Administrative Justice*.

The legislative and executive branches took the initiative of the politics of agency judicialization. As discussed earlier, research in legal studies has emphasized the role of lawyers and the judiciary in explaining the judicialization. While the courts made sure that agencies followed courtlike procedures in conducting hearings, it should be remembered that such a requirement had already been written in the statutes authorizing agencies to adjudicate. As for agency autonomy, another pillar of judiciality, the judiciary did not have much to say – until *Myers*. By making all agencies equally accountable to the presidency, the decision considerably altered the political landscape of state judiciality. In the long run, the decision that deprived ACs of their autonomy turned out to be a blessing in disguise for the judicialization of the ACs and the US administrative state.

5 The institutional consolidation of the independent regulatory commissions

"The United States is a government of commissions," Marshall Dimock, a pioneering scholar of public administration, commented shortly before the dawn of the New Deal.[1] His impression was not unfounded. ACs were already overseeing many prominent policy domains, and thanks to the *Myers* decision, the president was no longer opposed to the commissions. Still, their institutional stability was far from assured. The commissions' subordination to the president made them indistinguishable from the executive agencies in that respect, and although their courtlike procedures and the members' long and staggered tenures still made them different from executive agencies, the departments were quickly catching up, primarily through extended use of hearing examiners. If such a situation had continued, ACs could well have become marginalized in the administrative state.[2]

But another Supreme Court decision handed down in 1935 would radically change the outlook of the commissions. Restoring the autonomy of ACs, *Humphrey's Executor v. United States* not only changed the structure of the politics of state judiciality but induced President Franklin D. Roosevelt to pursue the abolishment of ACs by making it a major agenda of the Brownlow Committee he called to devise an executive reorganization scheme. The executivist challenge by the concerted effort of the popular chief executive and efficiency-oriented public administration experts became at once the most intellectually sophisticated and politically forceful attack on ACs in history. By overcoming the challenge, the commissions consolidated their status as representative agencies in the judicialized US administrative state.

Despite his training in law, FDR was clearly more dubious of the merits of judicialized ACs than his predecessor, who considered them the best administrative adjudicators. Upon assuming the presidency, he carried out extensive executive reorganization, which included abolishing the USSB and transferring its

1 Marshall E. Dimock, "The Development of American Administrative Law," *Journal of Comparative Legislation and International Law* 15 (1933): 36; James A. Stever, "Marshall Dimock's Deflective Organizational Theory," *Journal of Management History* 3 (1997): 317–327. Also see Marshall E. Dimock, "The Prospect for Administrative Tribunals," *California Law Review* 20 (1932): 162–166.

2 Musolf, *Federal Examiners*; Blachley and Oatman, *Administrative Legislation and Adjudication.*

functions to the Department of Commerce. While the action was based on the Economy Act of 1932, created with Hoover's initiative, the Republican would have opposed such a move out of deference to ACs' judiciality. FDR also aggressively sought to exercise control over ACs in various ways, thinking that they should be supervised by cabinet secretaries.[3] His efforts, though, often met with resistance from the commissions. Shortly after his inauguration, he summoned prominent members of ACs to the White House and requested that they report to him. While most attendees nodded in agreement, Joseph Eastman of the ICC refused, stating that the commission was "by law the creature of Congress" and that it was their "duty to report directly to it."[4]

Although FDR's lack of respect for ACs was apparent, *Myers* continued to affect their fate in his administration. This is why his first term saw the creation of several powerful ACs. The politics of regulation during the period was unprecedented in the dominance of the commission format in the institutional form of new regulation. While the immediate reason for the adoption of an AC differed from case to case, they had a common root – the president no longer had to brood about commission disobedience. FDR knew this from his own experience. In his first year in office, FDR dismissed a noncooperative Republican FTC commissioner, William E. Humphrey, when the president's repeated urging to resign voluntarily proved futile. In firing Humphrey, FDR did not specify a cause as stipulated in the FTC Act, although he could have easily concocted one. His decision to take full advantage of *Myers* was backed by Harvard law professor James Landis, a close advisor who had clerked for Justice Brandeis at the time of the ruling, to which he strenuously dissented.[5]

But the fast pace of the creation of ACs cannot be explained by the presidential factor alone. There had been a sizable opposition in Congress to the creation of additional ACs out of financial concerns. Now at the depth of the Depression, however, Congress, with a large Democratic majority, was ready to accept almost any policy proposal that might help pull the nation out of the economic crisis.

3 Executive Order 6166, June 10, 1933; Meriam, *Reorganization of the National Government*, Ch. 10; Polenberg, *Reorganizing Roosevelt's Government*, 9, 25; Angel Manuel Moreno, "Presidential Coordination of the Independent Regulatory Process," *Administrative Law Journal* 8 (1994): 484.

4 Claude Moore Fuess, *Joseph B. Eastman: Servant of the People* (New York: Columbia University Press, 1952), 245–246. Also see Eastman, "Place of the Independent Commission." FDR appointed Eastman the Federal Coordinator of Transportation in June 1933. Mark H. Rose, Bruce E. Seely, and Paul F. Barrett, *The Best Transportation System in the World: Railroads, Trucks, Airlines, and American Public Policy in the Twentieth Century* (Columbus: Ohio State University Press, 2006), 59; Polenberg, *Reorganizing Roosevelt's Government*, 11; Herring, *Public Administration and Public Interest*, 222–223.

5 Humphrey had irritated the progressives for his conservatism and pro-business attitude since his appointment to the commission in 1925. G. Cullom Davis, "The Transformation of the Federal Trade Commission, 1914–1929," *Mississippi Valley Historical Review* 49 (1962): 437–455; Donald A. Ritchie, *James M. Landis: Dean of the Regulators* (Cambridge, MA: Harvard University Press, 1980), 49.

Many of them judicialists, these New Deal–era lawmakers would not dare stand in the way of new ACs.[6]

The creation of the first two new major ACs in the FDR presidency illustrated the newfound tolerance of Congress and the president of additional ACs. Part of the emergency legislation passed during the first hundred days of the administration was the Securities Act, granting the FTC regulatory powers essential in improving the publicity and information of new securities issues. The subsequent effort to create a more comprehensive regulation led to another legislation in 1934. At the suggestion of the architects of the earlier act, including Landis and other protégés of Felix Frankfurter, his most trusted advisor, Roosevelt decided to assign additional regulatory authority to the FTC. At the same time, he was open to the idea of a separate securities commission – at least that was what Carter Glass, now the powerful chair of the Senate Appropriations Committee, told the press.[7] Distrustful of the New Dealers and fearing that the FRB, his brainchild, was going to be embroiled in securities regulation, Glass replaced the FTC in the legislative proposal with a new Securities Exchange Commission, in the Senate Banking Committee. The joint attempt by the president and his congressional allies to kill the commission provisions in the Senate bill failed. When the bill reached the conference committee, accusations that FDR was interfering with the appointment of conferees – the exclusion of Glass, to be specific – forced the president to retreat from the legislative process. In doing so, he stated to the press that the choice between the FTC and the proposed new commission was so "frightfully complicated" that he had not "gone into the details of it," but it was all right to him whichever way. While this undoubtedly was a bit of bravado, it was quite true that the president had a firm grip on the two ACs. The conference committee created the Securities and Exchange Commission, whose organic act was adopted in June 1934.[8]

The Communications Act, enacted less than two weeks after the 1934 Securities Exchange Act, also owed much to the tolerance of FDR and Congress to new ACs. The idea of integrating the regulation of telecommunications technologies – radio, telephone, and telegraph – into a single agency had already been proposed in the 1920s and gained popularity after the shift of the FRC to permanent status in 1929. Much interested in securing a radio regulator friendly to him, FDR took advantage of the public support for communications policy reform. In December 1933, he gave an instruction to investigate the best course of action to Secretary of Commerce Daniel Roper, who appointed an interdepartmental committee attended by executive officers and concerned congressional leaders. The committee's report submitted the next month recommended the

6 Arthur M. Schlesinger, Jr., *The Coming of the New Deal, 1933–1935* (1958; repr., New York: Houghton Mifflin Co., 2003), 7–10.

7 Ritchie, *Landis*, 55–57; Ralph F. De Bedts, *The New Deal's SEC: The Formative Years* (New York: Columbia University Press, 1964), 73–74.

8 Joel Seligman, *The Transformation of the Wall Street*, 3rd ed. (Frederick, MD: Aspen Publishers, 2003), 97–99; Franklin D. Roosevelt, *Complete Presidential Press Conferences of Franklin D. Roosevelt*, Vol. 3–4 (1934; repr., New York: Da Capo Press, 1972), 348–350.

implementation of communications policy either by a "communications commission of a quasi-judicial character" or a cabinet member with the aid of "a board of communication appeals whose function would be limited to issues involving equity." The two options were essentially identical to those the lawmakers faced in 1926 with radio regulation. In transmitting the report to Congress, Roosevelt attached a message suggesting the creation of a Federal Communications Commission, which Congress quickly did. Although FDR's preference for an AC over an executive officer has not been accounted for, it would be hard to explain without factoring in *Myers*.[9]

But even with combined executive-legislative support for new ACs, a proposed commission could still face a turf war with the executive department. Such was the case with the establishment of the National Labor Relations Board (NLRB). The New Deal labor relations policy had its origins in the National Labor Board FDR created in August 1933, to enforce Section 7(a) of the National Industrial Recovery Act guaranteeing collective bargaining rights to workers. It soon became apparent, however, that the board, composed of part-time, voluntary representatives of business, labor, and the government and lacking any power of enforcement was unfit to resolve labor disputes. The next year, FDR replaced the board with the (first) National Labor Relations Board. Aside from being a full-time board, it differed from its predecessor in its position in the federal government. The board was created "in connection with the Department of Labor" and was to rely on department staff for field assignments and help with the department's work. While this was an improvement on the National Labor Board, the new board's future remained uncertain due to lack of statutory foundation and constant clashes with the National Recovery Administration.[10]

The location of the labor relations agency within the government structure became a bone of contention in the legislation effort led by Sen. Robert Wagner (D-NY) to create an AC unaffiliated with any executive department. His idea of modeling it after the FTC enjoyed widespread support; attempts were made to name the new agency not NLRB but the "Federal Labor Commission" or "National Labor Commission," considering it "a parallel in the labor field with the Federal Trade Commission in the field of industry."[11] The proposal met

9 Rosen, *Modern Stentors*, 162–163; Committee on Interstate Commerce, *Study of Communications by an Interdepartmental Committee*, 73rd Cong., 2nd sess. (1934), 10; US Senate, *Message from the President of the United States Recommending that Congress Create a New Agency to Be Known as the Federal Communications Commission*, 73rd Cong., 2nd sess. (1934), S. Doc. 144; Robert W. McChesney, *Telecommunications, Mass Media, and Democracy: The Battle for the Control of U.S. Broadcasting, 1928–1935* (New York: Oxford University Press, 1993), Chs. 7 and 8.

10 Executive Order 6763, June 29, 1934; James A. Gross, *The Making of the National Labor Relations Board: A Study in Economics, Politics, and the Law* (Albany: State University of New York Press, 1974), Ch. 3; Peter H. Irons, *The New Deal Lawyers* (Princeton: Princeton University Press, 1982), Ch. 10.

11 J. Joseph Huthmacher, *Senator Robert F. Wagner and the Rise of Urban Liberalism* (New York: Atheneum, 1968), 190–197; Senate Committee on Education and Labor, *National Labor Relations Board*, 74th Cong., 1st sess. (1935), Pt. 3, 704–707; Alfred L. Bernheim

with resistance from the Department of Labor, however, especially from its head, Frances Perkins. She insisted that the new board be an independent commission inside her department just like the first NLRB, arguing that such an arrangement would both enhance the board's prestige and limit duplication of agency functions. Her opponents countered that the new board with quasi-judicial powers should be placed outside the department to win authority and respect. Labor leaders preferred, and business objected to, installing the board within the department, both groups believing that the board would be more amenable to workers that way. Curiously, FDR kept out of this debate despite his apparent support for Perkins's view. His silence no doubt contributed to the detachment of the three-member National Labor Relations Board, described by Wagner as "a form of industrial court," from the Department of Labor in the National Labor Relations Act enacted in May 1935.[12]

The creation of powerful ACs during the New Deal, along with the strengthening of existing ones through legislation, reinforced the commissions' presence in the administrative state. The *Myers* decision robbing ACs of their autonomy continued to contribute to their proliferation. It should be kept in mind, however, that such a development took place because of the ACs' loss of institutional distinctiveness. Given the adoption of courtlike procedures by executive agencies, ACs could have lost their institutional identity had the situation continued.[13]

A Supreme Court decision handed down shortly before the passage of the Wagner Act, however, prevented this. After being dismissed from the FTC in 1933, William Humphrey filed suit challenging FDR's action as a violation of the FTC Act's provision prescribing for-cause removal of commissioners. The Supreme Court unanimously ruled in favor of Humphrey, who had died a year earlier. The ruling in *Humphrey's Executor v. United States* clearly demarcated ACs from other government bodies. It overruled *Myers*, stating that the office of postmastership in question in the case was "so essentially unlike" the FTC commissionership that the decision could not serve as a clear precedent. The commission, which acted "in part quasi-legislatively and in part quasi-judicially," could not "in proper sense be characterized as an arm or an eye of the executive." Citing the legislative history of the FTC Act, the Court stressed the great weight the

and Dorothy Van Doren, eds., *Labor and the Government: An Investigation of the Role of the Government in Labor Relations* (New York: McGraw-Hill, 1935), 349–350; "Mr. William H. Davis," n.d., Folder 11, Box 1, National Labor Relations Board Subject Series, Leon Keyserling Papers, Georgetown University Library Booth Family Center for Special Collections.

12 Kirstin Downey, *Woman behind the New Deal: The Life of Frances Perkins, FDR's Secretary of Labor and His Moral Conscience* (New York: Doubleday, 2009), 220–222; Robert F. Wagner to John Banes, July 16, 1935, Folder 46, Box LA4, Robert F. Wagner Papers, Georgetown University Library Booth Family Center for Special Collections; Irons, *New Deal Lawyers*, 228–229; Irving Bernstein, *The New Deal Collective Bargaining Policy* (Berkeley: University of California Press, 1950); White, *Constitution and the New Deal*, 112–113; Ernst, *Tocqueville's Nightmare*, 62–63.

13 McCraw, *Prophets*, 210.

lawmakers gave to the independence of the commission, which was reflected in the provision fixing the commissioners' terms of office. Whether Congress could constitutionally limit the president's power of dismissal thus depended "upon the character of [the] office."[14]

By treating the ACs as a distinct category of government bodies, the *Humphrey's* decision considerably advanced the institutionalization of ACs. The Court clearly took a judicialist position in declaring that ACs conducting adjudications in the exercise of quasi-judicial and quasi-legislative powers must be autonomous from the president. In obiter dictum, the Court even hinted that the decision could extend to members of ACs created after *Myers* who did not enjoy statutory protection from removal. The ruling well deserves the title of "the fundamental constitutional charter" of ACs.[15]

The administration had received a serious blow. *Humphrey's* was one of the three anti-administration decisions handed down on "Black Monday," including the celebrated *Schechter* decision which also treated ACs as expert, courtlike bodies. But according to Robert Jackson, FDR's advisor and future Supreme Court justice, the president found *Humphrey's* the most repugnant of all Supreme Court decisions invalidating New Deal policy measures.[16] The president's wrath was understandable. In a single sweep, the ruling moved numerous agencies each overseeing major regulatory policy out of his reach. Even worse, Congress immediately indicated its concurrence with the court by adding a provision to the labor relations bill enumerating the possible causes for removing the members of the NLRB. Also, in the spirit of the Supreme Court decision, the Banking Act enacted the next month abolished the two ex-officio memberships of the FRB, further strengthened and renamed the Board of Governors of the Federal Reserve System.[17]

Although *Humphrey's* gave ACs a much firmer foothold in the administrative state, it cannot be concluded that the commissions became completely institutionalized as a result. This is because the president responded with a wholesale attack on the commissions, even attempting to eliminate them all. He had more than enough reason to do so. He now confronted more commissions than his predecessors had, partly because of his own administration's effort to install new ones. Worse, as illustrated in *Humphrey's*, most members of ACs were appointees of Republican presidents, owing to three consecutive Democratic defeats in presidential elections in the 1920s. FDR had simply had enough of recalcitrant ACs.

14 *Humphrey's Executor v. United States*, 295 U.S. 602 (1935), at 627–628, 631; White, *Constitution and the New Deal*, 108–114.

15 295 U.S. 602 (1935), at 632; Miller, "Independent Agencies," 94.

16 *A. L. A. Schechter Poultry Corp. v. United States*, 295 U.S. 495 (1935), at 539; Robert H. Jackson, *That Man: An Insider's Portrait of Franklin D. Roosevelt* (New York: Oxford University Press, 2003), 18–19. Also see Reuben Oppenheimer, "The Supreme Court and Administrative Law," *Columbia Law Review* 37 (1937): 1–42.

17 Cushman, *Independent Regulatory Commissions*, 366; Meltzer, *History of the Federal Reserve*, 1:484–485.

In March 1936, FDR announced the appointment of the President's Committee on Administrative Management, better known as the Brownlow Committee. The committee consisted of three authorities in public administration: Louis Brownlow, Luther Gulick, and Charles Merriam, with whom FDR had been discussing executive organization since assuming the presidency.[18] Ten months later, the Committee would present to him its well-known report on executive reorganization. As explained in the introduction, its goal in relation to ACs, now named "independent regulatory commissions" by the Committee, was particularly ambitious. Believing that ACs were inefficient and obstructed consistency of public policy because of their unaccountability to the president, the Committee proposed the absorption of ACs into executive departments in charge of relevant policy domains.[19]

The FDR administration's attack on the "headless 'fourth branch'" is crucial in the institutionalization of ACs in two ways. First, if any president could have succeeded in such radical reorganization of ACs, it was FDR. Winning an easy reelection after offering rapid succession of public policies to haul America up from the abyss of the Great Depression, he was as popular as any president could ever dream of being. This also meant that if ACs could survive this challenge, it could safely be said that they were fully rooted in the US administrative state. Second, the president's mobilization of public administration experts made the fight for AC reorganization not only political but intellectual, a direct confrontation between the judicialist and executivist visions of the administrative state. The *Humphrey's* decision was a powerful manifestation that the judicialist view of the state considering courtlike ACs default regulators had achieved the status of orthodoxy. Aimed at creating a more efficient and executive-centered state, the public administration experts gathered at the Committee threw down the gauntlet to the fairness-oriented judicialist state. If the executivists were to achieve their goal, they had to persuasively show why executive agencies ought to be prioritized over ACs. The Committee report, especially its denunciation of the ACs, has been regarded as the frontal attack by public administration experts on the prevailing judicialist view of the state.[20]

But curiously, little has been written on the Committee's AC proposal, described by the *Washington Evening Star* as "more revolutionary than any other part" of the report. Of the Committee's various proposals, the literature has paid much more attention to the enhancement of the president's organizational resources realized through the 1939 Executive Reorganization Act.[21] Other propositions, aimed at making administrative agencies more responsive to the president, have

18 Barry D. Karl, *Executive Reorganization and Reform in the New Deal: The Genesis of Administrative Management, 1900–39* (Cambridge, MA: Harvard University Press, 1963); For stylistic reasons, throughout this chapter, the Brownlow Committee is hereafter referred to as "the Committee."

19 *PCAM Report*, 5.

20 Sidney M. Milkis, *The President and the Parties: The Transformation of the American Party System since the New Deal* (New York: Oxford University Press, 1993), 110.

21 *Washington Evening Star*, Jan. 12, 1937; Arnold, *Managerial Presidency*; Herbert Emmerich, *Federal Organization and Administrative Management* (University: University of Alabama

been taken up in relation to the legislative battle that ended in failure in 1938. Altogether excluded from FDR's reorganization bills submitted to Congress, the AC proposal has been almost totally neglected. Its legislative failure has been casually attributed to strong congressional opposition, even though it was not even included in any congressional bill.[22]

In a rare work on the AC proposal, Peri Arnold analyzes the staff report on ACs Robert Cushman prepared for the Committee. After tracing the institutional development of ACs, Arnold presents the report as a frontal challenge to ACs inheriting many features of judicial courts. In his view, the Cushman report that formed the basis of the Committee's recommendation heralded the arrival of the vision of a new, executive-centered administrative state. This book joins Arnold in arguing that the Cushman report and FDR's reorganization attempt, of which it is a part, constitute a critical juncture in the development of US administrative state building. It also shares his characterization of ACs as courtlike agencies. However, it neither treats ACs as administrative agencies of the past that were to be overcome through the reorganization nor sees the AC proposal as "decisive," as Arnold does. This is because there are reasons to doubt the Committee's commitment to the reorganization of ACs. In stark contrast to the fiery rhetoric of the proposal in its final report, the Committee had explained to FDR that its report would not contain any proposal on ACs. Also, after the publication of the Committee report, the members and staff of the Committee were apparently noncommittal to the proposal and even removed the AC-related provisions from the executive reorganization bill the Committee drafted for the administration.[23]

What was behind the Committee's aversion to the reorganization of ACs? The rest of this chapter will show that although the Committee set out to reorganize the administrative state in a more efficient and executive-centered direction, it retreated when it realized the difficulty of theoretically legitimizing the replacement of ACs with executive agencies. The AC proposal was still included in the Committee's final report at FDR's insistence, but the Committee had little hope that ACs would be eliminated. If there was anything decisive about the AC proposal, it was the Committee's failure to justify the abolishment of judicialized commissions and the AC proposal's quiet death, which together signified the resilience of the judicialist administrative state against its executivist challengers.

When FDR created the Brownlow Committee, he was acutely aware of the hindrance ACs posed to effective presidential governance. He would bring the

---

Press, 1971); Matthew J. Dickinson, *Bitter Harvest: FDR, Presidential Power and the Growth of the Presidential Branch* (New York: Cambridge University Press, 1996).

22 Polenberg, *Reorganizing Roosevelt's Government*, 45; Louis Brownlow, "Developments since the Report of the President's Committee on Administrative Management," transcript of staff meeting of the Division of Administrative Management, Apr. 24, 1942, Folder 21.18, Box 21, Hugh Heclo Collection, Special Collections Library, George Mason University.

23 Peri E. Arnold, "The Brownlow Committee, Regulation, and the Presidency: Seventy Years Later," *Public Administration Review* 67 (2007): 1030; Polenberg, *Reorganizing Roosevelt's Government*, 25–26.

problem to the Committee shortly after its formation, already referring to ACs as "the Fourth Department" of the government. The Committee's members and staff took the suggestion seriously – so seriously that they would soon coin the term "independent regulatory commission." But they could not have ignored ACs even without such encouragement. To the prominent students of political science and public administration committed to efficient and responsive administration, ACs were problematic. Their multimember form blurred the locus of responsibility, complicated the division of labor, and slowed decision-making. Their courtlike procedures added to this sluggishness. The commissioners' long tenure and immunity from presidential removal didn't just make commissions unresponsive to the public; their autonomy could lead to inconsistent, even contradictory, policy outputs among agencies.[24]

There was a conundrum, however. As Louis Jaffe points out, ACs, the Committee's "bête noire," were the "darling" of lawyers who had been the primary guarantors of administrative agencies' legitimacy. The committee members were as cognizant of the prevailing judicialist vision, or paradigm, of public administration as any other experts. In *The Frontiers of Public Administration*, a collection of essays by leading public administration scholars published in the same year the committee was at work, Marshall Dimock outlined the paradigm's essence based on the supremacy of law and separation of powers. If an administrative body was to exercise legislative and judicial powers autonomously, he noted, "the best features of court procedure should be required in such administrative proceedings," as was the case in the ICC and other agencies. Dimock was no outlier among public administration experts; he would soon become a charter member of the American Society for Public Administration. As Dimock's case suggests, many public administration scholars of his time were either trained in, or at least influenced by, administrative law. Also, the early presidents of the American Political Science Association included prominent figures in administrative and public law such as Frank Goodnow, Ernst Freund, and Edward Corwin. Dimock wrote his doctoral dissertation under the direction of Goodnow, who had argued that the nature of administrators' position "should be much the same as that which we assign to judicial officers." In writing the first American textbook on public administration, Leonard White relied much on the thinking of Freund.[25]

But the members of the Brownlow Committee, also authorities of the discipline, were eager to present an alternative to the prevailing, judicialist view of public administration. According to Sidney Milkis, these experts were determined to

24 Minutes of Meeting of Members and Staff of President's Committee on Administrative Management, May 9 and 10, 1936, Folder A-II-22, Box 1, Papers of President's Committee on Administrative Management, Franklin D. Roosevelt Presidential Library (hereafter PCAM Papers).

25 Jaffe, "Independent Agency," 1068; Marshall E. Dimock, "The Rôle of Discretion in Modern Administration," in *The Frontiers of Public Administration*, ed. John M. Gaus, Leonard D. White, and Marshall E. Dimock (Chicago: University of Chicago Press, 1936), 63; Dimock, *Law and Dynamic Administration*, Ch. 7; Goodnow, *Politics and Administration*, 86; Kraines, *World and Ideas*, 97.

"move the political system from a governmental order based on *constitutionalism* to one emphasizing *public administration*" [emphasis in original]. Its members were about to challenge the paradigm by proposing a new, executivist paradigm of public administration. This is why the Committee report has often been hailed as the "high noon" of public administration orthodoxy due to its epoch-making role. It will be shown, however, that although the document boldly laid out the general theory in executivist terms, it turned out to be quite accommodating of the judicialist vision of the state in its specifics.[26]

There was no subject on which the contrast between the two camps of thought was starker than the status of ACs. As the representative administrative agencies in the judicialized state, the commissions were destined to attract much attention from the Committee. It was equally clear from the outset, however, that the Committee would not approach ACs, or administrative management in general, only from the social-scientific perspective. In a memorandum describing the work to be performed by the Committee written shortly before the announcement of its formation, Brownlow stated that the president needed to direct "fiscal, personnel, planning, and legal(?)" aspects of all agencies and hence their nature must be studied, suggesting that the analysis of the administrative management must include the jurisprudential perspective. Knowing that he would be attacking the judicialist paradigm, Brownlow was ambivalent about this decision. He knew that legal expertise must be utilized in the Committee's work in order to overcome the paradigm, but there also was the fear of being won over by it. In the end, he took the risk; in his memoir he took pride in his "sufficient foresight" to put the question mark after the word "legal" in the note.[27]

After the Committee got to work the next month, its members seemed more than willing to incorporate legal perspectives into their research. This was particularly true for the study on ACs. The Committee chose Robert Cushman, a Cornell political science professor, to conduct the AC study. While most of the staff were respected academics in political science and public administration, several of them, Cushman included, were also experts in public law. Cushman identified as a political scientist – he later became the president of the American Political Science Association – but his research method was strictly legal. He was then best known for annual commentaries on constitutional court cases in the *American Political Science Review* and, during his tenure as committee staff, even described himself as "a layman in the field of administration."[28]

26 Milkis, *President and the Parties*, 110; Stephanie P. Newbold and David H. Rosenbloom, "Brownlow Report Retrospective," *Public Administration Review* 67 (2007): 1006; Wallace Sayre, "The Trends of a Decade in Administrative Values," *Public Administration Review* 11 (1951): 1–9; Wallace Sayre, "Premises of Public Administration: Past and Emerging" *Public Administration Review* 18 (1958): 102–105. Milkis's work is very rich in details on the IRC proposal.

27 Louis Brownlow, *A Passion for Anonymity: The Autobiography of Louis Brownlow, the Second Half* (Chicago: University of Chicago Press, 1958), 334–335.

28 Cushman's commentaries were later published in book form, in multiple editions. Robert E. Cushman, *Leading Constitutional Decisions*, 12th ed. (New York: Appleton-Century-Crofts,

Why was Cushman hired for the AC study? The Committee was to complete its final report by the end of the year, which meant that its staff had only about six months for research and writing. So it recruited those who already had deep knowledge of their topic, who could "skim the cream off the top of their memories" in advising the Committee.[29] Cushman's earlier work on the history of federal police power, which had a close connection to the institutional development of ACs and regulation, made him a perfect choice. While his approach was decidedly legal, the Committee did not consider it a liability. This could be seen in the short list for the position that went to Cushman. Next to his name were those of Princeton's Edwin Corwin, the University of Michigan's I. L. Sharfman, and Frederick Blachly of the Brookings Institution, all well-known students of constitutional or administrative law. The Committee would take the judicialist paradigm fully into consideration in devising its executivist reorganization scheme that would bring efficiency and responsibility to regulation.[30]

But in recruiting its staff, the Committee did not just pay attention to the judicialist paradigm but accommodated it. The Committee sent to its newly appointed staff a document titled "Preliminary Outline of an Inquiry into Administrative Management of the Federal Government," containing instructions on each subject matter. On ACs, the manual stated that the staff were to analyze the merits of placing commission activities in executive departments to bring about coordination and control of administrative actions. Curiously, however, the staff member was to divide ACs' work into administrative and judicial aspects; the former could become "subject to central management," but the latter was to remain "removed from executive direction." Here, the autonomy of administrative adjudication – a pillar of agency judiciality – was treated as a given even though it was one of the biggest obstacles to the Committee's goal of the executive-centered state.[31]

The Committee's choice not to include the abolishment of ACs as part of their reorganization came from its view that the commissions were already too popular and established to be dismantled. Scholars of public administration had taken ACs' strength in adjudication for granted even before the *Humphrey's* decision. In 1933, the National Transportation Committee (NTC), organized by insurance companies, research universities, and philanthropic institutions, published its report on the political and economic problems in the nation's transportation system. The committee, a bipartisan group of distinguished figures including

1963); Robert E. Cushman to Joseph P. Harris, Nov. 1, 1936, Folder "M-Cushman, Robert," Box 18, PCAM Papers. Also see Stephanie P. Newbold and Larry D. Terry, "The President's Committee on Administrative Management: The Untold Story and the Federalist Connection," *Administration and Society* 38 (2006): 535.

29 Minutes of Meeting of Members and Staff of President's Committee on Administrative Management, May 9 and 10, 1936, PCAM Papers.

30 Robert E. Cushman, "The National Police Power under the Commerce Clause of the Constitution," *Minnesota Law Review* 3 (1918–1919): 289–319, 381–412, 452–483; Minutes of the Meeting of the Committee, Apr. 11, 1936, Folder A-II-14, Box 1, PCAM Papers.

31 "Preliminary Outline of an Inquiry into Administrative Management of the Federal Government," Folder A-II-17, Box 1, PCAM Papers.

ex-president Calvin Coolidge and Al Smith, the Democratic presidential candidate in 1928, partly blamed the courtlike passivity of the ICC for the deterioration of the American transportation network. Noting that the commission "sits and hears but has only a limited scope in which to inquire and plan and act," the NTC suggested the reorganization of the ICC into a hierarchical body similar to an executive department, arguing that it "speeds works" and "permits specialization" aside from enabling better use of policy expertise.[32] Although the NTC had plenty to say about the ICC's inefficiency and lack of expertise, however, it insisted that the commission was well customized to carry out "legislative and judicial action of the very highest order." The experts at the Brookings Institution who conducted research for the committee were even more supportive of the commission. Porter R. Taylor, who authored an analysis on possible reform of transportation policy, argued that the ICC was "clearly the logical federal agency to exercise control" over interstate transportation and even proposed that the transportation regulation should be reorganized around the commission.[33]

The judiciary's enunciation of its renewed commitment to the judiciality of administrative agencies as the Brownlow Committee worked on executive reorganization planning only strengthened its belief that the ACs were a political "third rail." Created in the aftermath of the *Humphrey's* decision, the Committee began its work with the Court's adherence to ACs in mind. A few weeks after the full Committee meeting, the Supreme Court handed down its opinion on *Morgan v. United States*, in which the Secretary of Agriculture's adjudicatory role prescribed in the Packers and Stockyards Act was disputed. The Court sided with the market agencies operating at the Kansas City Stockyards, who argued that Secretary Henry Wallace's failure to hold a full hearing as required in the act invalidated the maximum rate he issued. According to the Court, the proper hearing as part of the fulfillment of the quasi-legislative role of the secretary "has a quality resembling that of a judicial proceeding." The significance of the decision was not just in reaffirming the importance of overall judiciality in administrative adjudication but in emphasizing the gravity of courtlike procedures. While both department heads and AC commissioners had routinely relied on findings made by their subordinates, the Court reminded them that those with policy-making authority must themselves hold a "hearing in a substantial sense." This was because the secretary's duty to faithfully carry out such a hearing was "akin to that of a judge. The one who decides must hear." In making this argument, the Court referred to the procedures developed by the ICC as "good practice," and various agencies modified their procedures in accordance with the decision.[34]

32 Report of the National Transportation Committee, reproduced in Harold G. Moulton et al., *The American Transportation Problem* (Washington, DC: Brookings Institution, 1933), 32, 33. Also see Bernstein, *Regulating Business*, 59.

33 Report of the National Transportation Committee, l; Moulton et al., *American Transportation Problem*, 891–895; Also see Fuess, *Eastman*, 186–187.

34 *Morgan v. United States*, 298 U.S. 468 (1936), at 478, 480, 481. Also see Smith, "Practice and Procedure before the Interstate Commerce Commission." As is known, the case did not

In *Humphrey's* and *Morgan*, the Court declared that the two pillars of agency judiciality formed the basis of the constitutionality of the administrative state. "Looking back over the fifty years which have passed since the establishment of the Interstate Commerce Commission," Justice Harlan Stone stated at a conference held at Harvard in August 1936, "no one can now seriously doubt the possibility of establishing an administrative system which can be made to satisfy and harmonize the requirements of due process and the common law ideal of supremacy of law, on the one hand, and the demand, on the other, that government be afforded a needed means to function, freed from the necessity of strict conformity to the traditional procedure of the courts." The AC-centered judicialist administrative state, in the future chief justice's view, struck the right balance between efficiency and fairness.[35]

The Court's judicialist attitude severely restrained the Committee's scope of executive reorganization. Given the popularity of ACs and the judiciary's backing of them, emphasizing executive departments' efficiency and accountability was clearly insufficient in legitimizing the "departmentalization" of the commissions. To avoid being charged with executive encroachment, any intellectually serious recommendation of AC reorganization had to take the commissions' courtlike independence and procedures into account. But the Committee and its staff had no choice other than to accept them. In fact, there is reason to believe that they themselves were in partial support of the judicialist paradigm. The Committee members, determined to create a streamlined executive branch with the president at the helm, embraced it only reluctantly. In contrast, several staff members with legal expertise strongly internalized the paradigm. The Committee's AC proposal should therefore be viewed as a result of interaction among actors with varying degrees of commitment to the judicialist paradigm rather than a unified attack on it.

How did the Committee's AC proposal develop under such conditions? With most of the Committee staff having full-time jobs elsewhere, they conducted their research and writing independently but in regular touch with Joseph P. Harris, the Committee's research director. A full gathering of the Committee and its staff was held only once, in May. Its proceedings show how Cushman applied his expertise to the assignment from the Committee. The rough proposal

---

end with this decision. The Court reiterated its judicialist position on administrative procedures in a subsequent decision stating that "In administrative proceedings of a *quasi-judicial* character, the liberty and property of the citizen must be protected by the rudimentary requirements of fair play. These demand a fair and open hearing." [Emphasis in original.] *Morgan v. United States*, 304 U.S. 1 (1938), at 14; the court also stated that the hearings by the Department of Agriculture ought to meet "fundamental requirements of fairness which are of the essence of due process in a proceeding of a judicial nature." *Morgan v. United States*, 304 U.S. 1 (1938), at 19. Also see Kenneth C. Sears, "The Morgan Case and Administrative Procedure," *George Washington Law Review* 7 (1939): 726–739; Ernst, "Morgan and the New Dealers."

35 Harlan F. Stone, "The Common Law in the United States," *Harvard Law Review* 50 (1936): 16–17.

he prepared for the meeting already made the "broad problem" of "recognizing a 'fourth department' of the federal government" the central subject of his inquiry. He would address the desirability of ACs' autonomy from the president, the possible ways in which it could be delimited, and their legal implications.[36] In the meeting, Cushman tried to understand the Committee's intent so that he could closely follow it. He asked whether the staff were "free to suggest that the President should not have added power," or were to "consider expansion, status quo, or contraction of executive powers."[37]

In response, Committee members stressed the difficulty the autonomy of ACs posed to administrative management, but also emphasized that they were open to suggestions. They encouraged Cushman to ask whether quasi-judicial tasks should remain with, and continue to be committed to, ACs, repeatedly taking note of their multiplication over the years and the fact that the presidents had traditionally been held responsible for their actions despite their limited influence on them. At the same time, the Committee had no fixed conclusion in mind – at least that was what Cushman was told. According to Brownlow, the Committee was interested in finding out if the president could exert "managerial control" over ACs in some way and had "no prejudgments as to the *type* of administrative management to be proposed" [emphasis in original]. As Harris noted, however, Cushman was also welcome to suggest that "the judicial aspects of a bureau should be free of executive control," if he thought so.[38]

The Committee thus urged Cushman to investigate the possibility of merging ACs into the executive department, although without making him stick to the goal. Harris already felt that Cushman was "more sympathetic toward independence of regulatory bodies than toward bringing them under executive direction" and alerted Committee members. But thinking that the Committee report could diverge from Cushman's recommendations, they thought that was acceptable, as long as he did a "workmanlike job on the legal and administrative problems involved."[39]

A few points must be kept in mind to understand the Committee's willingness to accommodate Cushman's legal approach. For one, this was the first time the Committee members squarely faced the issue of ACs. While they had already had ample experience in state-level executive reorganization, there were few ACs with authority that matched that of their federal-level counterparts, and most of the

36 Robert E. Cushman, "Tentative Outline on Administrative Management," Folder A-II-39, Box 1, PCAM Papers.

37 Minutes of Meeting of Members and Staff of President's Committee on Administrative Management, May 9 and 10, 1936, PCAM Papers.

38 Minutes of Meeting of Members and Staff of President's Committee on Administrative Management, May 9 and 10, 1936, PCAM Papers.

39 Diary of Joseph P. Harris, May 22 to May 26, 1936, in Joseph P. Harris to Louis Brownlow, May 26, Folder "PCAM: Correspondence, Reports, Memoranda, Etc. 1936, 5/1936–5/29/1936," Box 47, Louis Brownlow Papers, John F. Kennedy Presidential Library. Also see Polenberg, *Reorganizing Roosevelt's Government*, 17.

time they could be departmentalized without much difficulty.[40] The Committee's tolerance, however, had an even more important reason: the members were not expecting that they could, or even should, instantly dispense with ACs. By this time, the Committee was in full agreement that the president's emphasis on the study of ACs was not in the "immediate urgency" of the problem but the "long-range importance." In other words, it was the trend toward more ACs, rather than individual commissions, that threatened the presidential management of administration.[41] This is why the Committee needed to treat ACs as a distinct *category* of agencies, now called "independent regulatory commissions." If this was so, ACs could even prove useful. Gulick, in a discussion with Cushman, advised that he ask whether ACs were "appropriate at one stage but not at another." Like many members of Congress in the 1920s, the Committee took issue not with individual commissions but with their proliferation, although for a very different reason.[42]

In investigating the possibility of ACs' assimilation into executive departments, Cushman could make full use of his legal expertise and needed to treat ACs only as a long-term threat, thanks to the constraints upon the Committee. It should then come as no surprise that his proposition turned out to be very moderate. By early August, he was already pondering the idea that would form the core of his final report to the Committee. In his progress report, Cushman stated that each AC ought to be transferred to a relevant executive department, split into an administrative section that was going to become a division of the department and an independent judicial section which was to be "in" but not "of" the department. There also was an important prerequisite to the transfer. There already had to be a "suitable department"; if none could be found, "the Commission *should remain independent*" [emphasis in original]. This would constitute a crucial difference between the AC proposals of Cushman and the Committee's final report.[43]

40 Luther H. Gulick. "Governmental Reorganization: Some Observations and Reflections on Administrative Reform," interview by James L. Garnett, November 30, 1976. I am grateful to Professor Garnett for sharing the transcript of the interview with me. Also see Schuyler Wallace, *Federal Departmentalization: A Critique of Theories of Organization* (New York: Columbia University Press, 1941).

41 Minutes of the Meeting of the Committee, Apr. 11, 1936, PCAM Papers. For instance, FDR had rejected the idea of creating an Air Commerce Commission to regulate air traffic offered by the Federal Aviation Commission, noting that "we should avoid the multiplication of separate regulatory agencies in the field of transportation," and recommended that the task be handled by the ICC. *Report of Federal Aviation Commission*, 74th Cong., 1st sess. (1935), S. Doc. 15, iv; Howard C. Westwood and Alexander E. Bennett, "A Footnote to the Legislative History of the Civil Aeronautics Act of 1938 and Afterword," *Notre Dame Lawyer* 42 (1967): 309–381.

42 Diary of Joseph P. Harris, entry for June 4 – July 9, 1936, Folder "PCAM: Correspondence, Reports, Memoranda, Etc. 1936, 6/2/1936–6/29/1936," Box 47, Brownlow Papers.

43 Robert E. Cushman, "Progress Report: Relation of Independent Regulatory Agencies to the President," Aug. 6, 1936, Folder A-II-31, Box 1, PCAM Papers.

With Harris's approval of the plan, Cushman proceeded to the final report, which he completed in mid-October. It showed that in pursuing the Committee's executive-centered administrative state, he utilized the core principles of the judicialist paradigm.[44]

Cushman's acceptance of the paradigm was most apparent in the way he presented the "problem of independent regulatory commissions" in American governance. He formulated it as a dilemma between two contradictory imperatives ACs were supposed to follow. In his succinct language, ACs were expected to be "both *politically responsible* and *judicially independent*" [emphasis in original] but were unable to achieve either.[45] Whereas political responsibility clearly was part of the executivist goal of the Committee, judicial independence was nothing but the reflection of the two principles at the heart of the fairness-oriented state. The report went on to analyze the clash of the two imperatives within ACs and sought a way out. According to Cushman, the proliferation of ACs had produced a "decentralized and chaotic administrative system" resulting in unaccountability. The president, supposedly the "general manager" of the United States, could not expect cooperation from ACs overseeing major regulatory policies. This made it impossible for him to fulfill his duty.[46]

At the same time, Cushman stressed that the quasi-judicial adjudication was the most important of all ACs' roles. Congress made ACs politically independent so that they could perform such duties to their fullest. While an AC's rule-making role compromised the commission's neutrality as an adjudicating body, the status quo clearly favored quasi-judicial independence at the cost of political responsibility. This was shown in the two legal limits to reform: the presidential inability to remove AC commissioners at will and the broad judicial review of ACs' decisions.[47]

What could be done? Because Cushman saw the problem as a dilemma involving the efficiency-fairness tradeoff, simply shifting the status quo toward more political responsibility was out of the question. He therefore strongly opposed an executivist reform of simply incorporating ACs into executive departments as regular bureaus, as it would sacrifice their independence essential to quasi-judicial work. Cushman was also against fitting ACs into executive departments while retaining their autonomy, however, as the gains from such a change would be too small to justify the resulting disruption.[48] This dilemma had to be squarely met and overcome, and this is why he proposed splitting each AC into administrative and judicial parts. The administrative section would be responsible for policy-determining functions and "housekeeping" inside a cabinet department; the judicial section would conduct the adjudication. Then, the former could be

44 Memorandum, Joseph P. Harris to Robert E. Cushman, Aug. 11, 1936, Folder A-II-31, Box 1, PCAM Papers.
45 Cushman, "The Problem," 219.
46 Cushman, "The Problem," 207.
47 Cushman, "The Problem," 216, 225–228.
48 Cushman, "The Problem," 238–239.

directed by the department head and be politically responsible. The latter could continue adjudicating outside the three branches.[49]

Cushman thus sought to meet the Committee's demand of making ACs more responsive to the chief executive. At the same time, he placed great, if not greater, weight upon upholding the judicialist paradigm in two ways. First, Cushman's plan to create an executive-centered government also looked out for a major judicialist concern about the administrative state. The reorganization would also resolve the prosecutor-judge-legislator combination in the commissions that had been criticized as violating the supremacy of law and separation of powers. If the ACs could be divided into two parts, their judicial sections would no longer engage in policy-determining quasi-legislative actions and could concentrate on quasi-judicial adjudication. Such an institutional arrangement, Cushman argued, also would allow the judicial sections to continue judicializing their procedures. He was so excited about the idea as to suggest in his report the prospect of the sections achieving administrative court status like the Board of Tax Appeals.[50]

Second, Cushman's recommendation was conditional. As noted above, he stressed that the partial merger of ACs into executive departments should be limited to the cases in which good commission-department matches were found; otherwise, ACs should remain as they were. Cushman also emphasized that decisions to reorganize the commissions ought to be made individually, after careful study. While these suggestions were only sensible given the complexity of the subject and the haste in which the report was produced, the tone of his recommendation was unmistakably in favor of the status quo. Essentially, all he proposed in the report was to begin discussing the possible merits of partial departmentalization of ACs, case by case. There could not have been a more modest proposal; Cushman had utterly no intention of providing a "decisive" solution to ACs.[51]

A clear illustration that Cushman was thinking in judicialist terms was the fact that his plan was practically identical to that presented by the Special Committee on Administrative Law of the American Bar Association, then a stronghold of conservative lawyers opposed to agency policy making. Created in 1933, the ABA committee was assigned the task of stopping illegitimate delegation of judicial power to the administrative agency that, according to its chair, "looks like a court and acts like a court but somehow escapes being classified as a court whenever you attempt to impose any limitations on its power." In its report in 1934, the ABA committee recommended that all ACs be abolished and "their executive and legislative functions should be transferred to the several executive departments."[52]

49 Cushman, "The Problem," 233.

50 Cushman analyzed quasi-legislative and quasi-judicial functions separately, as his assignment was to study ACs with focus on their latter function. The quasi-legislative function was analyzed by James Hart. "Preliminary Outline of an Inquiry," Folder A-II-17, Box 1, PCAM Papers; Cushman, "The Problem," 236.

51 Cushman, "The Problem," 229, 234.

52 American Bar Association, "Proceedings of the Fifty-Sixth Annual Meeting of American Bar Association," *Annual Report of the American Bar Association* 56 (1933), 197.

At the same time, the judicial function of each AC was to be transferred to an integrated administrative court or an individual tribunal whose role was limited to adjudication. Although facing diametrically opposite directions, one toward more efficiency and the other toward more fairness in policy implementation, Cushman and the ABA committee of extreme judicialists reached a very similar reform plan because of their common intellectual roots in the judicial paradigm and the shared goal of restraining ACs.[53]

One month after the submission of his report, Cushman wrote to Harris expressing "a great satisfaction" that his scheme was approved by the Committee that had just begun to prepare its own report to the president.[54] Because his was probably the first comprehensive analysis of ACs discussing their historical development and constitutional status, the Committee certainly appreciated Cushman's assessment of the AC problem.[55] This did not lead to the adoption of his proposition, but not because the Committee thought it too moderate. In his draft for the administrative management section of the Committee report, Gulick stated that the Committee would "make no recommendations for immediate action" regarding existing ACs. Brownlow followed suit with his memorandum of early November outlining the full Committee report, commenting that "the segregation of administrative duties from the quasi-judicial duties of the regular agencies now in existence" would be left untouched.[56]

Why did the Committee decide against offering a reform proposal for ACs? One thing is clear; the decision did not flow from its support for ACs. This was most evident from the Gulick draft of the Committee report which described the diversity of agencies as "chaotic." To Gulick, it was nothing short of "a miracle" that anything could be accomplished under the condition. Such a comment from him was unremarkable. In his famous "Notes on the Theory of Organizations" drafted in 1936 for distribution among the committee staff, Gulick placed paramount importance on the principle of "unity of command." ACs doubly defied it – by being independent of the president and also by having a collegial form. According to him, "nothing but confusion" would arise under multiple command.[57]

53 American Bar Association, "Report of the Special Committee on Administrative Law," *Annual Report of the American Bar Association* 57 (1934): 539–540; Ralph F. Fuchs, "Current Proposals for the Reorganization of the Federal Regulatory Agencies," *Texas Law Review* 16 (1938): 338–340. By 1936, the ABA committee had shifted from its position in 1934 of dividing each IRC into two to creating an administrative court to which most administrative adjudication would be referred. Cushman criticized the idea in the report for the inefficiency and excessive judicial intrusion it would entail. Cushman, "The Problem," 239.

54 Robert E. Cushman to Joseph P. Harris, Nov. 20, 1936, Folder "M-Cushman, Robert," Box 18, PCAM Papers.

55 Gulick, "Governmental Reorganization."

56 Gulick, "Departmental Reorganization," Folder C-I, Box 3, PCAM Papers; Brownlow, *Passion for Anonymity*, 377.

57 Gulick, "Departmental Reorganization," Folder C-I, Box 3, PCAM Papers; Luther Gulick, "Notes on the Theory of Organization, with Special Reference to Government in the United

If the Committee members were so hostile to ACs, why didn't they at least try to reorganize them? This was because their chief aim was, as noted, eliminating ACs in the long run; individual ACs were not the issue. In discussing the ACs, they emphasized that the commissions' *accumulation* was the heart of the problem. Gulick further argued that the creation of ACs and other independent agencies was perfectly legitimate when the government was to launch new activities, as "new purposes cannot be carried out without broad freedom to experiment." To "tie a totally new activity either to the regular bureau pattern or to the regular controls," in his view, "may defeat its purpose entirely."[58] Yet when the new activity became organized, Gulick noted, such agencies should be brought into "the normal structure of organization": in other words, executive departments. Otherwise, the continuing creation of ACs would result in what Brownlow called "the danger of the development of an irresponsible Fourth branch of the government." This could in the end, to again use Gulick's words, "dissipate and destroy the Executive authority." The Committee members decided against proposing an AC reform plan because the commissions were yet to have destructive impact on the administrative state. As stated in the final report, the "long-range problem" that "we keep on creating them [ACs]" was "of equal or even greater seriousness" to the immediate ones caused by existing commissions.[59]

The Committee members' acceptance of ACs, however conditional, may seem far fetched given their adhesion to the command-and-control structure of government bodies. It nonetheless was genuine. Gulick later wrote to Herbert Hoover, who shared his distaste for ACs, that "the long range consideration" had influenced the Committee the most in determining its proposals. As he had written earlier, he would "personally not be averse to the creation from time to time" of ACs when the government enters a new field of activity, although they eventually had to be "tied in" to executive departments.[60] From this perspective, Cushman's proposal seemed at once too limited in scope and too controversial to be worth fighting for. ACs already were so entrenched and respected that any presidential attempt to tamper with them would surely have provoked intense opposition. In such a situation, it made more sense to warn people of the long-term damage ACs could do to governance and encourage that regulatory functions would be "devolved upon the regular executive departments" in the future.[61]

Researchers into FDR's executive reorganization have gravely misunderstood the intention behind the Committee's fiery rhetoric against ACs. John Rohr has

---

States," in *Papers on the Science of Administration*, ed. Luther Gulick and L. Urwick (New York: Institute of Public Administration, 1937), 9.

58 Gulick, "Departmental Reorganization," Folder C-I, Box 3, PCAM Papers.

59 Brownlow Draft quoted in Brownlow, *Passion for Anonymity*, 377; Gulick, "Departmental Reorganization," Folder C-I, Box 3, PCAM Papers; *PCAM Report*, 41.

60 Luther Gulick to Herbert Hoover, Feb. 1, 1937, Folder J-I-9, Box 16, PCAM Papers; Peri E. Arnold, "The First Hoover Commission and the Managerial Presidency," *Journal of Politics* 38 (1976): 61.

61 Gulick, "Departmental Reorganization," Folder C-I, Box 3, PCAM Papers.

criticized the Committee's use of the expression "the headless 'fourth branch'" – the expression first appeared in Gulick's draft – as a "rhetorical blunder," suggesting that it unintentionally contributed to the delegitimization of ACs and of agencies in general. But it in fact was a deliberate act, designed to preclude further accumulation of ACs. Although the Committee members were strong proponents of efficiency in public administration, they were also aware of the efficiency-fairness tradeoff. Knowing that improving the efficiency of ACs would inevitably lead to the loss of procedural fairness, they decided to leave existing ACs alone and concentrated on deterring the creation of more commissions. The Committee's vicious attack on ACs, then, actually was a display of its limits. It is only ironic that the expression "fourth branch" is now widely used in reference to the entire administrative state – including executive agencies the Committee sought to promote – often in the context of its delegitimization.[62]

The Committee was content, even if not satisfied, with its recommendations until events took an unexpected turn. On November 14, 1936, Brownlow and Gulick discussed their plan with FDR, who had just secured reelection by a historic landslide in which he carried forty-six of the forty-eight states (except Maine and Vermont). In the point-by-point examination of recommendations, the president, who had once been comfortable in treating ACs as a long-term problem, expressed dissatisfaction with the AC non-proposal, asking, "Is this all you can say?" Despite the Committee members' explanation of the "strategy" behind the idea, he insisted on somehow "tying in" the commissions to executive departments.[63]

How did the Committee react to FDR's plea for an AC reorganization proposal? While the members certainly preferred their original idea, they shared FDR's preference for cabinet departments over commissions. As Gulick later commented, there was congruence between "his [FDR's] political needs and our theoretical analysis," which accurately describes the Committee's reversal of position. But if so, why did the Committee stop short of pursuing complete conversion of ACs into executive bureaus and settle on the partial absorption plan apparently based on the Cushman report? The decision to adopt the limited reorganization idea seemed to be made to minimize criticism from judicialists. After all, Cushman's was the only plan at hand that took the judicialist paradigm into account. As is already clear, the biggest theoretical obstacle to the departmentalization of ACs was the accepted norm that administrative adjudication had to be performed by courtlike agencies. Of course, this did not mean executive departments could not hear at all. As Cushman and the Committee both emphasized, they had already been adjudicating for a long time. But transforming an AC into

62 John A. Rohr, *To Run a Constitution*, 152–153; Gulick, "Departmental Reorganization," Folder C-I, Box 3, PCAM Papers; James W. Fesler, "The Brownlow Committee Fifty Years Later," *Public Administration Review* 47 (1987): 292.

63 Gulick memorandum quoted in Brownlow, *Passion for Anonymity*, 379; Polenberg, *Reorganizing Roosevelt's Government*, 20–21.

an executive bureau was an entirely different matter that would entail retrogression of the adjudication process.[64]

Although the Committee members were frustrated with Cushman's proposition, they knew that his view was in no way peculiar. Schuyler Wallace, another staff member with legal expertise, was in complete agreement with Cushman. In his detailed analysis on the status of ACs in his report on administrative reorganization, Wallace backed Cushman's conditional and partial AC departmentalization plan. He even argued that ACs' quasi-legislative functions should also remain independent from the executive ones. Such a view was only common sense for contemporary lawyers. Regardless of how strictly they adhered to the judicialist paradigm, they were invariably more apprehensive of adjudication by executive departments than by ACs.[65]

The Committee's AC proposal in the final report could only be understood against such a backdrop. Well aware that coming up with a rationale that would convince the judicialists into full AC departmentalization was impossible, the Committee initially only claimed against the increase in ACs, emphasizing its long-term negative consequences. But after FDR's intervention, something had to be proposed; the Committee then fell back on the Cushman plan, but removed all the conditions on AC reorganization. The Committee members thought the report would best serve its role as a policy paper that would maximize FDR's chance of reorganization; Gulick later described it as a "sales document" made to persuade the president, Congress, and the media to support the plan. The AC reorganization plan won FDR's strong approval.[66]

In the end, the development of the Committee report's AC proposal illustrates that the Committee itself accepted the basic tenets of the judicialist paradigm of the administrative state they sought to overcome. As already discussed, from the outset the Committee took the independence of administrative adjudication as a given. The Committee's portrayal of the "headless 'fourth branch'" in the final report exemplified its acknowledgment of the paradigm in two ways. First, the Committee actually praised ACs' multimember form for its appropriateness in fulfilling their quasi-judicial functions. While the board form of the organization was "cumbersome, wasteful, and ineffective in the conduct of administrative duties," it also was "extremely useful and necessary" for a variety of nonmanagerial activities, including quasi-judicial ones. Such a compliment to the autonomy and collegial form of ACs should be surprising given the Committee's antipathy toward them, but it makes perfect sense once paired with the Committee's initial non-proposal.[67]

64 Gulick, "Governmental Reorganization"; Cushman, "The Problem," 214–216; *PCAM Report*, 42.

65 Schuyler C. Wallace, "Administrative Reorganization in Relation to Administrative Management," Sep. 15, 1936, Folder C-II, Box 3, PCAM Papers. Also see "Progress Report of Staff Activities Covering the Period from June 22 to August 15," Folder 13, Box 262, President's Committee on Administrative Management, Charles E. Merriam Papers, Special Collections Research Center, University of Chicago Library.

66 Gulick, "Governmental Reorganization"; Polenberg, *Reorganizing Roosevelt's Government*, 15.

67 *PCAM Report*, 10, 32.

Second, even when it attacked the ACs, the Committee did not just measure them against its primary goals of efficiency and political responsibility; it strongly condemned the commissions for violating the separation of powers and noted that its proposal would do away with the prosecutor-judge combination that undermined "judicial fairness." While the criticism made sense in itself, it was very uncharacteristic of public administration scholars to make such an argument; it was more suited to extreme judicialists opposed to agency adjudication itself. After all, one could criticize ACs for constituting "the fourth branch" only if one thought that the government could have no more than the original three branches.[68]

The Committee's tributes to the principle valued by lawyers could be traced back to Cushman's report. The Committee's adoption of the views they were supposed to be attacking indicated how thoroughly the judicialist paradigm had seeped into the minds of political elites by the New Deal. It was unfortunate that the Committee's concession to the legal principles did not meet with the approval of legal experts, even those affiliated with the Committee. Soon after the release of the Committee report, Schuyler Wallace suggested to Joseph Harris that each AC receive separate treatment and be "integrated into departmental structure in varying degrees," just as proposed in the Cushman report. Cushman himself was predictably angry that the Committee had modified his plan. When it was later decided to publish his report alongside that of the Committee, he expressed gratitude at the chance to prove that he was "not proposing sweeping and immediate application of the proposed plan to all existing regulatory commissions."[69]

Although strongly influenced by the judicialist paradigm, the Committee's final proposal was widely perceived as radical and objectionable. This was because of its seemingly subtle but critical revisions of the Cushman plan. As mentioned, Cushman's conditional proposal would assimilate an AC into an executive department only when a "suitable" department already existed. Even if there was such a department, the degree and manner of assimilation were to be decided on an individual basis, after careful study. But the Committee's AC reorganization allowed no exception, even though the plan was presented only as a "possible solution" to the problem of ACs.[70]

In the end, the rigidity of the AC's proposal was what elicited vehement opposition from a broad range of actors. This was apparent the first time the president presented the Committee's recommendations to those outside the administration. Democratic leaders of Congress were briefed by FDR and the Committee on January 10, 1937. Sam Rayburn, newly elected House majority leader and chair of the Committee on Interstate Commerce, asked the president, "Does this

68 *PCAM Report*, 40; Arnold, *Making the Managerial Presidency*, 13–14; Rohr, *To Run a Constitution*, 138–139.

69 Schuyler Wallace to Joseph P. Harris, Jan. 15, 1937, Folder "M-Gulick, Luther," Box 18, PCAM Papers; Robert E. Cushman to Joseph P. Harris, March 15, 1937, Folder "M-Cushman, Robert," Box 18, PCAM Papers.

70 *PCAM Report*, 41.

apply to all the regulatory agencies? Is not the Interstate Commerce Commission, which is so popular and so successful, an exception?" Roosevelt's response that there would "be no exceptions, not one," was met with "shocked silence."[71]

Released to the public on the same day, the Brownlow Committee's AC proposal aroused a furor, especially among stakeholders of ACs. On January 11, FDR emphasized in a press conference the continuing independence of ACs' judicial section after absorption into an executive department. Still, fears about the plan mounted; there was no indication of how each AC would be restructured, and many commentators doubted the practicability of neatly separating the commissions' judicial activities from others. In this context, the *Washington Evening Star* noted that "the country has come to look up to" ACs like the ICC and FTC "largely because of their independence and their fairness" in policy making. In a statement published on January 19, the US Chamber of Commerce expressed concern with the way "freedom for impartial exercise of judicial and quasi-judicial functions" could be compromised by the reorganization and speculated that the AC proposal could "emerge as one of the most controversial" of the Committee's recommendations. Walter Lippmann reportedly called the proposal "the most dubious part" of the report. Members of various ACs also expressed opposition to the proposal and asked members of Congress for exemption from it. Without mentioning the Committee report, Joseph Eastman remarked in an address that because the work of the ICC "requires both impartiality and justice," the commission should be clear of "the slightest political tinge."[72]

To make matters worse for the administration, there was another source of uncertainty in reserve. Since late 1936, the Committee had been preparing a bill reflecting its recommendations. The draft bill's provisions on administrative agencies gave the president an unqualified power of reorganization, subject only to congressional veto; there was no reference to the splitting of ACs or the maintenance of the independence of the judicial section. Although such provisions had a clear precedent in the Economy Acts of 1932 and 1933, if made public, they were more than certain to add fuel to the fire. The Committee members quickly took note of the ominous atmosphere surrounding the AC proposal. A correspondent of Gulick's alerted him that the president of the Association of Interstate Commerce Practitioners was furious about the plan.[73] Having also picked up "views and gossip" in New York City, Gulick suggested to Brownlow

71 The Gulick memorandum reproduced in Brownlow, *Passion for Anonymity*, 391; Polenberg, *Reorganizing Roosevelt's Government*, 41–44.

72 Franklin D. Roosevelt, *Complete Presidential Press Conferences of Franklin D. Roosevelt*, Vol. 9–10 (1937; repr., New York: Da Capo Press, 1972), 84; *Washington Evening Star*, Jan. 15, 1937; Statement of the US Chamber of Commerce, Jan. 19, 1937, Folder J-III-1, Box 16, PCAM Papers; Lippman quoted in Lindsay Rogers, "The Independent Regulatory Commissions," *Political Science Quarterly* 52 (1937): 6; Polenberg, *Reorganizing Roosevelt's Government*, 91; *Washington Evening Star*, Jan. 21, 1937.

73 Reorganization Bill, Early Drafts, Dec. 17, 22, and 24, 1936, Folder B-II-4, Box 3, PCAM Papers. The 1933 act had expired in 1935. Louis G. Caldwell to Gulick, Jan. 15, 1937 (copy), Folder M-C, Box 18, PCAM Papers. Caldwell, former general counsel of the FRC,

that the "judicial phases" of ACs' activities at that point were left "wide open" in the bill. The recommendation was taken up, and the bill was immediately revised to safeguard quasi-judicial functions of ACs from presidential reorganization.[74]

On January 29, Joseph Harris wrote James Roosevelt, the president's son, who had just been appointed a liaison between FDR and ACs, advising that the administration should adopt the modification of the draft bill. Four days later, the Committee was informed that the administration would not use the proposed amendments "unless they were insisted upon later on." But the Committee's fear soon materialized. At a hearing of the Joint Committee on Government Organization in mid-February, the unrevised bill was attacked by legislators concerned with the fate of ACs. To reassure the congressional committee, Brownlow had to have a provision prescribing that ACs' quasi-judicial functions "may not be exercised by or supervised by any administrative or executive officer, but shall be exercised by a regulatory commission" inserted in the bill.[75]

The outlook of the AC proposal, now casually counted among the report's "vulnerable features" by a Committee staff member, continued to deteriorate.[76] The public backlash against FDR's plan to pack the Supreme Court with more compliant justices proposed in early February certainly made things worse. The administration finally conceded in April. To an inquiry on the fate of the ICC under the reorganization scheme, FDR stated that although he fully agreed with the Committee's recommendation, it "should be regarded as merely illustrative of one possible solution of the problem which might be suitable in the case of certain commissions" and was "not offered as a definite plan applicable alike to all of the independent regulatory agencies." If such a statement sounded awfully similar to Cushman's original idea, that was because the Committee had outsourced the drafting of the letter to him.[77]

The Brookings Institution's report on executive reorganization to the Senate, published on June 6, dealt the death blow to the Committee's plan. It proposed transferring many regulatory powers from executive departments to ACs, which

---

had also chaired the ABA's Special Committee on Administrative Law. Ernst, *Tocqueville's Nightmare*, 119.

74 Luther Gulick to Louis Brownlow, Jan. 20, 1937, Folder "M-Brownlow, Louis," Box 18, PCAM Papers; Polenberg, *Reorganizing Roosevelt's Government*, 44–45; Early Draft Bill, Jan. 29, 1937, Folder B-II-9, Box 3, PCAM Papers.

75 Journal of the Committee, Folder A-II-58a, Box 2, PCAM Papers; Dickinson, *Bitter Harvest*, 192; Polenberg, *Reorganizing Roosevelt's Government*, 43; The Committee bill is reproduced in US Congress, Joint Committee on Government Organization, *Reorganization of the Executive Departments*, 75th Cong., 1st sess. (1937), 8–12, 102.

76 John F. Miller to Luther Gulick, Feb. 20, 1937, Folder "M-Gulick, Luther," Box 18, PCAM Papers.

77 Joseph P. Harris to Marvin McIntyre, Mar. 31, 1937, Folder "M-Mc," Box 19, PCAM Papers; Memorandum, Louis Brownlow, Luther Gulick, and Charles E. Merriam, Mar. 17, 1937, Franklin D. Roosevelt Papers, Papers as President, Official File 285c, Folder "Reorganization, 1937 (2)," Box 5, Franklin D. Roosevelt Presidential Library. Also see Draft reply by Brownlow, Apr. 17, 1937, Franklin D. Roosevelt Papers, Papers as President, President's Personal File 4542, Franklin D. Roosevelt Presidential Library.

were arguably superior in conducting quasi-judicial functions.[78] The discussion, authored by Frederick Blachly, reflected the standard judicialist view on the subject and only could have undermined the prospects of the administration's plan. A few days later, the *Washington Post* ran an editorial comparing the AC-related recommendations of the Brownlow Committee and Brookings Institution and sided with the latter, noting that ACs were "not agents of the executive."[79]

The same day of the editorial, the administration's reorganization bill, considerably modified by the Senate Reorganization Committee, was released. The bill, S. 2700, sponsored by Majority Leader Joseph T. Robinson, placed all ACs beyond the reach of presidential reorganization. The House followed suit in its own bill, H.R. 8202, introduced in August. By this time, there was mounting opposition to FDR's court-packing plan, and cries against potential dictatorship had run their course, considerably diminishing the president's popularity.[80] The vulnerability of the AC proposal, combined with such a fraught political atmosphere, made the administration silently withdraw the plan. Subsequent reorganization bills also exempted major ACs from the presidential power of executive reorganization, and the Committee's AC reorganization plan was not revived during Roosevelt's presidency.[81]

"Sooner or later," Cushman wrote to Brownlow in late March 1937, the president must indicate that the Committee's AC proposal would "not be put into effect suddenly with one clap of thunder." The proposal's absence from the administration's executive reorganization bills easily would have made it the reorganization's biggest disappointment had the Committee been fully committed to it. But it wasn't. The members of the Committee were originally reluctant even to mention an AC proposal in its report. While this fact itself has been known, this chapter has shown the reason for the Committee's demur. Even though the Committee preferred making administrative agencies more efficient and responsive to the chief executive, it could not justify the promotion of its goals at the cost of judiciality and fairness. The Committee's challenge had gone down to defeat well before the publication of the report when its members decided against including any proposal on ACs.[82]

78 "Government Activities in the Regulation of Private Business Enterprises," in Select Committee to Investigate the Executive Agencies of the Government, *Investigation of Executive Agencies of the Government*, 75th Cong., 1st sess. (1937), S. Rep. 1275; *Washington Post*, June 7, 1937. On the debate and disagreements between the Committee and the Brookings Institution on executive reorganization, see Alasdair Roberts, "The Unassailable Principle: Why Luther Gulick Searched for a Science of Administration," *International Journal of Public Administration* 21 (1998): 255–259.

79 *Washington Post*, June 10, 1937.

80 *Washington Post*, June 11, 1937; S. 2700, 75th Congress; Polenberg, *Reorganizing Roosevelt's Government*, Ch. 3.

81 Joseph P. Harris, "The Progress of Administrative Reorganization in the Seventy-Fifth Congress," *American Political Science Review* 31 (1937): 862–870; Polenberg, *Reorganizing Roosevelt's Government*, 92.

82 Robert E. Cushman to Louis Brownlow, Mar. 24, 1937, Folder "M-Cushman, Robert," Box 18, PCAM Papers. Cushman offered a full rebuttal to the Brownlow Committee report

This analysis offers an important corrective to the dominant view on FDR's attempt to reorganize ACs and the Committee's part in it. Based on the Committee's "violent, unmeasured condemnation" of ACs and its seemingly radical proposal, the literature on reorganization has argued that the Committee was single-minded in its pursuit of the executivist administrative state. It should be clear, however, that the Committee not only took the judicialist paradigm seriously but also acquiesced to it despite its hostility to ACs. Believing that the only attainable goal under the circumstances was to prevent ACs from further proliferation, the Committee sought at least to stigmatize the commissions through criticism.[83]

The finding that the Committee was heavily influenced by the very judicialist paradigm it was challenging is a significant contribution to the scholarship on the Committee's position in the development of the field of public administration. Scholars such as Laurence Lynn and Alasdair Roberts have shattered the long-held myth that the Committee manifested the public administration orthodoxy. They substantiate their view by pointing out the intellectual heterogeneity of the contemporary public administration research, the conflict between the Committee and the Brookings Institution, and the disagreement between Committee members and staff. By pointing out the large presence of legal experts and their impact, this chapter has demonstrated that the Committee – and the then-fledgling discipline of public administration – took a balanced and flexible approach of accommodating the prevailing judicialist paradigm that had been developed by lawyers. As far as the reorganization of ACs was concerned, FDR was to blame for prematurely pushing a half-baked plan on a very delicate subject.[84]

As this case shows, an irony of the politics of ACs from the *Myers* decision to the Brownlow Committee report was that the presidents most openly hostile to ACs in the early twentieth century in the end made the biggest contribution to their institutionalization. Taft sought to bring ACs under the control of one of the three branches, both as the president and chief justice, and ended up helping to increase AC. Hoover and FDR assisted this, believing that *Myers* would be a binding precedent. In addition, FDR sowed the seeds of the restoration of AC autonomy by arbitrarily dismissing William Humphrey from the FTC. FDR's attack on the commissions after *Humphrey's* aided by leading public administration experts and its failure became the clearest reminder that the ACs were considered superior adjudicators to executive departments. The christening of the ACs by the president and the Committee, made to define their target, further entrenched "the independent regulatory commissions" in the US administrative

---

in the following article. "The Constitutional Status of the Independent Regulatory Commissions," *Cornell Law Quarterly* 24 (1939): 13–53, 163–197.

83 Louis L. Jaffe, "Invective and Investigation in Administrative Law," *Harvard Law Review* 52 (1939): 1242.

84 Laurence E. Lynn, Jr., "The Myth of the Bureaucratic Paradigm: What Traditional Public Administration Really Stood for," *Public Administration Review*, 61 (2001): 144–160; Alasdair Roberts, "Why the Brownlow Committee Failed: Neutrality and Partisanship in the Early Years of Public Administration," *Administration and Society* 28 (1996): 30–38; Roberts, "Unassailable Principle," 260.

state. The institutionalization of the ACs and the judicialization of the American state came full circle with FDR's executive reorganization and its failure, commemorating the semicentennial of the ICC.

The creation of ACs continued after the debacle of executive reorganization. The Brownlow Committee's stigmatization of ACs in its report was apparently insufficient in blocking further augmentation of the courtlike commissions. Sixteen months after the release of the report, the Civil Aeronautics Authority (CAA) was formed with the task of airspace regulation. The agency was created with the organizational scheme somewhat similar to the Committee's AC proposal. The five-member CAA was set up as an AC, but it also had an administrative officer answerable to the president. Two years later, however, it was split into two, with the adjudicatory section becoming the Civil Aeronautics Board (CAB), a full-fledged AC, while the rest of the CAA was absorbed into the Department of Commerce. While it has become increasingly popular to assign regulatory tasks to executive agencies, and no AC comparable to the "Big Six" – the ICC, CAB, FCC, FTC, FPC, and SEC – in prestige and authority has appeared since then, ACs have continued to thrive as an established category of government body.[85] ACs – now IRCs – are in the US administrative state to stay.

85 Joseph P. Harris to Clinton W. Hester, Dec. 2, 1937, Folder "M-Hester, Clinton W.," Box 19, PCAM Papers; Louis Brownlow to Franklin D. Roosevelt, Oct. 14, 1938, OF2955, Official File, Franklin D. Roosevelt Papers, Franklin D. Roosevelt Presidential Library. Westwood and Bennett, "Civil Aeronautics Act"; Bernard Schwartz, *Professor and the Commissions*, 23.

Conclusion

"The administrative process is, in essence, our generation's answer to the inadequacy of the judicial and the legislative processes." James Landis thus justified the growth of administrative agencies and their discretional policy implementation in *The Administrative Process*, published in 1938. In his view, the United States could no longer be governed without them, and the examples of agency activity in his highly acclaimed work were without exception those of IRCs, which "evolved from the very concept of administrative power."[1] Landis's predilection for the commissions is not surprising; he was a drafter of the 1933 and 1934 securities acts and a former member of the FTC and SEC. He also chaired the latter commission before recently returning to Harvard as the dean of the law school. Still, the declaration by a leading authority in administrative law and former counsel to FDR of the prominence of IRCs in US public administration – the book dismissed the Brownlow Committee's attack on the commissions as hysterical "numerology" blindly dwelling on the idea of tripartite government – symbolized the firm establishment of the commissions as a category of US agencies.[2]

While Landis had much faith in the fairness of IRCs, in his mind their true importance lay elsewhere. The development of the commissions was part of the American response to the rise of industrialism and democracy, and their mission was in infusing *efficiency* into governmental regulation, which was "the desperate need."[3] This could be achieved only by injecting policy expertise lacking in the government by judges, who tended to be "jacks-of-all-trades and master of none." Criticizing the attack on the exponential increase in the number of ACs

1 Landis, *Administrative Process*, 46, 111.

2 Landis, *Administrative Process*, 47; Ritchie, *Landis*, 85–87; Donald R. Brand, "The President as Chief Administrator: James Landis and the Brownlow Report," *Political Science Quarterly* 123 (2008): 69–93; Reuel E. Schiller, "The Era of Deference: Courts, Expertise, and the Emergence of New Deal Administrative Law," *Michigan Law Review* 106 (2007): 398–441. Landis was in approval of Cushman's analysis of the IRCs. James M. Landis to I. E. Drabkin, Apr. 17, 1941, Folder "Administrative Process," Box 171, James M. Landis Papers, Manuscript Division, Library of Congress.

3 Landis, *Administrative Process*, 7, 24. Also see Jessica Wang, "Imagining the Administrative State: Legal Pragmatism, Securities Regulation, and New Deal Liberalism," *Journal of Policy History* 17 (2005): 271–276.

since the Wilson administration, Landis argued that new regulations must accompany new agencies with relevant expertise.[4] There was a clear intent behind his emphasis on the merits of administrative agencies as promoters of government efficiency and expertise. By the time Landis gave the Storrs Lectures at Yale that formed the basis of the book, the biggest threat to IRCs and the judicialist state was no longer the executivist president and public administration scholars; it was powerful lawyers who resented agencies out of their extreme judicialism. Dismayed by the continued expansion of agency activities during the New Deal, the ABA's Special Committee on Administrative Law searched for a way to end what it saw as the illegitimate use of judicial power. The most popular suggestion was the creation of an appellate-level administrative court conducting adjudications in place of agencies.[5]

Soon after FDR's initial legislative effort for executive reorganization based on the Brownlow Committee report, the ABA began preparation for a direct attack on administrative agencies. Allying with congressional conservatives opposing FDR and the New Deal, the ABA launched its first fairness-oriented offensive against the IRC-centered judicialist administrative state. Its central figure was Roscoe Pound, Landis's predecessor at Harvard who had recently stunned the legal profession by transforming from an intellectual guardian of administrative tribunals into their worst enemy. He completed the conversion by assuming the chair of the ABA committee in 1938, determined to defeat "administrative absolutism."[6] After realizing the infeasibility of making the proposed administrative court handle agency hearings – the number of administrative adjudications was already estimated to be at least several times larger than that of judicial proceedings – Pound and his colleagues shifted their goal to turning agencies into de facto courts. Other reform ideas such as making judicial courts appoint experienced lawyers as administrative adjudicators were also considered.[7]

4 Landis, *Administrative Process*, 24–25, 31, 135.

5 White, *Constitution and the New Deal*, 114–126; O. R. McGuire, "Proposed Reforms in Judicial Reviews of Federal Administrative Action," *American Bar Association Journal* 19 (1933): 471–474; O. R. McGuire, "Sailing Close to the Wind, or the Need for a Federal Administrative Court," *American Bar Association Journal* 22 (1936): 853–859, 870. The administrative court bill drafted by the special committee was submitted to the 74th Congress but was not taken up. Robert M. Cooper, "The Proposed United States Administrative Court," *Michigan Law Review* 35 (1936): 193–252.

6 Arthur T. Vanderbilt, "The Place of the Administrative Tribunal in Our Legal System," *American Bar Association Journal* 24 (1938): 267–273; American Bar Association, "Report of the Special Committee on Administrative Law," 331–368; Ernst, *Tocqueville's Nightmare*, 108–115; Horwitz, *Transformation*, 217–220. Some authors emphasize continuity in Pound's thought, that he had always been critical of administrative adjudication or "executive justice." Peter Woll, *Administrative Law: The Informal Process* (Berkeley: University of California Press, 1963), 12–15; Joseph Postell, "The Anti-New Deal Progressive: Roscoe Pound's Alternative Administrative State," *Review of Politics* 74 (2012): 53–85; Grisinger, *Unwieldy American State*, 20–22.

7 Landis, *Administrative Process*, 19; Ernst, *Tocqueville's Nightmare*, 119–122.

Landis's defense of administrative tribunals in *The Administrative Process* was written against such a backdrop. Alarmed by the ABA's scheme to further judicialize agencies, he began his account of agencies by emphatically rejecting the idea that they were "merely courts." He went on to explain in detail how agency activities differed from those of the three constitutional branches and why multiple powers of the government must be exercised by a single body. Landis believed that the IRCs struck the best balance between efficiency and fairness in state building, and they ought to stay that way.[8]

In 1939, congressional conservatives submitted an administrative procedure reform bill drafted by the ABA committee. If enacted, the bill would have judicialized administrative procedures to the extent of paralyzing the agencies. Anyone aggrieved by an agency decision could ask for a formal hearing. Single-headed agencies were to organize an intra-agency board with three members for such adjudication, and at least one of its members had to be a lawyer. Curiously, however, many regulatory bodies, mostly IRCs, were exempted from the application of the bill, which signified the conservatives' acceptance of judicialized procedures – and the political clout – of these agencies.[9] Such a radical bill straitjacketing the administrative state would have had no chance of passage in FDR's first term. But there now was a sizable conservative opposition to the president in Congress, much of which owing to his abortive court-packing plan, the failed "purge" of conservative congressional candidates in the 1938 Democratic primaries, and the economic downturn of 1937. As a result, the Walter-Logan bill passed both houses late in 1940. Roosevelt vetoed it, stating in his message to Congress that the ongoing work of the committee headed by the attorney general studying administrative procedures ought to be completed before any reform could be seriously discussed.[10]

The series of attacks on the IRC-centered administrative state from the 1930s, the executivist one driven by FDR almost immediately followed by that from extreme judicialists, threw the intermediate, judicialist nature of the modern US administrative state into sharp relief; the same state that was too inefficient for executivists lacked procedural fairness in the eyes of extreme judicialists. In the legislative fight for the Walter-Logan bill, the same president who had sought to departmentalize IRCs a few years before ended up praising their efficiency in his veto message. The "administrative tribunals" that had originated with the ICC were characterized by "simple and non-technical hearings" and "informal

8 James M. Landis, "Crucial Issues in Administrative Law," *Harvard Law Review* 53 (1940): 1077–1102; Landis, *Administrative Process*, 19, 46.

9 For the political fight toward the adoption of the APA, see Shepherd, "Fierce Compromise"; James Edward Brazier, "Who Controls the Administrative State? Congress and the President Adopt the Administrative Procedure Act of 1946." (Ph.D. diss., Michigan State University, 1993); Grisinger, *Unwieldy American State*, 62–64.

10 Susan Dunn, *Roosevelt's Purge: How FDR Fought to Change the Democratic Party* (Cambridge, MA: Harvard University Press, 2012); Grisinger, *Unwieldy American State*, 65–72; Joanna L. Grisinger, "Law in Action: The Attorney General's Committee on Administrative Procedure," *Journal of Policy History* 20 (2008): 379–418.

proceedings." As such, the agencies supplemented the judiciary by "deciding issues on quantity production basis" and constituted the "very heart of modern reform administration."[11]

With the failure of an override, the battle over agency procedures was put to rest as the nation deepened its involvement in World War II. The conservative lawyers' quest for further judicialization of administrative procedures did not end with the Walter-Logan bill, though. They were much opposed to state intervention during the war, and their successive legislative efforts bore fruit in June 1946 in the Administrative Procedure Act, which set the standard procedures for all administrative agencies. In contrast to the tumultuous legislative battle earlier in the decade, the APA passed the two houses without fanfare by voice vote, and President Harry Truman signed it despite his strong belief in government efficiency.[12] With FDR's death in 1945, the issue of administrative state judicialization had lost much of its political heat. Also, it was widely thought that the APA, a compromise measure of the plans offered by the attorney general's committee generally supportive of the status quo and the conservative ABA, was essentially a codification of procedures already in use at major agencies.[13]

Although it did not immediately lead to substantial change, the APA, "an act to improve the administration of justice by prescribing *fair* administrative procedure" [emphasis added], nonetheless was a milestone in administrative state judicialization, for three reasons. First, Section Five of the act prescribed the requirements of formal hearings. Although formal hearings were to be used only when required by a statute or selected by the agency itself, the law opened the way for all agencies to conduct courtlike hearings. Second, the APA provided for examiners to preside over formal hearings. While many agencies had already hired examiners, the statute further institutionalized the office by limiting their duty to formal adjudication and reinforcing their autonomy from other agency officials. Third, in their search for model administrative procedures, the act's drafters heavily relied on the "better practices" of IRCs, especially those of the ICC and FTC.[14] This made much sense; unlike executive

11 Franklin D. Roosevelt, "Veto of a Bill Regulating Administrative Agencies," Dec. 8, 1940. Online by Gerhard Peters and John T. Woolley, The American Presidency Project, www.presidency.ucsb.edu/node/209411.

12 Grisinger, *Unwieldy American State*, Ch. 1; William E. Pemberton, *Bureaucratic Politics: Executive Reorganization during the Truman Administration* (Columbia: University of Missouri Press, 1979), 3. On the wartime state building see Bartholomew H. Sparrow, *From the Outside In: World War II and the American State* (Princeton: Princeton University Press, 1996).

13 Grisinger, *Unwieldy American State*, 11, 59, 61, 76–77; Brazier, "Fierce Compromise"; Woll, *Administrative Law*, 20–21; Reuel E. Schiller, "Reining-in the Administrative State: World War II and the Decline of Expert Administration," in *Total War and the Law: The American Home Front in World War II*, ed. Daniel Ernst and Victor Jew (Westport, CT: Praeger, 2002), 185–206; Peter Woll, "Administrative Law in the Seventies," *Public Administration Review* 32 (1972): 559–560; Vincent M. Barnett, Jr., "Judicialization of the Administrative Process," *Public Administration Review* 8 (1948): 126–133.

14 Musolf, *Federal Examiners*; Bradford Ross, "Federal Power Commission Practice and Procedure as Affected by the Administrative Procedure Act of 1946," in *The Federal Administrative*

departments that had been rebuked by the judiciary for inadequate adjudication, the procedures at IRCs withstood, however narrowly at times, judicial scrutiny throughout the 1930s. The APA at once perpetuating IRC-like procedures and vastly expanding their scope of application further judicialized the US administrative state.[15]

The politics of state judicialization enjoyed a rare equilibrium over the next decade. The atmosphere at the time was unmistakably in favor of maintaining agency judiciality. This owed much to the judicialist mood in Congress. Strongly committed to subordinating agencies to the supremacy of law, Congress engaged in building what David Rosenbloom calls "legislative-centered public administration." While the legislature by no means neglected efficiency and coordination, it was intent on securing agency compliance to such values as fairness and freedom from government intrusion.[16] The ABA kept on pushing for the continued judicialization of administrative procedures. The Supreme Court also occasionally signaled its interest in securing "the fundamentals of fair play" in administrative policy making, beginning with the 1940 *Pottsville* decision.[17]

It was not just the mostly judicialist lawmakers and the judiciary that stood behind courtlike agencies. Proposed by the Eightieth Congress in 1947 with a Republican majority and jointly appointed by Congress and Truman, the Commission on Organization of the Executive Branch of the Government headed by ex-president Hoover initially sought to devise a reorganization plan that would radically roll back the New Deal. But after the reelection of President Truman the following year, through whom the Commission's proposals would be submitted

---

Procedure Act and the Administrative Agencies, ed. George Warren (New York: New York University School of Law, 1947), 171; Grisinger, *Unwieldy American State*, 82.

15 Verkuil, "Emerging Concept"; Grisinger, *Unwieldy American State*, 22–24; Marian C. McKenna, *Franklin Roosevelt and the Great Constitutional War: The Court-Packing Crisis of 1937* (New York: Fordham University Press, 2002), 193–194; *Jones v. SEC*, 298 U.S. 1 (1936); *National Labor Relations Board v. Jones & Laughlin Steel Corporation*, 301 U.S. 1 (1937); Ernst, *Tocqueville's Nightmare*, 68–69; Charles H. Koch, Jr., "James Landis: The Administrative Process," *Administrative Law Review* 48 (1996): 426; The Attorney General's Committee on Administrative Procedure had concluded that the administrative adjudication, "far from being an encroachment upon the rule of law, is an extension of it." Attorney General's Committee on Administrative Procedure, *Final Report*, 77th Cong., 1st sess. (1941), S. Doc. 8, 2.

16 Grisinger, *Unwieldy American State*, 12, 108; Rosenbloom, *Building a Legislative-Centered Public Administration*, 36–37. The lawmakers' continued adherence to agency judiciality in the period was expressed in extreme form in the Taft-Hartley Act of 1947. Known for its anti-labor provisions, the act also separated the NLRB's adjudicatory and prosecutorial functions, making the board even more passive and courtlike. Ida Klaus, "The Taft-Hartley Experiment in Separation of NLRB Functions," *Industrial and Labor Relations Review* 11 (1958): 371–390.

17 Jeffrey S. Lubbers, "The ABA Section of Administrative Law and Regulatory Practice: From Objector to Protector of the APA," *Administrative Law Review* 50 (1998): 157–171; Thomas O. McGarity, "Regulatory Reform and the Positive State: An Historical Overview," *Administrative Law Review* 38 (1986): 412–415; Grisinger, *Unwieldy American State*, 226–227; *FCC v. Pottsville Broadcasting Co.*, 309 U.S. 134 (1940), at 143–144.

to Congress now with a Democratic majority, the (first) Hoover Commission shifted its goal to creating an efficient, president-centered executive branch. While the commission's proposals unveiled in 1949 had much in common with those of the Brownlow Committee, the two advisory committees' views on the IRCs differed substantially. The Hoover Commission did criticize IRCs for their inefficiency and pointed out deficiencies in individual commissions in its report. It still refrained from offering a critique of formal administrative procedures, and the commission's committee on IRCs declared that IRCs had "a proper place in the machinery of our Government." Truman successfully proposed several IRC reorganization plans based on the Hoover Commission's recommendations, but they stopped short of significantly dejudicializing IRCs.[18]

Unlike many of his predecessors, President Dwight Eisenhower was a conservative opposed to the strong administrative state. He saw little hope in dismantling it, however. As a result, the two advisory bodies on executive reorganization during his administration, the President's Advisory Committee for Government Organization and the second Hoover Commission both shied away from proposing a major IRC reform despite expressing an executivist preference. If anything, the lawyers who worked for the advisory boards enthusiastically argued in favor of further state judicialization. The second Hoover Commission's Task Force on Legal Services and Procedure went so far as to state that "[e]fficiency in the administrative process has no value unless the end result is due process and fair dealing for the individual citizen" and proposed the creation of an administrative court to which the agencies' adjudicatory functions were to be transferred.[19]

Despite such support from the three branches and their advisers, the judiciality of the US administrative state eroded in the long run. Most importantly, administrative adjudication became more informal. The change had begun well before World War II. A staff report to the Attorney General's Committee on Administrative Procedure already stated that "informal procedures constitute the vast bulk of administrative adjudication and are truly the life blood of the administrative process." Courtlike adjudication by top agency officials was considered a rarity by the mid-twentieth century.[20] In the 1970s, it was estimated that ninety

18 Commission on Organization of the Executive Branch of the Government, *Regulatory Commissions* (Washington, DC: Government Printing Office, 1949), 3; Pemberton, *Bureaucratic Politics*, Ch. 7; Grisinger, *Unwieldy American State*, Ch. 4. The modesty of the proposals partly owed to the fact that many of them came from James Landis. Ritchie, *Landis*, 175–176; Arnold, *Making the Managerial Presidency*, 146–147.

19 Robert Griffith, "Dwight D. Eisenhower and the Corporate Commonwealth," *American History Review* 87 (1982): 87–122; Grisinger, *Unwieldy American State*, 199, 215–217, 224; Woll, *Administrative Law*, 167; Commission on Organization of the Executive Branch of the Government, Task Force on Legal Services and Procedure, *Report on Legal Services and Procedure* (Washington, DC: Government Printing Office, 1955), 138.

20 Woll, *Administrative Law*, 25; Attorney General's Committee on Administrative Procedure, *Final Report*, 35; Rohr, *To Run a Constitution*, 158; Walter Gellhorn, *Federal Administrative Proceedings* (Baltimore: Johns Hopkins Press, 1941), Chs. 2 and 3. For figures on major agencies in 1940, see Chamberlin, Dowling, and Hays, *Judicial Function*, 9, n. 7; *Ramspeck v. Federal Trial Examiners Conference*, 345 U.S. 128 (1953), at 130.

percent of adjudication for individuals was informal. In addition, agencies' preferred mode of policy making changed from quasi-judicial adjudication to rulemaking. The enactment of the Federal Register Act in 1935 requiring agencies to publish their rules in the Federal Register signaled the transformation. While it had been customary for agencies to make rules through formal hearings until the mid-century, they have done so much less often since the 1960s. The Supreme Court decision in *United States v. Florida East Coast Railway Co.* in 1973 allowing agencies to use informal procedures unless otherwise instructed by written law was a catalyst.[21]

Why did such dejudicialization take place? As easily imagined, the exponential growth of agency work after World War II made extensive use of formal hearings unrealistic, even with the aid of hearing examiners. In 1963, Sen. Edward Long (D-MO), chair of the Judiciary Subcommittee on Administrative Practice and Procedure, assessed that administrative procedures were "tremendously complicated, often very lengthy, and usually terribly expensive." But pressure from workload was only part of the reason. As illustrated in the attacks on IRCs from the 1950s, agency judiciality itself became increasingly seen as ineffective from the pluralist perspective that was growing in popularity.[22] Both academics such as Samuel Huntington and Merver Bernstein and practitioners, including former members of IRCs, pointed out the commissions' vulnerability to industry capture and denounced their inefficiency, lack of expertise, and unresponsiveness to the public. According to the critics, case-by-case adjudication allowed the commissions to hand down inconsistent decisions sympathetic to regulated industries.[23] Upon resigning in disgust from the CAB in 1959 citing what he thought was the

21 Warner W. Gardner, "The Procedures by Which Informal Action Is Taken," *Administrative Law Review* 24 (1972): 155–166; Verkuil, "Study of Informal Adjudication Procedures"; McCraw, *Prophets*, 284–286; Levy and Shapiro, "Decline of the Trial," 481; Grisinger, *Unwieldy American State*, 253–255; Cane, *Controlling Administrative Power*, 317–318; *United States v. Florida East Coast Railway Co.*, 410 U.S. 224 (1973); Aaron L. Nielson, "In Defense of Formal Rulemaking," *Ohio State Law Journal* 75 (2014): 237–292; Barnett, "How the Supreme Court Derailed Formal Rulemaking"; William West, "Administrative Rulemaking: An Old and Emerging Literature," *Public Administration Review* 65 (2005): 655–668.

22 Levy and Shapiro, "Decline of the Trial," 479; Freedman, *Crisis and Legitimacy*, 161; Edward V. Long, "Administrative Proceedings: Their Time and Cost Can Be Cut Down," *American Bar Association Journal* 49 (1963): 833; Reuel E. Schiller, "Enlarging the Administrative Polity: Administrative Law and the Changing Definition of Pluralism, 1945–1970," *Vanderbilt Law Review* 53 (2000): 1410–1416; Theodore J. Lowi, *The End of Liberalism: The Second Republic of the United States*, 2nd ed. (New York: W. W. Norton, 1979), esp. 302–305.

23 Huntington, "Marasmus of the ICC"; Bernstein, *Regulating Business*; Kolko, *Triumph of Conservatism*; Grant McConnell, *Private Power and American Democracy* (New York: Alfred A. Knopf, 1966); Schwartz, *Professor and the Commissions*; Grisinger, *Unwieldy American State*, 227–243; Graham K. Wilson, *The Politics of Safety and Health: Occupational Safety and Health in the United States and Britain* (Oxford: Clarendon Press, 1985), 21–23; Bruce A. Ackerman and William T. Hassler, *Clean Coal/Dirty Air* (New Haven: Yale University Press, 1981). Also see Louis L. Jaffe, "Effective Limits"; Anne M. Kornhauser, *Debating the*

board's structural malaise, Louis Hector submitted a memorandum to President Eisenhower recommending the separation of the IRCs' executive and judicial functions so that the commissions could perform different tasks better. Former members of the FTC and FCC made similar suggestions.[24]

Taking advantage of IRCs' unpopularity, the chief executives became more aggressive in seeking executivist restructuring of commissions. Shortly after his election to the presidency, John F. Kennedy requested an IRC reform plan from James Landis, himself disillusioned with the commissions. Landis also came to believe that rulemaking was superior to quasi-judicial adjudication in bringing policy consistency and enabling long-term planning.[25] In addition to the organization of the ACUS, his report of December 1960 proposed the centralization of operation within IRCs to their chairs – many were by this time appointed by the president – together with the lengthening of the commissioners' terms. In his view, such a reconfiguration would improve both efficiency and interagency policy coordination without sacrificing IRCs' core judiciality. He was appointed special presidential assistant and given the mission of carrying out the proposals. Landis's effort fell victim to poor legislative maneuvering, however, and he left the administration in September 1961 in the wake of several personal scandals.[26]

While subsequent presidential efforts to reorganize IRCs would also prove unsuccessful, the commissions' dejudicialization continued. The proportion of lawyers among commissioners slowly decreased, as economists and scientists

---

American State: Liberal Anxieties and the New Leviathan, 1930–1970 (Philadelphia: University of Pennsylvania Press, 2015).

24 Woll, *Administrative Law*, 170–171; Emmette S. Redford, *National Regulatory Commissions: Need for a New Look* (College Park: University of Maryland, 1959); Louis J. Hector, "Problems of the CAB and the Independent Regulatory Commissions," *Yale Law Journal* 69 (1960): 931–964; Newton Minow, "Suggestions for Improvement of the Administrative Process," *Administrative Law Review* 15 (1963): 146–153; William L. Cary, *Politics and the Regulatory Agencies* (New York: McGraw-Hill, 1967). Philip Elman, "Administrative Reform of the Federal Trade Commission," *Georgetown Law Journal* 59 (1971): 777–860; Richard A. Harris and Sidney M. Milkis, *The Politics of Regulatory Change: A Tale of Two Agencies*, 2nd ed. (New York: Oxford University Press, 1996), 61, 66; Brian Balogh, "Reorganizing the Organizational Synthesis: Federal-Professional Relations in Modern America," *Studies in American Political Development* 5 (1991): 179; Brian Balogh, *Chain Reaction: Expert Debate and Public Participation in American Commercial Nuclear Power 1945–1975* (New York: Cambridge University Press, 1994).

25 Donald A. Ritchie, "Reforming the Regulatory Process: Why James Landis Changed His Mind," *Business History Review* 54 (1980): 283–302; Mariano-Florentino Cuéller, "James Landis and the Dilemmas of Administrative Government," *George Washington Law Review* 83 (2015): 1330–1357; Pestritto, "Progressive Origins," 34–36; Cane, *Administrative Tribunals and Adjudication*, 76; Grisinger, *Unwieldy American State*, 246–249. For a thorough analysis of the report, see Carl McFarland, "Landis' Report: The Voice of One Crying in the Darkness," *Virginia Law Review* 47 (1961): 373–438.

26 James Landis, *Report on Regulatory Agencies to the President-Elect* (Washington, DC: Government Printing Office, 1960); James M. Landis, "The Administrative Process: The Third Decade," *American Bar Association Journal* 47 (1961): 135–139; Richie, *Landis*, 177–186; Milton M. Carrow, "Dean Landis and the Regulatory Process," *George Washington Law Review* 29 (1961): 718–738; McCraw, *Prophets*, 207.

made their way into IRCs. With a few exceptions such as the NLRB, the number of examiners hired by IRCs steadily dropped, even when compared to some executive departments such as the Department of Labor. Such a change reflected the dwindling of formal hearings at the commissions.[27] Presidents have also managed to influence the workings of IRCs, including informally securing the resignations of the commissioners. As the two political parties became ideologically polarized from the late twentieth century, IRC commissioners themselves became more prone to fighting partisan and ideological battles. The independence of IRCs has been challenged through litigation in such cases as *Morrison v. Olson* and *Free Enterprise Fund v. Public Company Accounting Oversight Board*, although so far without success. It is therefore understandable that today's political scientists fail to recognize the IRCs' difference from executive agencies. America's judicialized administrative state organized around IRCs making policy through formal adjudication is now in the past.[28]

Diminishing administrative state judiciality, however, did not bring its demise. The formal hearing has not just remained an established mode of administrative decision-making but has expanded in certain policy areas. This is most visible in the dramatic increase of subordinate officers at agencies specializing in court-like hearings. After a rocky start, the hearing examiners rapidly gained visibility at many agencies. Their total number increased from 196 in 1947 to 1,068 in 1979.[29] Importantly, the Supreme Court came to respect them. In the 1951 ruling in the *Universal Camera* case reviewing a decision by the NLRB, the Court took into account the examiner's view that members of the board had overridden. In 1972, the Civil Service Commission renamed examiners as administrative law judges, recognizing their autonomy and the gravity of their mission. Congress confirmed this in the revision of the APA in 1978. As already noted, there also is

27 David Zaring, "Enforcement Adjudication at the SEC," in *Administrative Law from the Inside Out: Essays on Themes in the Work of Jerry L. Mashaw*, ed. Nicholas Parrillo (New York: Cambridge University Press, 2017), 271–294; McCraw, *Prophets*, 136–137; Florence Ann Heffron, "The Independent Regulatory Commissioners." (Ph.D. diss., University of Colorado, 1971); Grisinger, *Unwieldy American State*, 256–258; Jeffrey S. Lubbers, "A Unified Corps of ALJs: A Proposal to Test the Idea at the Federal Level," *Judicature* 65 (1981): 268.

28 Paul R. Verkuil, "Jawboning Administrative Agencies: Ex Parte Contacts by the White House," *Columbia Law Review* 80 (1980): 943–989; *Morrison v. Olson*, 487 U.S. 654 (1988); *Free Enterprise Fund v. Public Company Accounting Oversight Board*, 561 U.S. 477 (2010); Alvis, Bailey, and Taylor, *Removal Power*, 2–6 and Ch. 6; Berger and Edles, *Independent Agencies*, Ch. 3; Bressman and Thompson, "The Future of Agency Independence," 599–672; Ernst, *Tocqueville's Nightmare*, 7; Neal Devins and David E. Lewis, "Not-So Independent Agencies: Party Polarization and the Limits of Institutional Design," *Boston University Law Review* 88 (2008): 459–498; Peter L. Strauss, "The Place of Agencies in Government: Separation of Powers and the Fourth Branch," *Columbia Law Review* 84 (1984): 573–669.

29 Ralph F. Fuchs, "The Hearing Examiner Fiasco under the Administrative Procedure Act," *Harvard Law Review* 63 (1950): 737–768; Thomas C. Mans, "Selecting the 'Hidden Judiciary': How the Merit Process Works in Choosing Administrative Law Judges (Part I)," *Judicature* 63 (1980): 64.

a variety of non-ALJ adjudicators, or administrative judges, who do not enjoy the autonomy and status protection of ALJs but conduct courtlike adjudications.[30]

As is clear from the above, the judiciality of agencies has not been entirely lost. The administrative state's orientation toward fairness is still strong. In the face of strong criticism against regulatory capture from the 1950s, securing the participation of relevant actors grew in importance as a criterion of procedural fairness. As a result, some informal procedures such as notice-and-comment rulemaking came to be heavily used in order to ensure the involvement of the public. The creation of the Freedom of Information Act in 1966 also had the aim of controlling agencies through securing public access to their information. Court-like adjudication still thrives in areas where it is expected to best facilitate the participation of parties involved, and requirements for standing were loosened to expand participation.[31]

The Supreme Court made this point in the *Goldberg v. Kelly* decision in 1970, declaring that welfare service sustaining the recipients' living could be terminated only after an evidentiary hearing. Although the Court noted that such hearings "need not take the form of a judicial or quasi-judicial trial," formal hearings became the reference point in the "due process revolution" set off by the ruling that led to modification of procedures at many agencies.[32] While some of the Court's later decisions, such as *Mathews v. Eldridge* in 1976, have been more sympathetic to efficiency consideration in determining the degree of procedural formality, the judiciary has clearly viewed administrative procedures "as a function of the values of fairness, efficiency, and satisfaction."[33]

30 *Universal Camera Corp. v. NLRB*, 340 U.S. 474 (1951); Gerald M. Pops, "The Judicialization of Federal Administrative Law Judges: Implications for Policymaking," *West Virginia Law Review* 81 (1979): 169–206; Charles H. Koch, Jr., "Policymaking by the Administrative Judiciary," *Alabama Law Review* 56 (2005): 693–740; Jeffrey A. Wertkin, "Overruled: The Legalistic and Managerial Models of Administrative Adjudications." (Ph.D. diss., Georgetown University, 2008).

31 David L. Shapiro, "The Choice of Rulemaking or Adjudication in the Development of Administrative Policy," *Harvard Law Review* 78 (1965): 921–972; Richard B. Stewart, "The Reformation of American Administrative Law," *Harvard Law Review* 88 (1975): 1667–1813; Daniel B. Rodriguez and Barry R. Weingast, "The 'Reformation of Administrative Law' Revisited," *Journal of Law, Economics, and Organization* 31 (2015): 782–807; Michael Schudson, *The Rise of the Right to Know: Politics and the Culture of Transparency, 1945–1975* (Cambridge, MA: Harvard University Press, 2015); Robinson, *American Bureaucracy*, 126–129.

32 Cornelius M. Kerwin and Scott R. Furlong, *Rulemaking: How Government Agencies Write Law and Make Policy*, 4th ed. (Washington, DC: CQ Press, 2011), 175–180; Reuel E. Schiller, "Enlarging the Administrative Polity," 1434, 1444–1446; *Goldberg v. Kelly*, 397 U.S. 254 (1970), at 266; Mashaw, *Due Process in the Administrative State*; Mashaw et al., *Social Security Hearings and Appeals*.

33 *Mathews v. Eldridge*, 424 U.S. 319 (1976); Verkuil, "Emerging Concept," 280; Schwartz, "Administrative Law: The Third Century"; Levy and Shapiro, "Decline of the Trial," 494–502; Robinson, *American Bureaucracy*, 116–125; Friendly, "'Some Kind of Hearing'"; Willam T. Gormley, Jr., *Taming the Bureaucracy: Muscles, Prayers, and Other Strategies* (Princeton: Princeton University Press, 1989), 98–103; Guyora Binder, "Twentieth-Century

Agency autonomy has also been respected. The IRCs have had a smaller presence in social regulation from the 1960s; aside from some exceptions such as the Consumer Product Safety Commission created in 1972 to regulate consumer products, most new "independent" agencies such as the Environmental Protection Agency are not autonomous from the chief executive. While today's presidents certainly wish the IRCs to be aligned with other agencies, they have so far refrained from forcing the commissions into submission. In introducing the regulatory review of agency rulemaking by the Office of Informational and Regulatory Affairs, created in 1980 in the executive office as part of its effort at deregulation, the Reagan administration left independent agencies, including IRCs, out of the program. Although later administrations inherited and in some ways expanded such a scheme to aggressively oversee agencies regardless of party affiliation, they have so far also decided against abandoning the institutional distinction between executive and independent agencies and only encouraged the latter to voluntarily join the executivist regulatory scheme.[34]

The American administrative state has taken a decidedly executivist turn since the New Deal, but it has not become a Weberian state. The "hidden judiciary" continues to thrive, despite complaints of inefficiency and inconsistency. While the administrative state may no longer be sufficiently judicialized to impress many lawyers, it still stands between the positions taken by executivists and extreme judicialists. After his first presidential victory in 1968, Richard Nixon asked Roy Ash, a successful businessman, to create and head the President's Advisory Council on Executive Organization. Among other recommendations, the Ash Council produced a separate report on major IRCs in 1971. The document harshly criticized the commissions and recommended their reorganization into single-headed agencies. In the executivist council's view, the commissions were not just inefficient and unresponsive to both Congress and the president but *overjudicialized*, despite all the dejudicialization the commissions already had gone through since World War II.[35]

Legal Metaphors for Self and Society," in *Looking Back at Law's Century*, ed. Robert A. Kagan, Bryant Garth, and Austin Sarat (Ithaca: Cornell University Press, 2002), 165–166.

34 Eisner, *Regulatory Politics in Transition*, Ch. 6; Joanna Grisinger, "The (Long) Administrative Century: Progressive Models of Governance," in *The Progressives' Century: Political Reform, Constitutional Government, and the Modern American State*, ed. Stephen Skowronek, Stephen M. Engel, and Bruce Ackerman (New Haven: Yale University Press, 2016), 371–373; Moreno, "Presidential Coordination"; Alvis, Bailey, and Taylor, *Removal Power*, 190–191; Berger and Edles, *Independent Agencies*, 180–191; Eisner et al., *Contemporary Regulatory Policy*, 45–60; Elena Kagan, "Presidential Administration," *Harvard Law Review* 114 (2001): 2245–2385; Cary Coglianese, "Improving Regulatory Analysis at Independent Agencies," *American University Law Review* 67 (2018): 733–767. Also see Cass R. Sunstein, *After the Rights Revolution: Reconceiving the Regulatory State* (Cambridge, MA: Harvard University Press, 1990).

35 Arnold, *Making the Managerial Presidency*, 288–289; President's Advisory Council on Executive Reorganization, *A New Regulatory Framework: Report on Selected Independent Regulatory Agencies* (Washington, DC: Government Printing Office, 1971); Roger G. Noll, *Reforming Regulation: An Evaluation of the Ash Council Proposals* (Washington, DC: Brookings Institution Press, 1971). But also see Robinson, "Making of Administrative Policy";

The current political debate over the legitimacy of the US administrative state, however, clearly indicates that the state also is not judicialized enough to satisfy extreme judicialists. Since the late twentieth century, academics and lawyers drawing on the strict-constructionist reading of the Constitution have argued that administrative agencies exercising multiple powers of the government infringe on both the separation of powers and supremacy of law. The preceding loss of state judiciality, coupled with the judiciary's increasing deference to agency discretion as illustrated in the 1984 *Chevron* Supreme Court decision, undoubtedly set the stage for their fierce criticism that the administrative state should be dismantled or at least severely constrained.[36]

While extreme judicialists have followed a similar line of argument over the twentieth century, the contemporary debate is distinct in its close attention to history. Philip Hamburger has declared administrative law utterly unlawful after carefully tracing the history of the common law from its English origins. Joseph Postell has written a book-length history of the US bureaucracy from the founding era and argues that the constitutional principles including the separation of powers should and could serve as constraints upon the administrative state. These authors agree that the full-scale administrative state emerged in the United States in the early twentieth century when the progressives accepted the European notion of the bureaucratic state in promoting regulatory policies. Following the conventional wisdom on the cause of state judicialization, they argue that lawyers among the progressives played the key role in transplanting the Weberian state into the United States.[37]

But administrative states are not created equal, and they change over time. The critics of the US administrative state tend to equate it with the executivist, Weberian state. The fact that American administrative agencies operate differently from judicial courts, however, does not immediately mean they constitute a Weberian state. This book has shown that the modern American state has more domestic and judicialist origins than the above authors suggest. The IRCs took the form they did because the political elites greatly cared about the American institutional combination of the separation of powers and the common law. It is difficult to see the US administrative state organized around courtlike IRC as simply a European import. The modern American state emerged as a strongly judicialist one, and it has not lost its foundational orientation toward procedural fairness. Although a debate over the legitimacy of the US administrative state is outside the scope of

---

Glen O. Robinson, "On Reorganizing the Independent Regulatory Agencies," *Virginia Law Review* 57 (1971): 947–995.

36 *Chevron U.S.A., Inc. v. Natural Resources Defense Council, Inc.*, 467 U.S. 837 (1984).

37 Gary Lawson, "Rise and Rise of the Administrative State," *Harvard Law Review* 107 (1994): 1231–1254; Richard A. Epstein, *The Classical Liberal Constitution: The Uncertain Quest for Limited Government* (Cambridge, MA: Harvard University Press, 2014); Philip Hamburger, *Is Administrative Law Unlawful?* (Chicago: University of Chicago Press, 2014), esp. Chs. 22–24; Postell, *Bureaucracy in America*.

this book, its historical development should be taken into account in any discussion of the topic.[38]

A recent development in administrative state building exemplifies that the American state is not an imitation of its overseas counterparts; quasi-judicial agencies similar to IRCs have been popping up around the globe since the 1980s. The diffusion of regulation by independent agencies, often called "American-style regulation" in Europe, actually has a long tradition. A notable example is antitrust policy; the FTC is known as "the world's first 'independent' competition agency," and it has been a dominant model of regulation. The creation of "independent regulatory agencies" or "quasi-autonomous non-governmental organizations" (or QUANGOs), has accelerated as part of a worldwide movement in regulatory reform since the late twentieth century.[39]

As research by such scholars as Giandomenico Majone and David Levi-Faur has shown, the boom began in Europe, at both the national and European Union levels, but a similar development has been widely observed elsewhere around the world. These independent agencies, not a few of them employing courtlike procedures, are thought to be modeled upon American IRCs. Often considered peripheral and obsolete in the United States, IRCs are gaining relevance globally, now believed by many to be an effective type of institution to infuse policy expertise into the administrative process. The administrative states could be undergoing a convergence on the efficiency-fairness spectrum, approaching each other from different sides. In short, IRCs are no longer "American 'exceptionalism.'"[40]

38 See the following for powerful counterarguments. Freedman, *Crisis and Legitimacy*, Ch. 2; Rohr, *To Run a Constitution*, Ch. 3; Strauss, "Place of Agencies"; Ernst, *Tocqueville's Nightmare*, esp. Ch. 1.

39 Michael Moran, *The British Regulatory State: High Modernism and Hyper-Innovation* (New York: Oxford University Press, 2003), Ch. 1; Majone, *Regulating Europe*, 47, 49–56; Berger and Edles, *Independent Agencies*, Ch. 10; William E. Kovacic and Marc Winerman, "The Federal Trade Commission as an Independent Agency: Autonomy, Legitimacy, and Effectiveness," *Iowa Law Review* 100 (2015): 2087. Also see Majone, *Regulating Europe*, 50.

40 Majone, *Regulating Europe*; Giandomenico Majone, "The Rise of the Regulatory State in Europe," *West European Politics* 17 (1994): 92; David Levi-Faur, "The Global Diffusion of Regulatory Capitalism," *Annals of the American Academy of Political and Social Science* 598 (2005): 12–32; Fabrizio Gilardi, *Delegation in the Regulatory State: Independent Regulatory Agencies in Western Europe* (Cheltenham: Edward Elgar, 2008); Matthew Flinders, *Delegated Governance and the British State: Walking without Order* (New York: Oxford University Press, 2008); Christopher Pollitt and Colin Talbot, *Unbundled Government: A Critical Analysis of the Global Trend to Agencies, Quangos and Contractualisation* (London: Routledge, 2004); Susan Rose-Ackerman and Peter L. Lindseth, eds., *Comparative Administrative Law* (Cheltenham, UK: Edward Elgar, 2010), esp. Pt. 3; Damien Geradin, "The Development of European Regulatory Agencies: What the EU Should Learn from American Experience," *Columbia Journal of European Law* 11 (2004): 1–52; Mark Thatcher, "The Third Force? Independent Regulatory Agencies and Elected Politicians in Europe," *Governance* 18 (2005): 347–373; Miroslava Scholten, *The Political Accountability of EU and US Independent Regulatory Agencies* (Leiden: Brill, 2014); R. Daniel Kelemen, "The Politics of 'Eurocratic' Structure and the New European Agencies," *West European Politics* 25 (2002): 93–118; R. Daniel Kelemen, *Eurolegalism: The Transformation of Law and Regulation in the*

The worldwide diffusion of American-bred independent agencies means that the United States now shares not just the institutional apparatus but the difficulties posed by it with the rest of the world. The agencies have raised the thorny question of how their autonomy from elected officials can be legitimized in a democracy. Interestingly, those who have most recently tackled this conundrum have adopted a strategy of comparing the independent regulators to judicial courts, placing both types of institutions in the same category of "non-majoritarian institutions."[41] Because courts are the representative expert government bodies with a firm foundation in democracies, scholars have sought to learn from their experience in elucidating what it takes for independent agencies to get along with democracy. It should come as no surprise that fairness, along with expertise and professionalism, has been raised as a virtue of non-majoritarian institutions. The question has renewed importance today around the globe because of the spread of public mistrust in established knowledge. The Americans themselves are still searching for an answer. But there should be little doubt that the American debate on courtlike IRCs spanning three centuries provides rich food for thought on the role of judicialized, expert agencies in a democracy.[42]

European Union (Cambridge, MA: Harvard University Press, 2011); Francesca Bignami and R. Daniel Kelemen, "Kagan's Atlantic Crossing: Adversarial Legalsim, Eurolegalism, and Cooperative Legalism in European Regulatory Style," in *Varieties of Legal Order: The Politics of Adversarial and Bureaucratic Legalism*, ed. Thomas F. Burke and Jeb Barnes (New York: Routledge, 2018), 81–97; Navroz K. Dubash and Bronwen Morgan, *The Rise of the Regulatory State of the South: Infrastructure and Development in Emerging Economies* (Oxford: Oxford University Press, 2013).

41 Majone, *Regulating Europe*, Ch. 13; Martin Shapiro, "'Deliberative,' 'Independent' Technocracy v. Democratic Politics: Will the Globe Echo the E.U.?" *Law and Contemporary Problems* 68 (2005): 341–356; Frank Vibert, *The Rise of the Unelected: Democracy and the New Separation of Powers* (New York: Cambridge University Press, 2007); Paul Tucker, *Unelected Power: The Quest for Legitimacy in Central Banking and the Regulatory State* (Princeton: Princeton University Press, 2018); Eoin Carolan, *The New Separation of Powers: A Theory for the Modern State* (New York: Oxford University Press, 2009); Gül Sosay, "Consequences of Legitimizing Independent Regulatory Agencies in Contemporary Democracies," in *Delegation in Contemporary Democracies*, ed. Dietmar Braun and Fabrizio Gilardi (New York: Routledge, 2006), 171–190.

42 Majone, *Regulating Europe*, 285–286; Steven Brint, *In an Age of Experts: The Changing Role of Professionals in Politics and Public Life* (Princeton: Princeton University Press, 1994); Tom Nichols, *The Death of Expertise: The Campaign against Established Knowledge and Why It Matters* (New York: Oxford University Press, 2017).

Works cited

Manuscript collections

Louis Brownlow Papers, John F. Kennedy Presidential Library.
William Jennings Bryan Papers, Manuscript Division, Library of Congress.
Thomas M. Cooley Papers, Bentley Historical Library, University of Michigan.
Carter Glass Papers, Albert and Shirly Small Special Collections Library, University of Virginia.
Walter Q. Gresham Papers, Manuscript Division, Library of Congress.
Hugh Heclo Collection, Special Collections Library, George Mason University.
Papers of Herbert Hoover, Herbert Hoover Presidential Library.
Herbert Hoover Subject Collection, Hoover Institution, Stanford University.
Records of the Operating Division, Interstate Commerce Commission, Record Group 134, National Archives, College Park, MD.
Leon Keyserling Papers, Georgetown University Library Booth Family Center for Special Collections, Washington DC.
James M. Landis Papers, Manuscript Division, Library of Congress.
W. G. McAdoo Papers, Manuscript Division, Library of Congress.
Charles E. Merriam Papers, Special Collections Research Center, University of Chicago Library.
Francis Griffith Newlands Papers, Manuscripts and Archives, Yale University Library.
Papers of President's Committee on Administrative Management, Franklin D. Roosevelt Presidential Library.
John H. Reagan Papers, Dolph Briscoe Center for American History, University of Texas at Austin.
Franklin D. Roosevelt Papers, Papers as President, Franklin D. Roosevelt Presidential Library.
Robert F. Wagner Papers, Georgetown University Library Booth Family Center for Special Collections, Washington DC.
Wallace H. White Papers, Manuscript Division, Library of Congress.
John Sharp Williams Papers, Manuscript Division, Library of Congress.

Interview transcript

Gulick, Luther H. "Governmental Reorganization: Some Observations and Reflections on Administrative Reform." Interview by James L. Garnett, November 30, 1976.

Newspapers and magazines

Austin Weekly Statesman
Boston Globe
Chicago Tribune
New York Times
Railway and Corporation Law Journal
Statist (London)
Wall Street Journal
Washington Evening Star
Washington Post

Government and organization documents

American Bar Association, "Proceedings of the Fifty-Sixth Annual Meeting of American Bar Association." *Annual Report of the American Bar Association* 56 (1933): 41–212.

———. "Report of the Special Committee on Administrative Law." *Annual Report of the American Bar Association* 57 (1934): 539–564.

———. "Report of the Special Committee on Administrative Law." *Annual Report of the American Bar Association* 63 (1938): 331–368.

———. Commission on Law and the Economy. *Federal Regulation: Roads to Reform.* Chicago: American Bar Association, 1979.

Arnold & Porter LLP. *Reforming the Immigration System.* Washington, DC: American Bar Association Commission on Immigration, 2010.

Attorney General's Committee on Administrative Procedure. *Final Report.* Washington, DC: Government Printing Office, 1941.

Commission on Organization of the Executive Branch of the Government (Hoover Commission I). *Regulatory Commissions.* Washington, DC: Government Printing Office, 1949.

Commission on Organization of the Executive Branch of the Government (Hoover Commission II). Task Force on Legal Services and Procedure. *Report on Legal Services and Procedure.* Washington, DC: Government Printing Office, 1955.

Hoover, Herbert. "Annual Message to the Congress on the State of the Union." Dec. 3, 1929. Online by Gerhard Peters and John T. Woolley, The American Presidency Project www.presidency.ucsb.edu/node/209213

Interstate Commerce Commission. *First Annual Report of the Interstate Commerce Commission.* Washington, DC: Government Printing Office, 1887.

———. *Second Annual Report of the Interstate Commerce Commission.* Washington, DC: Government Printing Office, 1888.

———. *Fifth Annual Report of the Interstate Commerce Commission.* Washington, DC: Government Printing Office, 1891.

———. *Reports and Decisions of the Interstate Commerce Commission of the United States, April 5th, 1887 to April 5th, 1888.* New York: L. K. Strouse, 1888.

National Civic Federation. Department on Regulation of Interstate and Municipal Utilities. *Commission Regulation of Public Utilities: A Compilation and Analysis of Laws of Forty-Three States and of the Federal Government for the Regulation by Central Commissions of Railroads and Other Public Utilities.* New York: National Civic Federation, 1913.

President's Advisory Council on Executive Reorganization (Ash Council). *A New Regulatory Framework: Report on Selected Independent Regulatory Agencies.* Washington, DC: Government Printing Office, 1971.

President's Committee on Administrative Management (Brownlow Committee). *Report of the Committee, with Studies of Administrative Management in the Federal Government.* Washington, DC: Government Printing Office, 1937.

Roosevelt, Franklin D. "Veto of a Bill Regulating Administrative Agencies." Dec. 8, 1940. Online by Gerhard Peters and John T. Woolley, The American Presidency Project. www.presidency.ucsb.edu/node/209411

Roosevelt, Theodore. "Eighth Annual Message." Online by Gerhard Peters and John T. Woolley, The American Presidency Project. www.presidency.ucsb.edu/node/206223

Social Security Advisory Board. *Aspects of Disability Decision Making: Data and Materials.* 2012. www.ssab.gov/Details-Page/ArticleID/217/CHARTBOOK-Aspects-of-Disability-Decision-Making-Data-and-Materials-February-2012 (last accessed Dec. 4, 2018).

US Bureau of the Census. *Historical Statistics of the United States, Colonial Times to 1970, Bicentennial Edition.* Washington, DC: Government Printing Office, 1975.

US Congress. House of Representatives. Committee on Agriculture. *Federal Live Stock Commission.* 66th Cong., 3rd sess. 1921. House Rep. 1297.

US Congress. House of Representatives. Committee on the Merchant Marine and Fisheries. *Creating a Shipping Board, a Naval Auxiliary, and a Merchant Marine.* 64th Cong., 1st sess. 1916. Hearings on H.R. 10500.

US Congress. House of Representatives. Committee on Water Power. *Water Power.* 65th Cong., 2nd sess. 1919. Pts. 1–4.

US Congress. House of Representatives. Conference Committee. *Dams across Navigable Waters.* 65th Cong., 3rd sess. 1919. H. Rep. 1147.

———. *Meat-Packing Industry.* 67th Cong., 1st sess. 1921. House Rep. 324.

US Congress. House of Representatives. Committee on the Merchant Marine and the Fisheries. *To Regulate Radio Communication.* 69th Cong., 1st sess. 1926. Hearings on H.R. 5589.

US Congress. Joint Committee on Government Organization. *Reorganization of the Executive Departments.* 75th Cong., 1st sess. 1937. Committee Print.

US Congress. National Monetary Commission. *Report of the National Monetary Commission.* 62nd Cong., 2nd sess. 1912. S. Doc. 243.

US Congress. Senate. *Message from the President of the United States Recommending that Congress Create a New Agency to Be Known as the Federal Communications Commission.* 73rd Cong., 2nd sess. 1934. S. Doc. 144.

US Congress. Senate. *Report of Federal Aviation Commission*, 74th Cong., 1st sess. 1935. S. Doc. 15.

US Congress. Senate. Banking and Currency Committee. *Banking and Currency.* 63rd Cong., 1st sess. 1913. S. Doc. 232. Vols. 1–3.

US Congress. Senate. Committee on Commerce. *Creating a Shipping Board, a Naval Auxiliary, a Merchant Marine, and Regulating Carriers by Water Engaged in the Foreign and Interstate Commerce of the United States.* 64th Cong., 1st sess. 1916. S. Rep. 689.

US Congress. Senate. Committee on Education and Labor. *National Labor Relations Board.* 74th Cong., 1st sess. 1935. Hearings on S. 1958.

US Congress. Senate. Committee on Interstate Commerce. *Hearing[s] before the Committee on Interstate Commerce, United State Senate, Sixty-second Congress, pursuant to S. Res. 98, a resolution directing the Committee on interstate commerce to investigate and report desirable changes in the laws regulating and controlling corporations, persons, and firms, engaged in interstate commerce*, 62nd Cong. 1912. Committee Print.

———. *Federal Trade Commission*. 63rd Cong., 2nd sess. 1914. S. Rep. 597.

———. *Study of Communications by an Interdepartmental Committee*. 73rd Cong., 2nd sess. 1934. Committee Print.

US Congress. Senate. Select Committee on Interstate Commerce. *Report of the Senate Select Committee on Interstate Commerce*. 49th Cong., 1st sess. 1886. S. Rep. 46.

US Congress. Senate. Select Committee to Investigate the Executive Agencies of the Government. *Investigation of Executive Agencies of the Government*. 75th Cong., 1st sess. 1937. S. Rep. 1275.

US Department of Justice. Executive Office for Immigration Review. *Statistics Yearbook, Fiscal Year 2017*. www.justice.gov/eoir/statistical-year-book (last accessed Dec. 4, 2018).

US Government Accountability Office. *Social Security Disability: Additional Measures and Evaluation Needed to Enhance Accuracy and Consistency of Hearings Decisions*. Washington, DC: Government Accountability Office, 2017.

US Social Security Administration. *Leading the Hearings and Appeals Process into the Future: A Plan for Compassionate and Responsive Service*. Baltimore, MD: Social Security Administration.

Books and articles

Abinales, Patricio N. "Progressive-Machine Conflict in Early-Twentieth-Century U.S. Politics and Colonial-State Building in the Philippines." In *The American Colonial State in the Philippines: Global Perspectives*, edited by Julian Go and Anne L. Foster, 148–181. Durham: Duke University Press, 2003.

Ackerman, Bruce A., and William T. Hassler. *Clean Coal/Dirty Air*. New Haven: Yale University Press, 1981.

Adams, Henry Carter. "A Decade of Federal Railway Regulation." *Atlantic Monthly*, Apr. 1898, 433–443.

Aduddell, Robert M., and Louis P. Cain. "Public Policy toward 'The Greatest Trust in the World.'" *Business History Review* 55 (1981): 217–242.

Allen, Howard W., and Robert Slagter. "Congress in Crisis: Changes in Personnel and the Legislative Agenda in the U.S. Congress in the 1890s." *Social Science History* 16 (1992): 401–420.

Alvis, J. David, Jeremy D. Bailey, and F. Flagg Taylor, IV. *The Contested Removal Power, 1789–2010*. Lawrence: University Press of Kansas, 2013.

Arnold, Peri E. "The First Hoover Commission and the Managerial Presidency." *Journal of Politics* 38 (1976): 46–70.

———. *Making the Managerial Presidency: Comprehensive Reorganization Planning, 1905–1996*, 2nd ed. Lawrence: University of Kansas Press, 1998.

———. "The Brownlow Committee, Regulation, and the Presidency: Seventy Years Later." *Public Administration Review* 67 (2007): 1030–1040.

———. *Remaking the Presidency: Roosevelt, Taft, and Wilson, 1901–1916*. Lawrence: University Press of Kansas, 2009.

Asimow, Michael. *Adjudication Outside the Administrative Procedure Act*. Washington, DC: Administrative Conference of the Unite States, 2016.

Asimow, Michael, and Jeffrey S. Lubbers. "The Merits of 'Merits Review': A Comparative Look at the Australian Administrative Appeals Tribunal." *AIAL Forum* 67 (2011): 58–79.

Auerbach, Jerold S. *Unequal Justice: Lawyers and Social Change in Modern America.* New York: Oxford University Press, 1976.

Balogh, Brian. "Reorganizing the Organizational Synthesis: Federal-Professional Relations in Modern America." *Studies in American Political Development* 5 (1991): 119–172.

———. *Chain Reaction: Expert Debate and Public Participation in American Commercial Nuclear Power, 1945–1975.* New York: Cambridge University Press, 1994.

———. *A Government Out of Sight: The Mystery of National Authority in Nineteenth-Century America.* New York: Cambridge University Press, 2009.

Bamzai, Aditya. "Taft, Frankfurter, and the First Presidential for-cause Removal." *University of Richmond Law Review* 52 (2018): 691–748.

Barnett, Kent. "Why Bias Challenges to Administrative Adjudication Should Succeed." *Missouri Law Review* 81 (2016): 1023–1043.

———. "How the Supreme Court Derailed Formal Rulemaking." *George Washington Law Review Arguendo* 85 (2017): 1–24.

Barnett, Kent H., and Russell Wheeler. "Non-ALJ Adjudicators in Federal Agencies: Status, Selection, Oversight, and Removal," *Georgia Law Review* 53 (2019): 1–127.

Barnett, Vincent M., Jr. "Judicialization of the Administrative Process." *Public Administration Review* 8 (1948): 126–133.

Bates, Henry M. "Trends in American Government." In *Morrison Foundation Lectures*, edited by State Bar of California, 73–101. San Francisco: Alexander F. Morrison Lectureship Foundation, 1940.

Benjamin, Louise. "Working It Out Together: Radio Policy from Hoover to the Radio Act of 1927." *Journal of Broadcasting and Electronic Media* 42 (1998): 221–236.

Bensman, Marvin R. *The Beginning of Broadcast Regulation in the Twentieth Century.* Jefferson, NC: McFarland & Co., 2000.

Benson, Lee. *Merchants, Farmers, and Railroads: Railroad Regulation and New York Politics, 1850–1887.* Cambridge, MA: Harvard University Press, 1955.

Berk, Gerald. *Alternative Tracks: The Constitution of American Industrial Order, 1865–1917.* Baltimore: Johns Hopkins University Press, 1994.

———. *Louis D. Brandeis and the Making of Regulated Competition, 1900–1932.* New York: Cambridge University Press, 2009.

Berk, Gerald, and Dennis Galvan. "How People Experience and Change Institutions: A Field Guide to Creative Syncretism." *Theory and Society* 38 (2009): 543–580.

———. "Processes of Creative Syncretism: Experiential Origins of Institutional Order and Change." In *Political Creativity: Reconfiguring Institutional Order and Change*, edited by Gerald Berk, Dennis C. Galvan, and Victoria Hattam, 29–54. Philadelphia: University of Pennsylvania Press, 2013.

Bernheim, Alfred L., and Dorothy Van Doren, eds. *Labor and the Government: An Investigation of the Role of the Government in Labor Relations.* New York: McGraw-Hill, 1935.

Bernstein, Irving. *The New Deal Collective Bargaining Policy.* Berkeley: University of California Press, 1950.

Bernstein, Marver H. *Regulating Business by Independent Commission.* Princeton: Princeton University Press, 1955.

Bertelli, Anthony M., and Laurence E. Lynn, Jr. *Madison's Managers: Public Administration and the Constitution*. Baltimore: Johns Hopkins University Press, 2006.

Bignami, Francesca, and R. Daniel Kelemen. "Kagan's Atlantic Crossing: Adversarial Legalsim, Eurolegalism, and Cooperative Legalism in European Regulatory Style." In *Varieties of Legal Order: The Politics of Adversarial and Bureaucratic Legalism*, edited by Thomas F. Burke and Jeb Barnes, 81–97. New York: Routledge, 2018.

Binder, Guyora. "Twentieth-Century Legal Metaphors for Self and Society." In *Looking Back at Law's Century*, edited by Robert A. Kagan, Bryant Garth, and Austin Sarat, 151–183. Ithaca: Cornell University Press, 2002.

Binder, Sarah, and Mark Spindel. "Monetary Politics: Origins of the Federal Reserve." *Studies in American Political Development* 27 (2013): 1–13.

Blachly, Frederick F., and Miriam E. Oatman. *Federal Regulatory Action and Control*. Washington, DC: Brookings Institution, 1940.

Bolton, Alexander, and Sharece Thrower. "Legislative Capacity and Executive Unilateralism." *American Journal of Political Science* 60 (2016): 649–663.

Bowman, Harold M. "American Administrative Tribunals." *Political Science Quarterly* 21 (1906): 609–625.

Brand, Donald R. "The President as Chief Administrator: James Landis and the Brownlow Report." *Political Science Quarterly* 123 (2008): 69–93.

Brandeis, Louis D. *Letters of Louis D. Brandeis*, Vol. 3, *1913–1915: Progressive and Zionist*, edited by Melvin I. Urofsky and David W. Levy. New York: State University of New York Press, 1973.

Brazier, James Edward. "Who Controls the Administrative State? Congress and the President Adopt the Administrative Procedure Act of 1946." Ph.D. diss., Michigan State University, 1993.

Bregger, Marshall J., and Gary J. Edles. *Independent Agencies in the United States: Law, Structure, and Politics*. New York: Oxford University Press, 2015.

Bressman, Lisa Schultz, and Robert B. Thompson. "The Future of Agency Independence." *Vanderbilt Law Review* 63 (2010): 599–672.

Breyer, Stephen G., Richard B. Stewart, Cass R. Sunstein, Adrian Vermeule, and Michael Herz. *Administrative Law and Regulatory Policy: Problems, Text, and Cases*, 7th ed. New York: Aspen Publishers, 2011.

Brigman, William E. "The Executive Branch and the Independent Regulatory Agencies." *Presidential Studies Quarterly* 11 (1981): 244–261.

Brint, Steven. *In an Age of Experts: The Changing Role of Professionals in Politics and Public Life*. Princeton: Princeton University Press, 1994.

Brown, Rebecca L. "Separated Powers and Ordered Liberty." *University of Pennsylvania Law Review* 139 (1991): 1513–1566.

Brownlow, Louis. *A Passion for Anonymity: The Autobiography of Louis Brownlow, the Second Half*. Chicago: University of Chicago Press, 1958.

Buck, Solon. *The Granger Movement: A Study of Agricultural Organization and Its Political, Economic, and Social Manifestations, 1870–1880*. Cambridge, MA: Harvard University Press, 1913.

Calabresi, Steven G., and Christopher S. Yoo. *The Unitary Executive: Presidential Power from Washington to Bush*. New Haven: Yale University Press, 2008.

Calhoun, Charles W. *Gilded Age Cato: The Life of Walter Q. Gresham*. Lexington: University Press of Kentucky, 1988.

Campbell, Colin. "The Complex Organization of the Executive Branch: The Legacies of Competing Approaches to Administration." In *The Executive Branch*, edited by

Joel D. Aberbach and Mark A. Peterson, 243–282. New York: Oxford University Press, 2005.

della Cananea, Giacinto. *Due Process of Law Beyond the State*. New York: Oxford University Press, 2016.

Cane, Peter. *Administrative Tribunals and Adjudication*. Portland, OR: Hart Publishing, 2009.

———. "Judicial Review and Merits Review: Comparing Administrative Adjudication by Courts and Tribunals." In *Comparative Administrative Law*, edited by Susan Rose-Ackerman and Peter L. Lindseth, 426–448. Cheltenham, UK: Edward Elgar, 2010.

———. *Controlling Administrative Power: A Historical Comparison*. Cambridge: Cambridge University Press, 2016.

Carolan, Eoin. *The New Separation of Powers: A Theory for the Modern State*. New York: Oxford University Press, 2009.

Carpenter, Daniel P. *The Forging of Bureaucratic Autonomy: Reputations, Networks, and Policy Innovation in Executive Agencies*. Princeton: Princeton University Press, 2001.

———. *Reputation and Power: Organizational Image and Pharmaceutical Regulation at the FDA*. Princeton: Princeton University Press, 2010.

Carrington, Paul D. "Law and Economics in the Creation of Federal Administrative Law: Thomas Cooley, Elder to the Republic." *Iowa Law Review* 83 (1998): 363–390.

Carrow, Milton M. "Dean Landis and the Regulatory Process." *George Washington Law Review* 29 (1961): 718–738.

Cary, William L. *Politics and the Regulatory Agencies*. New York: McGraw-Hill, 1967.

Chamberlain, Joseph P., Noel T. Dowling, and Paul R. Hays. *The Judicial Function in Federal Administrative Agencies*. New York: Commonwealth Fund, 1942.

Chandler, Ralph Clark, ed. *A Centennial History of the American Administrative State*. New York: Free Press, 1987.

Chase, William C. *The American Law School and the Rise of Administrative Government*. Madison: University of Wisconsin Press, 1982.

Childs, William R. *The Texas Railroad Commission: Understanding Regulation in America to the Mid-Twentieth Century*. College Station: Texas A&M University Press, 2005.

Clark, Frederick C. "State Railroad Commissions and How They May Be Made Effective." *Publications of the American Economic Association* 6 (1891): 11–110.

Clemens, Elisabeth S. "Lineages of the Rube Goldberg State: Building and Blurring Public Programs, 1900–1940." In *Rethinking Political Institutions: The Art of the State*, edited by Ian Shapiro, Stephen Skowronek, and Daniel Galvin, 187–215. New York: New York University Press, 2006.

Clements, Kendrick A. *The Life of Herbert Hoover: Imperfect Visionary, 1918–1928*. New York: Palgrave Macmillan, 2010.

Coglianese, Cary. "Improving Regulatory Analysis at Independent Agencies." *American University Law Review* 67 (2018): 733–767.

Conover, Milton. *The Federal Power Commission: Its History, Activities and Organization*. Baltimore: Johns Hopkins Press, 1923.

Cooley, Thomas M. *A Treatise on the Constitutional Limitations Which Rest Upon the Legislative Power of the States of the American Union*, 3rd ed. Boston: Little, Brown, 1874.

———. *The General Principles of Constitutional Law in the United States of America.* Boston: Little, Brown, 1880.
Cooper, Robert M. "The Proposed United States Administrative Court." *Michigan Law Review* 35 (1936): 193–252.
Croly, Herbert. *The Promise of American Life.* 1909. Reprint, New York: Capricorn Books, 1964.
———. *Progressive Democracy.* New York: Macmillan, 1914.
Crowe, Justin. *Building the Judiciary: Law, Courts, and the Politics of Institutional Development.* Princeton: Princeton University Press, 2012.
Cuéller, Mariano-Florentino. "James Landis and the Dilemmas of Administrative Government." *George Washington Law Review* 83 (2015): 1330–1357.
Cullom, Shelby M. *Fifty Years of Public Service: Personal Recollections of Shelby M. Cullom.* 1911. Reprint, New York: Da Capo Press, 1969.
Cushman, Robert E. "The National Police Power under the Commerce Clause of the Constitution." *Minnesota Law Review* 3 (1918–1919): 289–319, 381–412, 452–483.
———. "The Problem of Independent Regulatory Commissions." In President's Committee on Administrative Management, *Report of the Committee, with Studies of Administrative Management in the Federal Government*, 205–243. Washington, DC: Government Printing Office, 1937.
———. "The Constitutional Status of the Independent Regulatory Commissions." *Cornell Law Quarterly* 24 (1939): 13–53 and 163–197.
———. *The Independent Regulatory Commissions.* New York: Oxford University Press, 1941.
———. *Leading Constitutional Decisions*, 12th ed. New York: Appleton-Century-Crofts, 1963.
Davidson, Alastair. *The Invisible State: The Formation of the Australian State, 1788–1901.* Melbourne: Cambridge University Press, 1991.
Davis, Frederick. "Judicialization of Administrative Law: The Trial-type Hearing and the Changing Status of the Hearing Officer." *Duke Law Journal* 1977 (1977): 389–408.
Davis, G. Cullom. "The Transformation of the Federal Trade Commission, 1914–1929." *Mississippi Valley Historical Review* 49 (1962): 437–455.
Davis, Kenneth Culp. *Administrative Law Treatise*, Vol. 1. St. Paul: West Publishing, 1958.
De Bedts, Ralph F. *The New Deal's SEC: The Formative Years.* New York: Columbia University Press, 1964.
DeCanio, Samuel. *Democracy and the Origins of the American Regulatory State.* New Haven: Yale University Press, 2015.
Devins, Neal, and David E. Lewis. "Not-So-Independent Agencies: Party Polarization and the Limits of Institutional Design." *Boston University Law Review* 88 (2008): 459–498.
Dicey, Albert V. *Lectures Introductory to the Study of the Law of the Constitution.* London: Macmillan, 1885.
Dickinson, John. *Administrative Justice and the Supremacy of Law in the United States.* New York: Russell and Russell, 1927.
Dickinson, Matthew J. *Bitter Harvest: FDR, Presidential Power and the Growth of the Presidential Branch.* New York: Cambridge University Press, 1996.

DiMaggio, Paul J., and Walter W. Powell. "The Iron Cage Revisited: Institutional Isomorphism and Collective Rationality in Organizational Fields." *American Sociological Review* 48 (1983): 147–160.

Dimock, Marshall E. "The Prospect for Administrative Tribunals." *California Law Review* 20 (1932): 162–166.

———. *British Public Utilities and National Development.* London: G. Allen & Unwin, 1933.

———. "The Development of American Administrative Law." *Journal of Comparative Legislation and International Law* 15 (1933): 35–46.

———. "The Rôle of Discretion in Modern Administration." In *The Frontiers of Public Administration*, edited by John M. Gaus, Leonard D. White, and Marshall E. Dimock, 145–165. Chicago: University of Chicago Press, 1936.

———. *Law and Dynamic Administration.* New York: Praeger, 1980.

Dix, George E. "The Death of the Commerce Court: A Study in Institutional Weakness." *American Journal of Legal History* 8 (1964): 238–260.

Dodd, Lynda G., ed. *The Rights Revolution Revisited: Institutional Perspectives on the Private Enforcement of Civil Rights in the U.S.* New York: Cambridge University Press, 2018.

Doern, G. Bruce, Michael J. Prince, and Richard J. Schultz. *Rules and Unruliness: Canadian Regulatory Democracy, Governance, Capitalism, and Welfarism.* Montreal: McGill-Queen's University Press, 2014.

Donovan, William J., and Ralstone R. Irvine. "The President's Power to Remove Members of Administrative Agencies." *Cornell Law Quarterly* 21 (1936): 215–248.

Downey, Kirstin. *Woman behind the New Deal: The Life of Frances Perkins, FDR's Secretary of Labor and His Moral Conscience.* New York: Doubleday, 2009.

Dubash, Navroz K., and Bronwen Morgan. *The Rise of the Regulatory State of the South: Infrastructure and Development in Emerging Economies.* Oxford: Oxford University Press, 2013.

Dunn, Susan. *Roosevelt's Purge: How FDR Fought to Change the Democratic Party.* Cambridge, MA: Harvard University Press, 2012.

Eastman, Joseph B. "The Place of the Independent Commission." *Constitutional Review* 12 (1928): 95–102.

Edles, Gary J. "The ICC Hearing Process: A Cost-Benefit Approach to Administrative Agency Alternative Dispute Resolution." *Transportation Law Journal* 16 (1987): 99–105.

Eisner, Mark Allen. *From Warfare State to Welfare State: World War I, Compensatory State Building, and the Limits of Modern Order.* University Park: Pennsylvania State University Press, 2000.

———. *Regulatory Politics in Transition*, 2nd ed. Baltimore: Johns Hopkins University Press, 2000.

Eisner, Mark Allen, Jeff Worsham, Evan J. Ringquist, and Franchesca Nestor. *Contemporary Regulatory Policy*, 3rd ed. Boulder: Lynne Rienner, 2018.

Ellis, Ron. *Unjust by Design: Canada's Administrative Justice System.* Vancouver: UBC Press, 2013.

Elman, Philip. "Administrative Reform of the Federal Trade Commission." *Georgetown Law Journal* 59 (1971): 777–860.

Ely, James W., Jr. *Railroads and American Law.* Lawrence: University Press of Kansas, 2001.

Emmerich, Herbert. *Federal Organization and Administrative Management.* University: University of Alabama Press, 1971.
Epstein, David, and Sharyn O'Halloran. *Delegating Powers: A Transaction Cost Approach to Policy Making under Separate Powers.* New York: Cambridge University Press, 1999.
Epstein, Richard A. *The Classical Liberal Constitution: The Uncertain Quest for Limited Government.* Cambridge, MA: Harvard University Press, 2014.
Ernst, Daniel R. "Law and the State, 1920–2000: Institutional Growth and Structural Change." In *The Cambridge History of Law in America*, Vol. 3, *The Twentieth Century and After (1920–)*, edited by Michael Grossberg and Christopher Tomlins, 1–33. New York: Cambridge University Press, 2008.
———. "Morgan and the New Dealers." *Journal of Policy History* 20 (2008): 447–481.
———. *Tocqueville's Nightmare: The Administrative State Emerges in America, 1900–1940.* New York: Oxford University Press, 2014.
Evans, Peter B., Dietrich Rueschemeyer, and Theda Skocpol, eds. *Bringing the State Back In.* Cambridge, MA: Cambridge University Press, 1985.
Farhang, Sean. *The Litigation State: Public Regulation and Private Lawsuits in the U.S.* Princeton: Princeton University Press, 2010.
Fellmeth, Robert C. *The Interstate Commerce Omission, the Public Interest and the ICC: The Ralph Nader Study Group Report on the Interstate Commerce Commission.* New York: Viking Press, 1970.
Fesler, James W. "The Brownlow Committee Fifty Years Later." *Public Administration Review* 47 (1987): 291–296.
Finegold, Kenneth, and Theda Skocpol. *State and Party in America's New Deal.* Madison: University of Wisconsin Press, 1995.
Fiorina, Morris P. "Legislative Choice of Regulatory Forms: Legal Process or Administrative Process?" *Public Choice* 39 (1982): 33–66
———. "Legislator Uncertainty, Legislative Control, and the Delegation of Legislative Power." *Journal of Law, Economics, and Organization* 2 (1986): 32–51.
Fisher, Louis. *The Politics of Shared Power: Congress and the Executive*, 4th ed. College Station: Texas A&M University Press, 1998.
Flinders, Matthew. *Delegated Governance and the British State: Walking without Order.* New York: Oxford University Press, 2008.
Forbath, William E. "The Long Life of Liberal America: Law and State-Building in the U.S. and England." *Law and History Review* 24 (2006): 179–192.
———. "Politics, State Building, and the Courts, 1870–1920." In *The Cambridge History of Law in America*, Vol. 2, *The Long Nineteenth Century (1789–1920)*, edited by Michael Grossberg and Christopher Tomlins, 643–696. New York: Cambridge University Press, 2008.
Foster, C. D. *Privatization, Public Ownership and the Regulation of Natural Monopoly.* Oxford: Blackwell, 1992.
Frankfurter, Felix. *A Selection of Cases under the Interstate Commerce Act.* Cambridge, MA: Harvard University Press, 1915.
Frankfurter, Felix, and James M. Landis. *The Business of the Supreme Court: A Study in the Federal Judicial System.* New York: Macmillan, 1928.
Frederickson, H. George. *Social Equity and Public Administration: Origins, Developments, and Applications.* Armonk, NY: M. E. Sharpe, 2010.
Freedman, James O. *Crisis and Legitimacy: The Administrative Process and American Government.* New York: Cambridge University Press, 1978.

Freund, Ernst. “Legislative Problems and Solutions.” *American Bar Association Journal* 7 (1921): 656–658.

Freyer, Tony Allan. *Forums of Order: The Federal Courts and Business in American History.* Greenwich, CT: JAI Press, 1979.

Friedman, Lawrence M. *A History of American Law*, 3rd ed. New York: Touchstone, 2005.

Friendly, Henry J. “Some Kind of Hearing.” *University of Pennsylvania Law Review* 123 (1975): 1267–1317.

Fuchs, Ralph F. “Current Proposals for the Reorganization of the Federal Regulatory Agencies.” *Texas Law Review* 16 (1938): 335–358

———. “The Hearing Examiner Fiasco under the Administrative Procedure Act.” *Harvard Law Review* 63 (1950): 737–768.

———. “Fairness and Effectiveness in Administrative Agency Organization and Procedures.” *Indiana Law Journal* 36 (1960): 1–50.

Fuess, Claude Moore. *Joseph B. Eastman: Servant of the People.* New York: Columbia University Press, 1952.

Gajduschek, Gyorgy. “Bureaucracy: Is It Efficient? Is It not? Is That the Question? Uncertainty Reduction: An Ignored Element of Bureaucratic Rationality.” *Administration and Society* 34 (2003): 700–723.

Galligan, D. J. *Due Process and Fair Procedures: A Study of Administrative Procedures.* New York: Oxford University Press, 1996.

Gardner, Warner W. “The Procedures by Which Informal Action Is Taken.” *Administrative Law Review* 24 (1972): 155–166.

Gellhorn, Walter. *Federal Administrative Proceedings.* Baltimore: Johns Hopkins Press, 1941.

Geradin, Damien. “The Development of European Regulatory Agencies: What the EU Should Learn from American Experience.” *Columbia Journal of European Law* 11 (2004): 1–52.

Gibson, Andrew, and Arthur Donovan. *The Abandoned Ocean: A History of United States Maritime Policy.* Columbia: University of South Carolina Press, 2000.

Gilardi, Fabrizio. *Delegation in the Regulatory State: Independent Regulatory Agencies in Western Europe.* Cheltenham: Edward Elgar, 2008.

Gillman, Howard. “How Political Parties Can Use the Courts to Advance Their Agendas: Federal Courts in the United States, 1875–1891.” *American Political Science Review* 96 (2002): 511–524.

Glass, Carter. *An Adventure in Constructive Finance.* 1927. Reprint, New York: Arno Press, 1975.

Glock, Judge. “The Forgotten Visitorial Power: The Origins of Administrative Subpoenas and Modern Regulation.” *Review of Banking and Financial Law* 37 (2017): 205–266.

Godfrey, Donald G., and Val E. Limburg. “The Rogue Elephant of Radio Legislation: Senator William E. Borah.” *Journalism Quarterly* 67 (1990): 214–224.

Goodman, Leonard S. “Getting Started: Organization, Procedure and Initial Business of the ICC in 1887.” *Transportation Law Journal* 16 (1987): 7–34.

Goodman, Mark, and Mark Gring. “The Ideological Fight over Creation of the Federal Radio Commission in 1927.” *Journalism History* 26 (2000): 117–124.

Goodnow, Frank J. *Politics and Administration.* New York: Macmillan, 1900.

Goodsell, Charles T., and Ceferina C. Gayo. “Appointive Control of Federal Regulatory Commissions.” *Administrative Law Review* 23 (1971): 291–303.

Gormley, Willam T., Jr. *Taming the Bureaucracy: Muscles, Prayers, and Other Strategies*. Princeton: Princeton University Press, 1989.

Gould, Lewis L. *The Presidency of Theodore Roosevelt*. Lawrence: University Press of Kansas, 1991.

———. *The William Howard Taft Presidency*. Lawrence: University Press of Kansas, 2009.

Greer, C. Stuart. "Expanding the Judicial Power of the Administrative Law Judge to Establish Efficiency and Fairness in Administrative Adjudication." *University of Richmond Law Review* 103 (1992): 103–130.

Griffith, Robert. "Dwight D. Eisenhower and the Corporate Commonwealth." *American History Review* 87 (1982): 87–122.

Grisinger, Joanna Lynn. "Reforming the State: Reorganization and the Federal Government, 1937–1964." Ph.D. diss., University of Chicago, 2005.

———. "Law in Action: The Attorney General's Committee on Administrative Procedure." *Journal of Policy History* 20 (2008): 379–418.

———. *The Unwieldy American State: Administrative Politics since the New Deal*. New York: Cambridge University Press, 2012.

———. "Law and the Administrative State." In *A Companion to American Legal History*, edited by Sally E. Hadden and Alfred L. Brophy, 367–386. Chichester, UK: Wiley-Blackwell, 2013.

———. "The (Long) Administrative Century: Progressive Models of Governance." In *The Progressives' Century: Political Reform, Constitutional Government, and the Modern American State*, edited by Stephen Skowronek, Stephen M. Engel, and Bruce Ackerman, 360–381. New Haven: Yale University Press, 2016.

Gross, James A. *The Making of the National Labor Relations Board: A Study in Economics, Politics, and the Law*. Albany: State University of New York Press, 1974.

Grossman, David Michael. "Professors and Public Service, 1885–1925: A Chapter in the Professionalization of the Social Sciences." Ph.D. diss., Washington University, 1973.

Grussendorf, Paul. *My Trials: Inside America's Deportation Factories*, 2nd ed. North Charleston, SC: CreateSpace Publishing, 2012.

Gulick, Luther. "Notes on the Theory of Organization, with Special Reference to Government in the United States." In *Papers on the Science of Administration*, edited by Luther Gulick and L. Urwick, 1–45. New York: Institute of Public Administration, 1937.

Guthrie, Chris, Jeffrey J. Rachlinski, and Andrew J. Wistrich. "The 'Hidden Judiciary': An Empirical Examination of Executive Branch Justice." *Duke Law Journal* 2009 (2009): 1477–1530.

Haber, Samuel. *Efficiency and Uplift: Scientific Management in the Progressive Era, 1890–1920*. Chicago: University of Chicago Press, 1964.

Haley, John O. *Antitrust in Germany and Japan: The First Fifty Years, 1947–1998*. Seattle: University of Washington Press, 2001.

Hamburger, Philip. *Is Administrative Law Unlawful?* Chicago: University of Chicago Press, 2014.

Hamlin, Rebecca. *Let Me Be a Refugee: Administrative Justice and the Politics of Asylum in the United States, Canada, and Australia*. New York: Oxford University Press, 2014.

Harris, Joseph P. "The Progress of Administrative Reorganization in the Seventy-Fifth Congress." *American Political Science Review* 31 (1937): 862–870.

Harris, Richard A., and Sidney M. Milkis. *The Politics of Regulatory Change: A Tale of Two Agencies*, 2nd ed. New York: Oxford University Press, 1996.
Harrison, Robert. *Congress, Progressive Reform, and the New American State.* New York: Cambridge University Press, 2004.
Hayes, Lauffer T., and Frank J. Ruff. "The Administration of the Federal Food and Drugs Act." *Law and Contemporary Problems* 1 (1933): 16–35.
Hector, Louis J. "Problems of the CAB and the Independent Regulatory Commissions." *Yale Law Journal* 69 (1960): 931–964.
Henderson, George C. *The Federal Trade Commission: A Study in Administrative Law and Procedure.* New Haven: Yale University Press, 1924.
Herring, E. Pendleton. *Public Administration and the Public Interest.* New York: McGraw-Hill, 1936.
Hirschl, Ran. "The Judicialization of Politics." In *The Oxford Handbook of Political Science*, edited by Robert E. Goodin, 253–274. New York: Oxford University Press, 2011.
Hoffer, Williamjames Hull. *To Enlarge the Machinery of Government: Congressional Debates and the Growth of the American State, 1858–1891.* Baltimore: Johns Hopkins University Press, 2007.
Hoffman, Susan. *Politics and Banking: Ideas, Public Policy, and the Creation of Financial Institutions.* Baltimore: Johns Hopkins University Press, 2001.
Holt, W. Stull. *The Federal Trade Commission: Its History, Activities, and Organization.* New York: D. Appleton and Co., 1922.
Hoogenboom, Ari. *Outlawing the Spoils: A History of the Civil Service Reform Movement, 1865–1883.* Urbana: University of Illinois Press, 1961.
Hoogenboom, Ari, and Olive Hoogenboom. *A History of the ICC: From Panacea to Palliative.* New York: W. W. Norton, 1976.
Horwitz, Morton J. *The Transformation of American Law, 1870–1960: The Crisis of Legal Orthodoxy.* New York: Oxford University Press, 1992.
Howell, William G. *Thinking about the Presidency: The Primacy of Power.* Princeton: Princeton University Press, 2013.
Huber, John D., and Charles R. Shipan, *Deliberate Discretion? The Institutional Foundations of Bureaucratic Autonomy.* New York: Cambridge University Press, 2002.
Huntington, Samuel P. "The Marasmus of the ICC: The Commission, the Railroads, and the Public Interest." *Yale Law Journal* 61 (1952): 467–509.
Huthmacher, J. Joseph. *Senator Robert F. Wagner and the Rise of Urban Liberalism.* New York: Atheneum, 1968.
Irish, Kerry E. *Clarence C. Dill: The Life of a Western Politician.* Pullman: Washington State University Press, 2000.
Irons, Peter H. *The New Deal Lawyers.* Princeton: Princeton University Press, 1982.
Jackson, Robert H. *That Man: An Insider's Portrait of Franklin D. Roosevelt.* New York: Oxford University Press, 2003.
Jaffe, Louis L. "Invective and Investigation in Administrative Law." *Harvard Law Review* 52 (1939): 1201–1245.
———. "The Effective Limits of the Administrative Process: A Reevaluation." *Harvard Law Review* 67 (1954): 1105–1135.
———. "The Independent Agency: A New Scapegoat." *Yale Law Journal* 65 (1956): 1068–1076.
James, Scott C. *Presidents, Parties, and the State: A Party System Perspective on Democratic Regulatory Choice, 1884–1936.* New York: Cambridge University Press, 2000.

Jones, Alan. "Thomas M. Cooley and the Interstate Commerce Commission: Continuity and Change in the Doctrine of Equal Rights." *Political Science Quarterly* 81 (1966): 602–627.

———. "Thomas M. Cooley and 'Laissez-Faire Constitutionalism': A Reconsideration." *Journal of American History* 53 (1967): 751–771.

Kagan, Elena. "Presidential Administration." *Harvard Law Review* 114 (2001): 2245–2385.

Kagan, Robert A. *Adversarial Legalism: The American Way of Law*. Cambridge, MA: Harvard University Press, 2001.

———. "Varieties of Bureaucratic Justice: Building on Mashaw's Typology." In *Administrative Law from the Inside Out: Essays on Themes in the Work of Jerry L. Mashaw*, edited by Nicholas R. Parrillo, 247–270. New York: Cambridge University Press, 2017.

Kahn, Jonathan. *Budgeting Democracy: State Building and Citizenship in America, 1890–1928*. Ithaca: Cornell University Press, 1997.

Karl, Barry D. *Executive Reorganization and Reform in the New Deal: The Genesis of Administrative Management, 1900–39*. Cambridge, MA: Harvard University Press, 1963.

———. *The Uneasy State: The United States from 1915 to 1945*. Chicago: University of Chicago Press, 1983.

Kazin, Michael. *A Godly Hero: The Life of William Jennings Bryan*. New York: Alfred A. Knopf, 2006.

Kelemen, R. Daniel. "The Politics of 'Eurocratic' Structure and the New European Agencies." *West European Politics* 25 (2002): 93–118.

———. *Eurolegalism: The Transformation of Law and Regulation in the European Union*. Cambridge, MA: Harvard University Press, 2011.

Keller, Morton. *Regulating a New Economy: Public Policy and Economic Change in America, 1900–1933*. Cambridge, MA: Harvard University Press, 1990.

Kerwin, Cornelius M., and Scott R. Furlong. *Rulemaking: How Government Agencies Write Law and Make Policy*, 4th ed. Washington, DC: CQ Press, 2011.

Kessler, Amalia D. *Inventing American Exceptionalism: The Origins of American Adversarial Legal Culture, 1800–1877*. New Haven: Yale University Press, 2017.

King, Desmond, and Robert C. Lieberman. "The American State." In *The Oxford Handbook of American Political Development*, edited by Richard M. Valelly, Suzanne Mettler, and Robert C. Lieberman, 231–258. New York: Oxford University Press, 2016.

Klaus, Ida. "The Taft-Hartley Experiment in Separation of NLRB Functions." *Industrial and Labor Relations Review* 11 (1958): 371–390.

Koch, Charles H., Jr. "James Landis: The Administrative Process." *Administrative Law Review* 48 (1996): 419–433.

———. "Policymaking by the Administrative Judiciary." *Alabama Law Review* 56 (2005): 693–740.

Kolko, Gabriel. *The Triumph of Conservatism: A Reinterpretation of American History, 1900–1916*. 1963. Reprint, Chicago: Quadrangle Books, 1967.

———. *Railroads and Regulation, 1877–1916*. New York: W. W. Norton, 1965.

Kornhauser, Anne M. *Debating the American State: Liberal Anxieties and the New Leviathan, 1930–1970*. Philadelphia: University of Pennsylvania Press, 2015.

Kovacic, William E., and Marc Winerman. "The Federal Trade Commission as an Independent Agency: Autonomy, Legitimacy, and Effectiveness." *Iowa Law Review* 100 (2015): 2085–2113.

Kraines, Oscar. *The World and Ideas of Ernst Freund: The Search for General Principles of Legislation and Administrative Law*. Tuscaloosa: University of Alabama Press, 1974.

Krent, Harold J., and Scott Morris. *Achieving Greater Consistency in Social Security Disability Adjudication: An Empirical Study and Suggested Reforms.* Washington, DC: Administrative Conference of the United States, 2013.

Landis, James M. *The Administrative Process.* New Haven: Yale University Press, 1938.

———. "Crucial Issues in Administrative Law." *Harvard Law Review* 53 (1940): 1077–1102.

———. *Report on Regulatory Agencies to the President-Elect.* Washington, DC: Government Printing Office, 1960.

———. "The Administrative Process: The Third Decade." *American Bar Association Journal* 47 (1961): 135–139.

Laughlin, J. Laurence. "Currency Reform." *Journal of Political Economy* 15 (1907): 603–610.

Lawson, Gary. "Rise and Rise of the Administrative State." *Harvard Law Review* 107 (1994): 1231–1254.

Lee, Mordecai. *Institutionalizing Congress and the Presidency: The U.S. Bureau of Efficiency, 1916–1933.* College Station: Texas A&M Press, 2006.

Leonard, Thomas C. *Illiberal Reformers: Race, Eugenics and American Economics in the Progressive Era.* Princeton: Princeton University Press, 2016.

Letwin, William. *Law and Economic Policy in America: The Evolution of the Sherman Antitrust Act.* Chicago: University of Chicago Press, 1965.

Levi-Faur, David. "The Global Diffusion of Regulatory Capitalism." *Annals of the American Academy of Political and Social Science* 598 (2005): 12–32.

Levy, Richard E., and Sidney A. Shapiro. "Administrative Procedure and the Decline of the Trial." *University of Kansas Law Review* 51 (2003): 473–508.

Lewis, David E. *Presidents and the Politics of Agency Design: Political Insulation in the United States Government Bureaucracy*, 1946–1997. Palo Alto: Stanford University Press, 2003.

Light, Paul C. *The Tides of Reform: Making Government Work, 1945–1995.* New Haven: Yale University Press, 1997.

Link, Arthur S. *Wilson: The New Freedom.* Princeton: Princeton University Press, 1956.

Litwak, Jeffrey B., ed. *A Guide to Federal Agency Adjudication*, 2nd ed. Chicago: American Bar Association, 2012.

Livingston, James. *Origins of the Federal Reserve System: Money, Class, and Corporate Capitalism, 1890–1913.* Ithaca: Cornell University Press, 1986.

Long, Edward V. "Administrative Proceedings: Their Time and Cost Can Be Cut Down." *American Bar Association Journal* 49 (1963): 833–836.

Loughlin, Martin. "Procedural Fairness: A Study of the Crisis in Administrative Law Theory." *University of Toronto Law Journal* 28 (1978): 215–241.

Lowi, Theodore J. *The End of Liberalism: The Second Republic of the United States*, 2nd ed. New York: W. W. Norton, 1979.

Lubbers, Jeffrey S. "Federal Administrative Law Judges: A Focus on Our Invisible Judiciary." *Administrative Law Review* 33 (1981): 109–131.

———. "A Unified Corps of ALJs: A Proposal to Test the Idea at the Federal Level." *Judicature* 65 (1981): 266–276.

———. "The ABA Section of Administrative Law and Regulatory Practice: From Objector to Protector of the APA." *Administrative Law Review* 50 (1998): 157–171.

Lutton, Larry S. "History and American Public Administration." *Administration and Society* 31 (1999): 205–221.

Lynn, Laurence E., Jr. "The Myth of the Bureaucratic Paradigm: What Traditional Public Administration Really Stood for." *Public Administration Review* 61 (2001): 144–160.

MacAvoy, Paul W., ed. *The Crisis of the Regulatory Commissions: An Introduction to a Current Issue of Public Policy* (New York: W. W. Norton, 1970).

Madison, James, Alexander Hamilton, and John Jay, *The Federalist Papers.* 1788. Reprint, New York: Penguin Books, 1987.

Majone, Giandomenico. "The Rise of the Regulatory State in Europe." *West European Politics* 17 (1994): 77–101.

———. *Regulating Europe.* London: Routledge, 1996.

Mans, Thomas C. "Selecting the 'Hidden Judiciary': How the Merit Process Works in Choosing Administrative Law Judges (Part I)." *Judicature* 63 (1980): 60–73.

Mashaw, Jerry L. *Bureaucratic Justice: Managing Social Security Disability Claims.* New Haven: Yale University Press, 1983.

———. *Due Process in the Administrative State.* New Haven: Yale University Press, 1985.

———. "The American Model of Federal Administrative Law: Remembering the First One Hundred Years." *George Washington Law Review* 78 (2010): 975–992.

———. *Creating the Administrative Constitution: The Lost One Hundred Years of American Administrative Law.* New Haven: Yale University Press, 2012.

Mashaw Jerry L., Charles J. Goetz, Frank I. Goodman, Warren F. Schwartz, Paul R. Verkuil, and Milton M. Carrow, *Social Security Hearings and Appeals: A Study of the Social Security Administration Hearing System.* Lexington, MA: Lexington Books, 1978.

McChesney, Robert W. *Telecommunications, Mass Media, and Democracy: The Battle for the Control of U.S. Broadcasting, 1928–1935.* New York: Oxford University Press, 1993.

McConnell, Grant. *Private Power and American Democracy.* New York: Alfred A. Knopf, 1966.

McCraw, Thomas K. *Prophets of Regulation: Charles Francis Adams, Louis D. Brandeis, James M. Landis, Alfred E. Kahn.* Cambridge, MA: Belknap Press of Harvard University Press, 1984.

McCubbins, Mathew D., Roger G. Noll, and Barry R. Weingast. "Administrative Procedures as Instruments of Political Control." *Journal of Law, Economics, and Organization* 3 (1987): 243–277.

——— (McNollgast). "The Political Origins of the Administrative Procedure Act." *Journal of Law, Economics, and Organization* 15 (1999): 180–217.

McCulley, Richard T. *Banks and Politics during the Progressive Era: The Origins of the Federal Reserve System, 1897–1913.* New York: Garland, 1992.

McFarland, Carl. *Judicial Control of the Federal Trade Commission and the Interstate Commerce Commission, 1920–1930: A Comparative Study in the Relations of Courts to Administrative Commissions.* Cambridge, MA: Harvard University Press, 1933.

———. "Landis' Report: The Voice of One Crying in the Darkness." *Virginia Law Review* 47 (1961): 373–438.

McGarity, Thomas O. "Regulatory Reform and the Positive State: An Historical Overview." *Administrative Law Review* 38 (1986): 399–425.

McGuire, O. R. "Proposed Reforms in Judicial Reviews of Federal Administrative Action." *American Bar Association Journal* 19 (1933): 471–474.

———. "Sailing Close to the Wind, or the Need for a Federal Administrative Court." *American Bar Association Journal* 22 (1936): 853–859.

McKenna, Marian C. *Franklin Roosevelt and the Great Constitutional War: The Court-Packing Crisis of 1937.* New York: Fordham University Press, 2002.

McLean, S. J. "The English Railway and Canal Commission of 1888." *Quarterly Journal of Economics* 20 (1905): 1–58.

Mechem, John Leland. "Procedure and Practice before the Federal Trade Commission." *Michigan Law Review* 21 (1922): 125–159.

Meltzer, Allan H. *A History of the Federal Reserve, Vol. 1, 1913–1951.* Chicago: University of Chicago Press, 2003.

Meriam, Lewis, and Laurence F. Schmeckebier, *Reorganization of the National Government: What Does It Involve?* Washington, DC: Brookings Institution, 1939.

Merkel, Philip L. "The Origins of an Expanded Federal Court Jurisdiction: Railroad Development and the Ascendancy of the Federal Judiciary." *Business History Review* 58 (1984): 336–358.

Milkis, Sidney M. *The President and the Parties: The Transformation of the American Party System since the New Deal.* New York: Oxford University Press, 1993.

———. "William Howard Taft and the Struggle for the Soul of the Constitution." In *Toward an American Conservatism: Constitutional Conservatism during the Progressive Era*, edited by Joseph Postell and Johnathan O'Neill, 63–93. New York: Palgrave Macmillan, 2013.

Miller, Banks, Linda Camp Keith, and Jennifer S. Holmes. *Immigration Judges and U.S. Asylum Policy.* Philadelphia: University of Pennsylvania Press, 2015.

Miller, Clarence A. "The Interstate Commerce Commissioners: The First Fifty Years: 1887–1937." *George Washington Law Review* 5 (1937): 580–700.

Miller, Geoffrey P. "Independent Agencies." *Supreme Court Review* 1986 (1986): 41–97.

Minow, Newton. "Suggestions for Improvement of the Administrative Process." *Administrative Law Review* 15 (1963): 146–153.

Moe, Terry M. "Regulatory Performance and Presidential Administration." *American Journal of Political Science* 26 (1982): 197–224.

Moran, Michael. *The British Regulatory State: High Modernism and Hyper-Innovation.* New York: Oxford University Press, 2003.

Moreno, Angel Manuel. "Presidential Coordination of the Independent Regulatory Process." *Administrative Law Journal* 8 (1994): 461–477.

Morgan, Douglas F., Kent A. Kirwan, John A. Rohr, David H. Rosenbloom, and David Lewis Schaefer. "Recovering, Restoring, and Renewing the Foundations of American Public Administration." *Public Administration Review* 70 (2010): 621–633.

Mosher, Frederick C. *The GAO: The Quest for Accountability in American Government.* Boulder: Westview Press, 1979.

Moulton, Harold G., and associates. *The American Transportation Problem.* Washington, DC: Brookings Institution, 1933.

Mulroy, Quinn. "Public Regulation through Private Litigation: The Regulatory Power of Private Lawsuits and the American Bureaucracy." Ph.D. diss., Columbia University, 2012.

Murphy, William. "Theodore Roosevelt and the Bureau of Corporation: Executive-Corporate and the Advancement of the Regulatory State." *American Nineteenth Century History* 14 (2013): 73–111.
Musolf, Lloyd D. *Federal Examiners and the Conflict of Law and Administration.* Baltimore: Johns Hopkins Press, 1953.
Nash, Gerald D. "Origins of the Interstate Commerce Act of 1887." *Pennsylvania History* 24 (1957): 181–190.
Nelson, Michael. "A Short, Ironic History of American National Bureaucracy." *Journal of Politics* 44 (1982): 747–778.
Newbold, Stephanie P., and David H. Rosenbloom. "Brownlow Report Retrospective." *Public Administration Review* 67 (2007): 1006–1009.
———, eds. *The Constitutional School of American Public Administration.* New York: Routledge, 2017.
Newbold, Stephanie P., and Larry D. Terry. "The President's Committee on Administrative Management: The Untold Story and the Federalist Connection." *Administration and Society* 38 (2006): 522–555.
Nichols, Tom. *The Death of Expertise: The Campaign against Established Knowledge and Why It Matters.* New York: Oxford University Press, 2017.
Nielson, Aaron L. "In Defense of Formal Rulemaking." *Ohio State Law Journal* 75 (2014): 237–292.
Noll, Roger G. *Reforming Regulation: An Evaluation of the Ash Council Proposals.* Washington, DC: Brookings Institution Press, 1971.
Nonet, Philippe. *Administrative Justice: Advocacy and Change in a Government Agency.* New York: Russell Sage Foundation, 1969.
Novak, William J. "Making the Modern American Legislative State." In *Living Legislation: Durability, Change, and the Politics of American Lawmaking*, edited by Jeffery A. Jenkins and Eric M. Patashnik, 20–43. Chicago: University of Chicago Press, 2012.
———. "A Revisionist History of Regulatory Capture." In *Regulatory Capture: Special Interest Influence and How to Limit It*, edited by Daniel Carpenter and David A. Moss, 25–48. New York: Cambridge University Press, 2014.
———. "The Public Utility Idea and the Origins of Modern Business Regulation." In *Corporations and American Democracy*, edited by Naomi R. Lamoreaux and William J. Novak, 139–176. Cambridge, MA: Harvard University Press, 2017.
Okun, Arthur. *Equality and Efficiency: The Big Tradeoff.* Washington, DC: Brookings Institution, 1975.
Oppenheimer, Reuben. "The Supreme Court and Administrative Law." *Columbia Law Review* 37 (1937): 1–42.
Osbourne, David, and Ted Gaebler. *Reinventing Government: How the Entrepreneurial Spirit Is Transforming the Public Sector.* Reading, MA: Addison-Wesley, 1993.
Ostrom, Vincent. *The Intellectual Crisis in American Public Administration*, 3rd ed. Tuscaloosa: University of Alabama Press, 2008.
Overeem, Patrick. *The Politics-Administration Dichotomy: Toward a Constitutional Perspective*, 2nd ed. Boca Raton, FL: CRC Press, 2012.
Parrillo, Nicholas R. *Against the Profit Motive: The Salary Revolution in American Government, 1780–1940.* New Haven: Yale University Press, 2013.
———, ed. *Administrative Law from the Inside Out: Essays on Themes in the Work of Jerry L. Mashaw.* New York: Cambridge University Press, 2017.

Parris, Henry. *Government and the Railways in Nineteenth-Century Britain*. London: Routledge & Kegan Paul, 1965.

———. *Constitutional Bureaucracy: The Development of British Central Administration since the Eighteenth Century*. London: George Allen & Unwin, 1969.

Pemberton, William E. *Bureaucratic Politics: Executive Reorganization during the Truman Administration*. Columbia: University of Missouri Press, 1979.

Pestritto, Ronald J. "The Progressive Origins of the Administrative State: Wilson, Goodnow, and Landis." *Social Philosophy and Policy* 24 (2007): 16–54.

Peters, B. Guy. "Administrative Traditions and the Anglo-American Democracies." In *Civil Service Systems in Anglo-American Countries*, edited by John Halligan, 10–26. Cheltenham, UK: Edward Elgar, 2003.

Pinkett, Harold T. "The Keep Commission, 1905–1909: A Rooseveltian Effort for Administrative Reform." *Journal of American History* 52 (1965): 297–312.

Pisani, Donald J. *Water and American Government: The Reclamation Bureau, National Water Policy, and the West, 1902–1935*. Berkeley: University of California Press, 2006

———. "Water Planning in the Progressive Era: The Inland Waterways Commission Reconsidered." *Journal of Policy History* 18 (2006): 389–418.

Polenberg, Richard. *Reorganizing Roosevelt's Government: The Controversy over Executive Reorganization, 1936–1939*. Cambridge, MA: Harvard University Press, 1966.

Pollitt, Christopher, and Colin Talbot. *Unbundled Government: A Critical Analysis of the Global Trend to Agencies, Quangos and Contractualisation*. London: Routledge, 2004.

Pops, Gerald M. "The Judicialization of Federal Administrative Law Judges: Implications for Policymaking." *West Virginia Law Review* 81 (1979): 169–206.

Porter, Kirk H. and Donald Bruce Robinson, comp. *National Party Platforms, 1840–1964*. Urbana: University of Illinois Press.

Postell, Joseph. "The Anti-New Deal Progressive: Roscoe Pound's Alternative Administrative State." *Review of Politics* 74 (2012): 53–85.

———. *Bureaucracy in America: The Administrative State's Challenge to Constitutional Government*. Columbia: University of Missouri Press, 2017.

Pound, Roscoe. "The Causes of Popular Dissatisfaction with the Administration of Justice." *American Law Review* 40 (1906): 1–25.

———. "Executive Justice." *American Law Register* 55 (1907): 137–146.

———. *The Spirit of the Common Law*. Francetown, NH: Marshall Jones Co., 1921.

Purcell, Edward A., Jr. "Ideas and Interests: Businessmen and the Interstate Commerce Act." *Journal of American History* 54 (1967): 561–578.

Rabin, Robert L. "Federal Regulation in Historical Perspective." *Stanford Law Review* 38 (1986): 1188–1326.

Ramji-Nogales, Jaya, Andrew I. Schoenholtz, and Philip G. Schrag. *Refugee Roulette: Disparities in Asylum Adjudication and Proposals for Reform*. New York: New York University Press, 2009.

Redford, Emmette S. *National Regulatory Commissions: Need for a New Look*. College Park: University of Maryland, 1959.

Remini, Robert V. *The House: The History of the House of Representatives*. New York: HarperCollins, 2006.

Ritchie, Donald A. *James M. Landis: Dean of the Regulators*. Cambridge, MA: Harvard University Press, 1980.

———. "Reforming the Regulatory Process: Why James Landis Changed His Mind." *Business History Review* 54 (1980): 283–302.
Roberts, Alasdair. "Why the Brownlow Committee Failed: Neutrality and Partisanship in the Early Years of Public Administration." *Administration and Society* 28 (1996): 3–38.
———. "The Unassailable Principle: Why Luther Gulick Searched for a Science of Administration." *International Journal of Public Administration* 21 (1998): 235–274.
Robinson, Glen O. "The Making of Administrative Policy: Another Look at Rulemaking and Adjudication and Administrative Procedural Reform." *University of Pennsylvania Law Review* 118 (1970): 485–539.
———. "On Reorganizing the Independent Regulatory Agencies." *Virginia Law Review* 57 (1971): 947–995.
———. *American Bureaucracy: Public Choice and Public Law*. Ann Arbor: University of Michigan Press, 1991.
Rockwell, Stephen J. *Indian Affairs and the Administrative State in the Nineteenth Century*. New York: Cambridge University Press, 2010.
Rodriguez, Daniel B., and Barry R. Weingast. "The 'Reformation of Administrative Law' Revisited." *Journal of Law, Economics, and Organization* 31 (2015): 782–807.
Rogers, Lindsay. "The Independent Regulatory Commissions." *Political Science Quarterly* 52 (1937): 1–17.
Rohr, John A. *To Run a Constitution: The Legitimacy of the Administrative State*. Lawrence: University Press of Kansas, 1986.
———. *Civil Servants and Their Constitutions*. Lawrence: University Press of Kansas, 2002.
Roman, Andrew J. "Regulatory Law and Procedure." In *The Regulatory Process in Canada*, edited by G. Bruce Doern, 68–93. Toronto: Macmillan, 1978.
Roosevelt, Franklin D. *Complete Presidential Press Conferences of Franklin D. Roosevelt*, Vol. 3–4. 1934. Reprint, New York: Da Capo Press, 1972.
———. *Complete Presidential Press Conferences of Franklin D. Roosevelt*, Vol. 9–10. 1937. Reprint, New York: Da Capo Press, 1972.
Roosevelt, Theodore. *An Autobiography*. New York: Charles Scribner's Sons, 1926.
Root, Elihu. "Public Service by the Bar." *Annual Report of the American Bar Association* (1916): 355–374.
Rose, Mark H., Bruce E. Seely, and Paul F. Barrett. *The Best Transportation System in the World: Railroads, Trucks, Airlines, and American Public Policy in the Twentieth Century*. Columbus: Ohio State University Press, 2006.
Rose-Ackerman, Susan, and Peter L. Lindseth, eds. *Comparative Administrative Law*. Cheltenham, UK: Edward Elgar, 2010.
Rosenbloom, David H. "Public Administrative Theory and the Separation of Powers." *Public Administration Review* 43 (1983): 219–227.
———. *Building a Legislative-Centered Public Administration: Congress and the Administrative State, 1946–1999*. Tuscaloosa: University of Alabama Press, 2000.
———. "Retrofitting the Administrative State to the Constitution: Congress and the Judiciary's Twentieth-Century Progress." *Public Administration Review* 60 (2000): 39–46.
———. *Public Administration and Law*, 3rd ed. Boca Raton, FL: CRC Press, 2010.
Ross, Bradford. "Federal Power Commission Practice and Procedure as Affected by the Administrative Procedure Act of 1946." In *The Federal Administrative*

Procedure Act and the Administrative Agencies, edited by George Warren, 170–195. New York: New York University School of Law, 1947.
Rueschemeyer, Dietrich. *Lawyers and Their Society: A Comparative Study of the Legal Profession in Germany and in the United States.* Cambridge, MA: Harvard University Press, 1973.
Salyer, Lucy E. *Laws Harsh as Tigers: Chinese Immigrants and the Shaping of Modern Immigration Law.* Chapel Hill: University of North Carolina Press, 1995.
Sanders, Elizabeth. *Roots of Reform: Farmers, Workers, and the American State, 1877–1917.* Chicago: University of Chicago Press, 1999.
Sayre, Wallace. "The Trends of a Decade in Administrative Values." *Public Administration Review* 11 (1951): 1–9.
———. "Premises of Public Administration: Past and Emerging." *Public Administration Review* 18 (1958): 102–105.
Schauer, Frederick F. "English Natural Justice and American Due Process: An Analytical Comparison." *William and Mary Law Review* 18 (1976): 47–72.
Schiller, Reuel E. "Enlarging the Administrative Polity: Administrative Law and the Changing Definition of Pluralism, 1945–1970." *Vanderbilt Law Review* 53 (2000): 1389–1453.
———. "Reining in the Administrative State: World War II and the Decline of Expert Administration." In *Total War and the Law: The American Home Front in World War II*, edited by Daniel Ernst and Victor Jew, 185–206. Westport, CT: Praeger, 2002.
———. " 'Saint George and the Dragon': Courts and the Development of the Administrative State in Twentieth-Century America." *Journal of Policy History* 17 (2005): 110–124.
———. "The Era of Deference: Courts, Expertise, and the Emergence of New Deal Administrative Law." *Michigan Law Review* 106 (2007): 398–441.
———. "The Historical Origins of American Regulatory Exceptionalism." In *Comparative Law and Regulation*, edited by Francesca Bignami and David Zaring, 55–72. Cheltenham, UK: Edward Elgar, 2016.
Scholten, Miroslava. *The Political Accountability of EU and US Independent Regulatory Agencies.* Leiden: Brill, 2014.
Schreckhise, William D., Daniel E. Chand, and Nicholas P. Lovrich. "Decision Making in the Hidden Judiciary: Institutions, Recruitment, and Responsiveness Among U.S. Administrative Law Judges." *Administrative Theory and Praxis* 40 (2018): 119–142.
Schudson, Michael. *The Rise of the Right to Know: Politics and the Culture of Transparency, 1945–1975.* Cambridge, MA: Harvard University Press, 2015.
Schultz, Richard. "Regulatory Agencies and the Dilemmas of Delegation." In *The Administrative State in Canada: Essays in Honour of J. E. Hodgetts*, edited by O. P. Dwivedi, 89–106. Toronto: University of Toronto Press, 1982.
Schwartz, Bernard. *American Administrative Law.* London: Sir Isaac Pitman & Sons, 1950.
———. *The Professor and the Commissions.* New York: Alfred A. Knopf, 1959.
———. *Administrative Law.* Boston: Little, Brown, 1976.
———. "Administrative Law: The Third Century." *Administrative Law Review* 29 (1977): 291–319.
Schwartz, Bernard, and H. W. R. Wade. *Legal Control of Government: Administrative Law in Britain and the United States.* Oxford: Clarendon Press, 1972.

Sears, Kenneth C. "The Morgan Case and Administrative Procedure." *George Washington Law Review* 7 (1939): 726–739.

Seligman, Joel. *The Transformation of the Wall Street*, 3rd ed. Frederick, MD: Aspen Publishers, 2003.

Shamir, Ronen. *Managing Legal Uncertainty: Elite Lawyers in the New Deal.* Durham: Duke University Press, 1995.

Shapiro, David L. "The Choice of Rulemaking or Adjudication in the Development of Administrative Policy." *Harvard Law Review* 78 (1965): 921–972.

Shapiro, Martin. "'Deliberative,' 'Independent' Technocracy v. Democratic Politics: Will the Globe Echo the E.U.?" *Law and Contemporary Problems* 68 (2005): 341–356.

Sharfman, I. L. *The Interstate Commerce Commission: A Study in Administrative Procedure.* 4 vols. New York: Commonwealth Fund, 1931–1937.

Shefter, Martin. *Political Parties and the State: The American Historical Experience.* Princeton: Princeton University Press, 1994.

Shepard, George B. "Fierce Compromise: The Administrative Procedure Act Emerges from New Deal Politics." *Northwestern University Law Review* 90 (1996): 1557–1683.

Shipan, Charles R. *Designing Judicial Review: Interest Groups, Congress, and Communications Policy.* Ann Arbor: University of Michigan Press, 2000.

Shook, Dale N. *William G. McAdoo and the Development of National Economic Policy, 1913–1918.* New York: Garland Publishing, 1987.

Shugerman, Jed Handelsman. "The Dependent Origins of Independent Agencies: The Interstate Commerce Commission, the Tenure of Office Act, and the Rise of Modern Campaign Finance." *Journal of Law and Politics* 31 (2015): 139–186.

Sicotte, Richard. "Economic Crisis and Political Response: The Political Economy of the Shipping Act of 1916." *Journal of Economy History* 59 (1999): 861–884.

Silberman, Bernard S. *Cages of Reason: The Rise of the Rational State in France, Japan, the United States, and Great Britain.* Chicago: University of Chicago Press, 1993.

Silbey, Joel H. *The American Political Nation, 1838–1893.* Palo Alto: Stanford University Press, 1991.

Simon, Herbert. *Administrative Behavior: A Study of Decision-Making Processes in Administrative Organizations*, 4th ed. New York: Free Press, 1997.

Sklar, Martin J. *The Corporate Reconstruction of American Capitalism, 1900–1916: The Market, the Law, and Politics.* New York: Cambridge University Press, 1988.

Skoler, Daniel L. "The Administrative Law Judiciary: Change, Challenge, and Choices." *Annals of the American Academy of Political and Social Science* 462 (1982): 34–47.

Skoler, Daniel L., and Cynthia E. Weixel. "Social Security Adjudication in Five Nations." *Administrative Law Review* 33 (1981): 269–284.

Skowronek, Stephen. *Building a New American State: The Expansion of National Administrative Capacities, 1877–1920.* New York: Cambridge University Press, 1982.

Slotten, Hugh R. *Radio and Television Regulation: Broadcast Technology in the United States, 1920–1960.* Baltimore: Johns Hopkins University Press, 2000.

Smith, Elmer A. "Practice and Procedure before the Interstate Commerce Commission." *George Washington Law Review* 5 (1937): 404–461.

Smith, Loren A. "Judicialization: The Twilight of Administrative Law." *Duke Law Journal* 1985 (1985): 427–466.

Smith, Rixey, and Norman Beasley. *Carter Glass: A Biography*. New York: Longmans, Green and Co., 1939.

Sosay, Gül. "Consequences of Legitimizing Independent Regulatory Agencies in Contemporary Democracies." In *Delegation in Contemporary Democracies*, edited by Dietmar Braun and Fabrizio Gilardi, 171–190. New York: Routledge, 2006.

Sparrow, Bartholomew H. *From the Outside In: World War II and the American State*. Princeton: Princeton University Press, 1996.

Staszak, Sarah. *No Day in Court: Access to Justice and the Politics of Judicial Retrenchment*. New York: Oxford University Press, 2015.

Stebbings, Chantal. *Legal Foundations of Tribunals in Nineteenth-Century England*. Cambridge: Cambridge University Press, 2006.

Stephenson, Nathaniel Wright. *Nelson W. Aldrich: A Leader in American Politics*. New York: Charles Scribner's Sons, 1930.

Stever, James A. "Marshall Dimock's Deflective Organizational Theory." *Journal of Management History* 3 (1997): 317–327.

Stewart, Richard B. "The Reformation of American Administrative Law." *Harvard Law Review* 88 (1975): 1667–1813.

———. "Administrative Law in the Twenty-First Century." *New York University Law Review* 78 (2003): 437–460.

Stillman, Richard J., II. "The Constitutional Bicentennial and the Centennial of the American Administrative State." *Public Administration Review* 47 (1987): 4–8.

Stone, Harlan F. "The Common Law in the United States." *Harvard Law Review* 50 (1936): 4–26.

Strauss, Peter L. "The Place of Agencies in Government: Separation of Powers and the Fourth Branch." *Columbia Law Review* 84 (1984): 573–669.

Strum, Philippa. *Louis D. Brandeis: Justice for the People*. Cambridge, MA: Harvard University Press, 1984.

Sunstein, Cass R. *After the Rights Revolution: Reconceiving the Regulatory State*. Cambridge, MA: Harvard University Press, 1990.

Svara, James H., and James R. Brunet. "Social Equity Is a Pillar of Public Administration." *Journal of Public Affairs Education* 11 (2005): 253–258.

Thatcher, Mark. "The Third Force? Independent Regulatory Agencies and Elected Politicians in Europe." *Governance* 18 (2005): 347–373.

Thomas, Robert. *Administrative Justice and Asylum Appeals: A Study of Tribunal Adjudication*. Oxford: Hart Publishing, 2011.

Timberlake, Richard H. *Monetary Policy in the United States: An Intellectual and Institutional History*. Chicago: University of Chicago Press, 1993.

Tollefson, Martin. "Judicial Review of the Decisions of the Interstate Commerce Commission." *George Washington Law Review* 5 (1937): 503–542.

Trask, Roger R. *The General Accounting Office, 1921–1966*. Washington, DC: Ross and Perry, 2001.

Tucker, Paul. *Unelected Power: The Quest for Legitimacy in Central Banking and the Regulatory State*. Princeton: Princeton University Press, 2018.

Tulis, Jeffrey. *The Rhetorical Presidency*. Princeton: Princeton University Press, 1987.

Urofsky, Melvin I. *Louis D. Brandeis: A Life*. New York: Schocken Books, 2009.

Vanderbilt, Arthur T. "The Place of the Administrative Tribunal in Our Legal System." *American Bar Association Journal* 24 (1938): 267–273.

Veeder, Henry. "The Federal Trade Commission and the Packers." *Illinois Law Review* 15 (1921): 485–503.

Verkuil, Paul R. "A Study of Informal Adjudication Procedures." *University of Chicago Law Review* 43 (1976): 739–796.
———. "The Emerging Concept of Administrative Procedure." *Columbia Law Review* 78 (1978): 258–329.
———. "Jawboning Administrative Agencies: Ex Parte Contacts by the White House." *Columbia Law Review* 80 (1980): 943–989.
———. "A Study of Immigration Procedures." *UCLA Law Review* 31 (1984): 1141–1207.
———. "The Purposes and Limits of Independent Agencies." *Duke Law Journal* 1988 (1988): 257–279.
———. "Separation of Powers, the Rule of Law and the Idea of Independence." *William and Mary Law Review* 30 (1989): 301–341.
———. "Reflections upon the Federal Administrative Judiciary." *UCLA Law Review* 39 (1992): 1341–1363.
———. "Meeting the Mashaw Test for Consistency in Administrative Decision-Making." In *Administrative Law from the Inside Out: Essays on Themes in the Work of Jerry L. Mashaw*, edited by Nicholas R. Parrillo, 239–246. New York: Cambridge University Press, 2017.
Vibert, Frank. *The Rise of the Unelected: Democracy and the New Separation of Powers.* New York: Cambridge University Press, 2007.
Wade, H. W. R. *Towards Administrative Justice.* Ann Arbor: University of Michigan Press, 1963.
Waldo, Dwight. *The Administrative State: A Study of the Political Theory of American Public Administration.* 1948. Reprint, New York: Routledge, 2017.
Wallace, Schuyler. *Federal Departmentalization: A Critique of Theories of Organization.* New York: Columbia University Press, 1941.
Wang, Jessica. "Imagining the Administrative State: Legal Pragmatism, Securities Regulation, and New Deal Liberalism." *Journal of Policy History* 17 (2005): 257–293.
Webb, Ross A. *Benjamin Helm Bristow, Border State Politician.* Lexington: University Press of Kentucky, 1969.
Weber, Max. *The Theory of Social and Economic Organization*, translated by A. M. Henderson and Talcott Parsons. New York: Oxford University Press, 1947.
———, trans. *From Max Weber: Essays in Sociology*, edited by H. H. Gerth and C. Wright Mills. New York: Routledge, 2009.
Weinstein, James. *The Corporate Ideal in the Liberal State, 1900–1918.* Boston: Beacon Press, 1968.
Wertkin, Jeffrey A. "Overruled: The Legalistic and Managerial Models of Administrative Adjudications." Ph.D. diss., Georgetown University, 2008.
West, Robert Craig. *Banking Reform and the Federal Reserve, 1863–1923.* Ithaca: Cornell University Press, 1974.
West, William. "Administrative Rulemaking: An Old and Emerging Literature." *Public Administration Review* 65 (2005): 655–668.
Westwood, Howard C. and Alexander E. Bennett. "A Footnote to the Legislative History of the Civil Aeronautics Act of 1938 and Afterword." *Notre Dame Lawyer* 42 (1967): 309–381.
White, Eugene N. " 'To Establish a More Effective Supervision of Banking': How the Birth of the Fed Altered Bank Supervision." In *The Origins, History, and Future of the Federal Reserve: A Return to Jekyll Island*, edited by Michael D. Bordo and William Roberds, 7–54. New York: Cambridge University Press, 2013.

White, G. Edward. *Intervention and Detachment: Essays in Legal History and Jurisprudence*. New York: Oxford University Press, 1994.

———. *The Constitution and the New Deal*. Cambridge, MA: Harvard University Press, 2000.

White, Leonard D. *Introduction to the Study of Public Administration*. New York: Macmillan, 1926.

———. *The Jacksonians: A Study in Administrative History, 1829–1861*. New York: Macmillan, 1954.

———. *The Republican Era: 1869–1901: A Study in Administrative History*. New York: Macmillan, 1958.

White, Richard D., Jr. "More than an Analytical Tool: Examining the Ideological Role of Efficiency." *Public Productivity and Management Review* 23 (1999): 8–23.

Wicker, Elmus. *The Great Debate on Banking Reform: Nelson Aldrich and the Origins of the Fed*. Columbus: Ohio State University Press, 2005.

Willis, Henry Parker. *The Federal Reserve System: Legislation, Organization and Operation*. New York: Ronald Press, 1923.

Wilson, Graham K. *The Politics of Safety and Health: Occupational Safety and Health in the United States and Britain*. Oxford: Clarendon Press, 1985.

Wilson, James Q. *Bureaucracy: What Government Agencies Do and Why They Do It*. New York: Basic Books, 1989.

Wilson, Thomas. *The Power "to Coin" Money: The Exercise of Monetary Powers by the Congress*. Armonk, NY: M. E. Sharpe, 1992.

Wilson, Woodrow. "The Study of Administration." *Political Science Quarterly* 2 (1887): 197–222.

———. *The New Freedom: A Call for the Emancipation of the Generous Energies of a People*. Garden City: Doubleday, Page and Co., 1921.

———. *The Papers of Woodrow Wilson*, edited by Arthur S. Link. 69 vols. Princeton: Princeton University Press, 1966–1994.

Woll, Peter. *Administrative Law: The Informal Process*. Berkeley: University of California Press, 1963.

———. "Administrative Law in the Seventies." *Public Administration Review* 32 (1972): 557–564.

Woodward, C. Vann. "The Age of Reinterpretation." *American Historical Review* 66 (1960): 1–19.

Wraith, R. E., and P. G. Hutchesson. *Administrative Tribunals*. London: George Allen and Unwin, 1973.

Young, Gordon G. "Public Rights and the Federal Judicial Power: From *Murray's Lessee* through *Crowell* to *Schor*." *Buffalo Law Review* 35 (1986): 765–869.

Zaring, David. "Enforcement Adjudication at the SEC." In *Administrative Law from the Inside Out: Essays on Themes in the Work of Jerry L. Mashaw*, edited by Nicholas R. Parrillo, 271–294. New York: Cambridge University Press, 2017.

Zeppos, Nicholas S. "The Legal Profession and the Development of Administrative Law." *Chicago-Kent Law Review* 72 (1997): 1119–1157.

Web Pages

Transactional Records Access Clearinghouse, Syracuse University. "Average Time Pending Cases Have Been Waiting in Immigration Courts." http://trac.syr.edu/phptools/immigration/court_backlog/apprep_backlog_avgdays.php (last accessed Dec. 26, 2018).

———. "Backlog of Pending Cases in Immigration Courts." http://trac.syr.edu/phptools/immigration/court_backlog/apprep_backlog.php (last accessed Dec. 26, 2018).
US Office of Personnel Management. "Administrative Law Judges." www.opm.gov/services-for-agencies/administrative-law-judges/#url=ALJs-by-Agency (last accessed Dec. 26, 2018).

Index

For Product Safety Concerns and Information please contact our EU
representative GPSR@taylorandfrancis.com
Taylor & Francis Verlag GmbH, Kaufingerstraße 24, 80331 München, Germany

www.ingramcontent.com/pod-product-compliance
Ingram Content Group UK Ltd.
Pitfield, Milton Keynes, MK11 3LW, UK
UKHW021720240926
475702UK00029BA/1667
9781032092669